GODS MUST BE CRAZY!

Farmer ↔ Hunter

Century of Humiliation ↔ Century of AI Rejuvenation

SAJI MADAPAT

A Satirical Odyssey Through the Gloriously Unhinged
Funhouse Mirror of Global Capitalism

"Victory comes from finding opportunities in problems."
— Sun Tzu, Art of War

*Proceeds from this book will be donated to the Mother Teresa Mission
(Missionaries of Charity) or similar missions.*

DEDICATION

"Every gun that is made, every warship launched, every rocket fired signifies, in the final sense, a theft from those who hunger and are not fed, those who are cold and are not clothed.

This world in arms is not spending money alone. It is spending the sweat of its laborers, the genius of its scientists, the hopes of its children. The cost of one modern heavy bomber is this: a modern brick school in more than 30 cities. It is two electric power plants, each serving a town of 60,000 population. It is two fine, fully equipped hospitals. It is some fifty miles of concrete pavement. We pay for a single fighter with a half-million bushels of wheat. We pay for a single destroyer with new homes that could have housed more than 8,000 people. . . . This is not a way of life at all, in any true sense. Under the cloud of threatening war, it is humanity hanging from a cross of iron."

— President Dwight D. Eisenhower
Supreme Commander, Allied Expeditionary Force (WWII)

*What Eisenhower warned of in iron, this book traces in silicon,
in supply chains, in the quiet arithmetic of who builds and who buys.*

Saji Madapat is the ultimate contrarian insider. His journey traces one of the most improbable arcs in modern finance—from a boatman's son in the below-sea-level paddies of Kuttanad, Kerala, to the CFO's office of a Fortune 10 "World's Most Admired Company". As a Big Four financial transformation architect, Madapat led enterprise strategies across forty-plus countries. In a Singapore boardroom in 2006, he sat in the room where eleven thousand manufacturing jobs were offshored to Shenzhen. When a junior analyst asked, "What happens when they don't need us anymore?", the room went silent for four seconds. That silence echoes through every chapter of this book.

He did not merely observe the Farmer-Hunter dynamic from the outside; he helped create the conditions that made it decisive. A Clinton Global Initiative Fellow, Madapat brings a rare dual vision to geopolitical analysis: the deployment literacy of someone who has read supply chains across forty nations, and the narrative literacy of someone who spent decades inside the financial complex that obscures them. He is the author of over a dozen bestselling books and a Kala Sreshta laureate in ancient Theyyam ritual traditions, where a human performer is painted into a deity through trance and fire. This cultural inheritance provides his unique "inner vision" (ullil kaanal). Writing from the position of the Boatman, he reads both currents at the halocline, committed to neither, honest about both. He lives on the banks of the Mississippi—still reading the undercurrent.

Kala Sreshta (Most Accomplished Artist) Award
(Prof. MN Karasseri to Saji & Subhash Chandran(Chief Editor Mathrubhumi))
-Sculpture by Kanayi Kunhiraman

In the backwaters of Kerala, two currents flow through the same channel. The brackish tide pushes inland from the Arabian Sea, and the freshwater descends from the Western Ghats. They coexist in the same body of water, each governed by its own logic, meeting without mixing. The boatmen do not choose between currents. They read both.

— From the oral traditions of the Kuttanad boatmen

Contents

A NOTE TO THE READER

On the Book's Architecture

This book is structured around the three stages of a Theyyam ritual—a sacred performance tradition from northern Kerala, India, in which a human performer is progressively transformed into a deity through paint, costume, and trance. The three stages provide the book's architecture:

Part I: Thottam (The Invocation) — Chapters 1–4. The performer has not yet been painted. The songs are sung, the deity's genealogy is recited, and the ground is prepared. In the book, these chapters establish the two systems—the Farmer's patient deployment and the Hunter's reactive frenzy—and introduce the analytical framework (halocline, Field vs. Forest, the Interdependency Web) through which the competition will be read. Chapter 3 documents the fourteenth domain—algorithmic polarization and social cohesion—that determines whether the Hunter can respond to the Farmer's deployment at all. Chapter 4 maps the Hunter's broken bow: the social infrastructure erosion that prevents the Hunter's magnificent arrows from flying.

Part II: Vellatam (The Transformation) — Chapters 5–10. The face is being painted. Each color, each line, brings the deity closer to manifestation. These are the domain chapters—the innovation paradox, tariffs and rare earths, military-industrial capacity, semiconductors, the industries of daily life, the dollar and digital alternatives—each one adding a stroke to the portrait of two civilizations in asymmetric competition.

Part III: Mukhathezhuthu (The Sacred Face) — Chapters 11–12 and Epilogue. The mask is complete. The deity arrives. The human vanishes. These chapters deliver the assessment: the Farmer's vulnerabilities, the Surprise that reframes the competition, the Rooseveltian prescription, and the author's unmasked voice.

On Narrative Method

This book employs scenario-based extrapolation grounded in observable economic, geopolitical, and technological trajectories as of early 2026. Events and developments referenced in the near future are projections drawn from current data, policy direction, and institutional momentum—not predictions. Where specific dates or events are cited, they represent the author's informed assessment of trajectory, not certainty of outcome. The analytical framework and its conclusions do not depend on any single projected event proving exactly correct. The reader should engage with the scenarios as disciplined extrapolation—the same methodology used in defense intelligence assessments, corporate strategic planning, and the scenario work of institutions like the RAND Corporation.

On Analytical Posture

This book is written as a corrective—a corrective to the systematic underestimation of Chinese deployment capacity that has characterized Western analysis for over two decades. As a corrective, it deliberately foregrounds the data points that the conventional narrative misses or minimizes. It documents the Farmer's harvest with a thoroughness that may, at times, read as advocacy. It is not. It is the other side of a ledger that has been unbalanced for twenty years. Chapter 11 applies the same analytical rigor to the Farmer's vulnerabilities—demographics, property, trust, legitimacy, and the structural fragilities that no amount of industrial capacity alone can overcome. The reader should weigh accordingly.

On the Boatman's Ledger

Each chapter concludes with a "Boatman's Ledger"—a running analytical tool designed for investors, business leaders, and policy practitioners who want to translate the chapter's geopolitical analysis into portfolio and strategic implications. The Ledger's scenario allocations, risk frameworks, and strategic actions are illustrative and educational.

They do not constitute financial, investment, or legal advice. Readers should consult qualified professionals before making investment decisions based on any framework in this book.

DRAMATIS PERSONAE

The human-scale characters who carry the book's thesis in their hands

THE FARMER'S WORLD

Chen Yue (陈越) An engineer from Anhui province whose cracked knuckles became keyboard strokes—the intergenerational arc from rural poverty to semiconductor ambition. Introduced in Chapter 1.

Zhang Mei (张梅) A welder at the Jiangnan Shipyard, whose thermos and whose daughter's drawing ("Mama welds the world") ground the shipbuilding data in maternal labor. Introduced in Chapter 7.

Liu Jing (刘静) A process engineer in a Chinese semiconductor fabrication facility, working in a bunny suit under eleven minutes of ultraviolet light. The human face of the silicon self-reliance campaign. Introduced in Chapter 8.

Chen Liling (陈丽玲) A grandmother in Wuhan who takes a robotaxi to visit her granddaughter on an ordinary Tuesday—the moment deployment becomes invisible. Introduced in Chapter 9.

Wei Lin (魏林) A thirty-four-year-old professional in Beijing who has chosen not to have children. Her hotpot dinner with friends is the demographic crisis made personal. Introduced in Chapter 11.

Wang Sufen (王素芬) A trade-finance manager processing cross-border payments through CIPS at 6:47 PM—the dedollarization thesis in a single transaction. Introduced in Chapter 10.

THE HUNTER'S WORLD

Marcus Chen A Westchester-based portfolio manager of Chinese-American heritage, whose assumptions about markets, nations, and his own identity are progressively dismantled across the book. The reader's analytical surrogate. Appears in every chapter.

Sarah Kowalski Owner of a home goods boutique on West Federal Street in Youngstown, Ohio, whose ceramics inventory and kiln-technology supply chain are hostage to tariff policy. The impact on American small businesses has become tangible. Introduced in the Prologue; expanded arc in Chapter 4.

Kevin Marcus's analyst and skeptical foil, who voices the conventional Western objections—"government program wearing a corporate mask"—that the book systematically addresses. Introduced in Chapter 2.

Diane Kessler A former managing editor of a regional newspaper in Mahoning County, Ohio, whose twenty-three-year career was consumed by the attention harvest—the algorithm that extinguished the community's torchbearer. The fourteenth domain's human face. Introduced in Chapter 3.

Maria Delgado A sixty-one-year-old uninsured warehouse worker in Youngstown, Ohio, whose monthly metformin arithmetic—$52 for a molecule that costs $3.80 at source, embodies the broken bow's healthcare crack. Introduced in Chapter 4.

Gerald A retired postal worker in Youngstown, whose arthritic knees are the last piece of informal social infrastructure connecting Maria Delgado to her medication. The orumuttu in human form. Introduced in Chapter 4.

THE SPACE BETWEEN

Klaus Reinhardt A German industrial executive navigating between the two currents—the embodiment of the "osmoregulation" framework for nations caught between the Farmer and the Hunter. Introduced in Chapter 6.

Maria Delgado (Monterrey) A Mexican automotive-parts supplier whose factory floor tells the story of supply-chain rerouting, tariff arbitrage, and the human cost of trade-war geography. Introduced in Chapter 6.

Note: *Two characters share the name, Maria Delgado. Sarah's neighbor in Youngstown is the Maria, whose arc runs through Chapters 4, 8, 9, and the Epilogue. The Monterrey automotive supplier appears in Chapter 6's tariff forensics and the Epilogue. Context distinguishes them throughout.*

PREFACE

The Coke Bottle and the Boatman

Before dawn in northern Malabar, when the torches are still unlit, and the compound is silent, the Theyyam performer squats in darkness, breathing. No paint on his face. No crown. No divine mask. Just a man in the dark, his lungs filling with something the audience cannot yet see. The transformation has not begun, but the air already carries its charge—the way monsoon air carries rain fifteen minutes before the first drop falls. When the drumbeats start, the face paint dries, and the crown descends, the performer will see with ullil kaanal—inner vision—and the human being will vanish into the deity. But here, in the predawn silence, everything is still possible, and nothing has yet been revealed.

• • •

The title nods to the 1980 satire The Gods Must Be Crazy, in which a pilot's discarded Coca-Cola bottle lands in a Kalahari village, is first hailed as a gift from the Gods and then becomes a fuse for internecine havoc.

• • •

Let me confess before the global economic politburo.

I am the prodigal capitalistic cowboy, the corporate arsonist, the financial termite with an MBA and a conscience that arrived thirty years late—happily gnawing through the structural beams of Western capitalism while wearing a suit that cost more than my father's entire house. An unlikely export from Kerala, India—a place so idyllically verdant and politically perplexing it's called "God's Own Country." One assumes this is because even omniscient deities appreciate a front-row seat to the irony of political arrangements that defy conventional analysis. This is my confession. This is my field report. This is the Theyyam performer's breathing changing before the deity arrives.

But first—the bottle.

In Jamie Uys's 1980 film *The Gods Must Be Crazy*, a bush pilot flying over the Kalahari Desert finishes a Coca-Cola and tosses the empty bottle out of his cockpit window. It falls through hot silence—glass catching equatorial light—and lands, intact, in the middle of a San Bushman settlement that has never encountered manufactured glass. The villagers examine it with wonder. It is harder than anything they possess. It can grind grain, flatten hides, and make music when you blow across its mouth. It is, by any rational measure, a marvel—a technological gift from the heavens.

Then the trouble begins. Because there is only one bottle and many hands that want it, the gift becomes a source of envy, conflict, and violence—emotions the San had managed to avoid for millennia through their egalitarian social architecture. The bottle has not changed them. It has revealed fault lines that abundance conceals, and scarcity exposes. The elder Xi, watching his community unravel over a piece of curved glass, makes the only rational decision available: he walks to what he believes is the edge of the earth and hurls the bottle into the void. The gods, he concludes, must be crazy to have sent such a gift.

I have spent thirty years holding that bottle.

Not a Coca-Cola bottle. Something shinier, more intoxicating, and far more dangerous: the promise of American capitalism—a gift that arrived in Kuttanad, Kerala, not from the sky but from the pages of Western travelogues in my father's college library, and that carried me from a TV-free household to the CFO's office of a Fortune 10 corporation named by *Fortune* as the World's Most Admired Company. The journey from Kuttanadan rice paddies to the glass towers of American enterprise is the Coke Bottle parable made flesh. The bottle is beautiful. The bottle is useful. The bottle can save you half a billion dollars in portfolio optimization. And the bottle, if you are not careful, will shatter your community, hollow your institutions, and leave you standing in rubble, wondering why the gods thought this was a good idea.

I held the bottle. I profited from the bottle. I watched the bottle shatter communities on four continents. And now I'm the man standing at the edge of the world, deciding whether to throw it into the void or finally read the bill of materials etched in the glass.

. . .

The Rice Paddy and the Bloomberg Terminal

I am from Kuttanad, the rice bowl of Kerala, where farmers cultivate below sea level in a landscape shaped by monsoons, tides, and the perpetual negotiation between salt water and fresh water. The paddies stretch to the horizon like a green meditation, interrupted only by coconut palms that lean into the wind as if eavesdropping on the water's secrets. The air tastes of brine and possibility. The earth is so low that the sea is always whispering threats, and the farmers are always whispering back: *not today*.

My parents were teachers—committed socialists in a state so politically distinctive that Communists have been democratically elected for over half a century, thanks to Catholic schools established by European missionaries. Kerala presents the fascinating paradox of maintaining 99% literacy rates, the highest life expectancy in India, and robust social welfare systems while operating within a democratic communist framework—a statistical unicorn that gives global policy wonks both hope and throbbing migraines.

We did not own a television. My school holidays were spent navigating my father's library, devouring Western travelogues that, in retrospect, were colonial marketing brochures with excellent production values. The sole cinematic experience deemed worthy of theatrical viewing was *Gandhi*—a film about a man who defeated an empire while dressed in a bedsheet and practicing radical minimalism. It is a miracle I did not attempt to negotiate Wall Street bonuses through hunger strikes.

But we had the backwaters. And in the backwaters, we had the *halocline*—the invisible boundary where freshwater and saltwater meet but do not mix. To the untrained eye, the water looks uniform. To the boatman who has spent his life reading undercurrents, the halocline is as visible as a wall. He sees where the fresh current runs and where the salt will poison the crop. He reads what the surface conceals.

Here is what the textbooks miss: life *concentrates* at the halocline. The shrimp, the prawns, the pearl-spot fish—they gather at the boundary layer where the two waters meet, because that is where the nutrients are richest. The richest ecology in Kuttanad exists not in the freshwater or the saltwater but in the thin, unstable zone between them. The boatman knows this. He sets his nets at the halocline. He harvests where the two currents collide. The analytical implication would take me thirty years to understand: the deepest insights come not from being firmly in one current or the other, but from reading both simultaneously—from living in the boundary layer where the biology is richest and the vision is clearest.

The boatman does not argue with the water. He does not write op-eds about the water. He does not convene a bipartisan panel to study the water's intentions. He reads the current, adjusts his oar, and arrives alive. The Bloomberg terminal operator, by contrast, stares at a screen full of prices stripped of harvests, data stripped of dirt, numbers stripped of the civilizational logic that produced them, and calls this "information." The boatman would call it *māyā*— the beautiful illusion that drowns those who mistake the surface for the depth.

I did not know it then, but the backwaters were teaching me to read a different kind of halocline—the one between narrative and deployment, between what markets say and what factories produce, between what Bloomberg terminals display and what Chinese shipyards launch. That education would take thirty years, four continents, and a journey through the most sophisticated *māyā*-generating machinery in human history before I understood what the boatman had been showing me all along.

• • •

The Tiger Ride: From Communist Classrooms to Gordon Gekko's Boardroom

Kerala's peculiar brand of democratic communism produced extraordinary literacy and life expectancy, but it also produced an industrial desert so barren that its most reliable export was its own children. After an Industrial Engineering degree—with a profoundly ironic specialization in Total Quality Management, a discipline about optimizing systems in a state that had optimized the art of producing nothing to optimize—I migrated to Bombay, India's chaotic commercial capital.

There, I discovered that my career prospects beyond the factory floor were severely constrained by my dark skin as a "lungi-wearing Kala Madrasi"—a discriminatory label demonstrating how societies worldwide invent creative hierarchies when more obvious distinctions prove insufficient. Facing this career ceiling, I obtained an MBA in Finance, survived the 1996 stock market crash, and rode the Y2K wave into the ERP gold rush.

A word about that Y2K wave, because it matters to this book's thesis. The Year 2000 bug was arguably the most profitable catastrophe in the history of services globalization—the moment the world's most advanced technological civilization discovered it had hard-coded a two-digit apocalypse into every legacy database on the planet and needed it fixed yesterday. India became the cognitive equivalent of what China was to manufacturing: essential, invisible, and delightfully inexpensive. We were "Cyber Coolies"—deployed in the thousands to resurrect dead mainframes and patch doomsday code. Y2K created the world's first mass-production assembly line for intellectual labor, and I was a cog in its machinery.

I was a Cyber Coolie before I was a corporate arsonist before I was a Kuttanadan boatman. Each identity prepared me to see what the others could not.

The ERP gold rush proved to be my golden ticket to the United States. The universe, possessing what economists might call "asymmetric irony distribution," positioned me as a global EPM architect at AMC Theatres—the world's premier purveyor of escapist entertainment, owned by what was then China's richest man. This is capitalism's signature magic trick: transforming the offspring of socialist teachers into a high priest of corporate finance faster than you can say "dialectical materialism has cash flow problems."

I reached the pinnacle of this improbable ascent as an advisor to the CFO's office at a Fortune 10 "World's Most Admired Company," where I established their Project Portfolio Management Office and saved them approximately half a billion dollars. In the grand tradition of corporate America—where no good deed goes unpunished—I became a victim of my own financial engineering when the 2008 tsunami washed away my job along with much of the global financial system.

I confess to having metaphorical blood on my hands.

I participated in C-level "financial engineering" at some of the world's largest corporations, including North America's second-largest private equity firm. We were the self-proclaimed architects of shareholder value. I remember the exact moment the mask slipped. Singapore, 2006. A marble-floored boardroom overlooking Marina Bay. The McKinsey partners had just finished presenting the "optimization roadmap"—three hundred slides recommending the transfer of eleven thousand manufacturing jobs to Shenzhen. The CFO nodded. I nodded. Everyone in the room nodded because the quarterly math was flawless. Then a junior analyst, barely three years out of Wharton, asked the question that no one in the room wanted to hear: "What happens when they don't need us anymore?" The room went silent for precisely four seconds. Then someone changed the slide.

That four-second silence has echoed through every chapter of this book.

Financial engineering "termites" like myself have systematically infested Western capitalism's structural foundation. The edifice now sways with the structural integrity of a soufflé in an earthquake.

Here is the personal paradox that is this book's thesis in miniature. My parents, steadfast in their socialist principles, spent nearly three decades accumulating 97% of the construction cost for their modest dream home. The remaining 3% required another three decades to repay at 30% interest to "alternative financial service providers" who preferred not to be called loan sharks despite remarkably similar collection methodologies. I, their prodigal capitalist offspring, channeled my inner Gordon Gekko during the 2008 crisis and acquired two North American properties valued at over a million dollars—financed on 97% mortgages, refinanced to extract more than ten times my initial investment, at interest rates so negligible they resembled a mathematical rounding error.

My parents saved for thirty years to own a house. I leveraged someone else's panic to own two in six months. The system my parents trusted demanded patience and punished it with usurious interest. The system I exploited rewarded audacity and called it "smart money."

In retrospect, my mother's gold bangles—part of India's 25,000 tons of privately held gold, more than the Federal Reserve, the European Central Bank, and the Bank of England combined—may have constituted a more rational investment thesis than anything I ever assembled on a Bloomberg terminal. When rural Indian women are sitting on

a larger gold reserve than the Fed, the ECB, and the Bank of England combined, you begin to wonder who's really running the show.

* * *

The Existential Awakening: Cambodia's Killing Fields and the Edge of the World

Finding myself unemployed in 2009—a condition affecting approximately 8.7 million other Americans, though few with my particular Kuttanadan-to-Fortune-10 backstory—I packed my bags for the Cambodian jungles. My quest was the Clinton Global Young Executive Leadership initiative through the Chinese GIFT program—searching for answers from the bottom of the economic pyramid.

Amidst the ghostly echoes of Pol Pot's agrarian experiment, a question coiled around my consciousness: *How could these resource-rich nations remain so catastrophically poor?* Hernando de Soto had already calculated that developing nations possess more latent wealth than all twelve major Western stock markets combined. Yet here they languished—first before their colonial masters, now genuflecting toward China's economic empire—while Western charities fluttered about, attempting to greenwash historical guilt with microloans and heart-tugging Instagram campaigns.

But it was the killing fields themselves that delivered the real education.

Here, where ideology had murdered millions in the name of agrarian purity, I—an executive who had spent a decade advising corporations on how to extract maximum value from "human resources"—stood in red soil thick with the memory of bones. The killing fields killed quickly. Corporate optimization kills slowly, with dental coverage. The killing fields had a madman with an ideology. Corporate extraction has a consulting deck with bullet points. The methodology differs; the mathematics of dehumanization rhymes.

Standing in that red soil, I understood for the first time that I was not merely an observer of systemic failure—I was one of its architects. The financial engineering tools I had wielded in Fortune 10 boardrooms were the polite, PowerPoint-enabled cousins of every extractive system in history. The difference was scale, not species. The quarterly earnings call is the genteel grandchild of the colonial extraction report. Same algebra. Better catering.

It was there—not in a boardroom, not on a Bloomberg terminal, not in a McKinsey deck—that the halocline became visible. I was standing at the intersection of two civilizational currents that the surface narrative could not reveal. One current was the patient, compounding, deployment-driven ascent of Chinese industrial power across every domain that matters—backed by a state-owned enterprise ecosystem so vast it constitutes the largest single concentration of productive capital in human history, planting not seven flashy trees but thousands of quiet seedlings across every sector of the economy. The other was the spectacular, self-inflicted, financially engineered hollowing of the very system I had spent two decades serving—a system now dominated by seven corporate principalities whose combined market capitalization exceeds $20 trillion but whose combined contribution to actual, physical, put-it-on-a-barge-and-export-it production shrinks with each passing earnings call.

And I—the Kuttanadan boatman's son who had become a Fortune 10 financial engineer—could see both currents because I had swum in both.

· · ·

The War Zone at Home: Plywood, Pledges, and the Rooseveltian Imperative

"Unless there is security here at home, there cannot be lasting peace in the world."

— Franklin Delano Roosevelt

I returned from the killing fields to the City of Broad Shoulders—now more accurately the City of Strategically Deployed Plywood—where a peculiar brand of urban renewal was underway. According to the dulcet tones captured on a Chicago City Council recording, my neighborhood had morphed into "a virtual war zone." The minutes detailed "gang members armed with AK-47s threatening to shoot black people" and, in a rather bold HR move, "shooting at the police."

Staring at the plywood fortifications now adorning my own centennial home—a structure that had stoically weathered actual wars—I understood that this was the third halocline. Cambodia had shown me the halocline between civilizations: the Farmer's patient deployment flowing beneath the Hunter's surface narrative. The backwaters had shown me the halocline between fresh and salt water. But Chicago showed me the halocline *within* a civilization: the invisible density gradient separating the institutional America I had believed in—the America of Roosevelt's arsenal, of the GI Bill, of the Marshall Plan—from the plywood-fortified America I was actually living in. Two realities occupy the same geographic space, unable to mix, each denying the other's existence.

Yet it is precisely this escalating pattern—from the surreal cosplay of the January 6th insurrection to the institutional hollowing I had witnessed in Fortune 10 boardrooms to the literal hollowing I was witnessing through my boarded-up windows, from the spectacle of Tomahawk missiles raining down on empty bunkers while a President selects the next Supreme Leader of a sovereign nation via cable news—that dragged me back to the page. Cambodia showed me that civilizational collapse has a pattern. Chicago showed me that the pattern had come home. The Middle East showed me that the Hunter cannot stop hunting, even when the quarry is a sandcastle.

The Farmer plants while the Hunter boards up his windows and argues with himself about whose fault it is.

· · ·

The Bottle Shatters

In the film, Xi walks to the edge of the world to throw the Coke bottle away. The edge turns out to be a cliff above a cloud bank. He hurls the bottle into the mist, and it disappears. Problem solved—for the San. But the bottle still exists somewhere. It did not cease to be dangerous simply because it left one community.

Our era's Coke bottle glints brighter—AI supremacy, e-yuan wallets, trillion-dollar deficits, semiconductor dependencies, algorithmic polarization machines—"blessings" that corrode the civic bedrock even as they dazzle. And this time, the bottle cannot be thrown over a cliff. It is embedded in every supply chain, every trade route, every GPU cluster, every autonomous vehicle navigating the streets of Wuhan at 3 a.m. while American test vehicles sit parked in Phoenix, awaiting regulatory clearance that may never come.

The bottle is now held by seven pairs of hands—Apple, Microsoft, Nvidia, Amazon, Alphabet, Meta, Tesla—the "Magnificent Seven" whose combined market capitalization exceeds $20 trillion, whose combined employee count is smaller than the population of Wyoming, and whose combined influence over the daily lives of eight billion humans exceeds that of most sovereign governments. They are the Coke Bottle industrialized—quasi-sovereign principalities whose market valuations eclipse the GDPs of actual countries. Chapter 2 will anatomize each one. Here, what matters is the pattern: from purported engines of innovation to sprawling, Gilded Age empires built on extraction, surveillance, and the kind of unchecked corporate power that makes historic monopolies look like lemonade stands.

Meanwhile, China watches with the patient focus of a civilization that has planted more than 5,000 AI companies since 2023, each applying artificial intelligence to a specific domain: logistics, agriculture, manufacturing, healthcare, education, and municipal governance. They are deploying AI across every sector simultaneously—backed by a state-owned enterprise ecosystem that constitutes the largest single concentration of productive capital in human history. The Farmer does not need to storm the gate. The Farmer digs around it.

The pattern is not new. The Dutch East India Company, valued at approximately $10 trillion in contemporary terms, followed a 200-year arc from innovation to financialization to decline. The British East India Company, at $5 trillion, traced the same trajectory. The American corporate empire—built on Roosevelt's industrial foundation, financialized under Friedman's doctrine, hollowed by the very shareholder-value theology I once preached—is roughly 250 years into the same cycle. The Coke Bottle is not a metaphor. It is a pattern, and the pattern has a clock.

This book is what happens when the Kuttanadan boatman's son picks up the Coke bottle, turns it in the light, and reads what is etched in the glass—not the brand name, not the marketing slogan, but the bill of materials, the supply chain, the thirteen interlocking domains that determine whether a civilization harvests or hallucinates. It is written from the halocline—the position between two currents where you can see both and belong fully to neither. It is written by someone who helped build the system this book critiques, who watched the Farmer's strategy from inside the Hunter's boardrooms, and who carries the Theyyam performer's *ullil kaanal*—the inner vision—not as metaphor but as inheritance.

I do not pretend to objectivity. Objectivity is what Bloomberg terminals sell—numbers stripped of context, prices stripped of harvest, data stripped of the civilizational logic that produced them. What I offer instead is the boatman's vision: the ability to read undercurrents that the surface cannot reveal, honed by three decades of swimming in both waters.

The gods are not crazy. They are running a civilizational experiment across thirteen domains, and the Coke bottle they dropped—on America's lawn, on the global trading system, on the assumptions that undergird every portfolio on Wall Street—is shattering. This book is the field report from the man who held the bottle, profited from the bottle, boarded up his windows when the bottle's consequences arrived on his own doorstep, and finally understood what the boatman knew all along: the price of the gift is the community it destroys, unless you learn to read what the surface conceals.

Like Xi marching to the edge of the world, this book charts a Rooseveltian trek to haul America—call it a bruised republic or a woozy empire—back from the brink before the shards fly. Whether the Hunter can learn to plant, whether the bottle can be repurposed rather than merely discarded, whether the halocline clarity this book offers arrives in time—these are the questions that carried me from the Cambodian killing fields, through the plywood fortifications of Chicago, and back to the page.

The performer's breathing has changed. The *ullil kaanal* is opening. Something is approaching.

Turn the page. Meet the Boatman. Read the undercurrent.

RITUAL STAGE MARKER

The air is still. No costume. No paint. But the performer's breathing has changed. The drummers feel it first—a shift in the predawn silence, like the moment before a monsoon breaks. Something is approaching.

PROLOGUE

Two Harvests

"The supreme art of war is to subdue the enemy without fighting."

— Sun Tzu, The Art of War, Chapter III

The Theyyam performer closes his eyes. The compound smells of coconut oil and crushed turmeric. When he opens them, he sees not with mortal sight but with ullil kaanal—inner vision. The drums have not yet started, but the air already trembles.

• • •

October 18, 1860

The smoke rose from the Yuanmingyuan for three days.

It rose not as smoke rises from a cooking fire or a funeral pyre—purposeful, contained, grieved over—but as smoke rises from a civilization being taught its place in someone else's hierarchy. It smelled of burning silk and lacquered cedar and something sweeter, sicker—the scent of ten thousand scrolls of calligraphy converting irreversibly to carbon. Porcelain cracked in the heat with a sound like knuckles breaking. Jade, which cannot burn, lay in the ashes glowing a color that no jeweler had ever seen and no jeweler would ever reproduce. This was the kind of smoke that enters the nostrils of schoolchildren a century and a half later and never leaves. The kind that becomes doctrine.

The Old Summer Palace—a complex of gardens, pavilions, temples, and libraries spanning 860 acres northwest of Beijing, built over a century and a half by the greatest artisans of the Qing dynasty—was put to the torch on the orders of Lord Elgin, the British High Commissioner to China. The French had already looted what they could carry: jade, porcelain, silks, cloisonné, bronzes from the Zodiac fountain, and astronomical instruments calibrated by Jesuit missionaries who had served the Qing court for generations. What could not be carried was burned. The fire was not incidental. It was pedagogical.

Victor Hugo, writing from exile, called it what it was: "One day, two bandits entered the Summer Palace. One plundered; the other burned." The two bandits were France and England. He predicted that history would judge. History judged. But history's judgment does not rebuild libraries. It does not restore the thousands of irreplaceable volumes from the *Siku Quanshu* that turned to ash in the October wind. It does not re-carve the jade or re-engineer the hydraulic fountains designed by Giuseppe Castiglione in a fusion of Baroque and Chinese aesthetics that existed nowhere else on Earth and would never exist again.

What the burning did engineer was something far more durable than any palace: a memory. A scar tissue of civilizational humiliation that calcified into strategic doctrine. The ruins were deliberately left unrestored. They stand today as a national monument—not to what was built, but to what was taken. Chinese schoolchildren on field trips visit the broken marble columns, stand before them, and learn, in the wordless language of rubble, the foundational lesson of modern Chinese statecraft: *This is why we will never be weak again.*

The Century of Humiliation is not a chapter in a history textbook. It is the BIOS—the basic input/output system of Chinese strategic consciousness, the code that runs before any application loads. From the First Opium War in 1839 to the founding of the People's Republic in 1949, the lesson was etched into the motherboard of national identity: brilliance at invention means nothing without the power to defend the harvest. Paper, gunpowder, the compass, movable type—four gifts to the world, each turned into a weapon against the giver. The scar did not fade. The scar became firmware.

When, 165 years later, a hedge fund quant in Hangzhou trained a frontier AI model for $5.6 million in compute costs, the GPU cluster's total cost of ownership approached $100 million, but the *training efficiency*, requiring only 2.788 million H800 GPU hours, is what shattered the American pricing premise—the reaction in Beijing was not surprise. It was recognition. DeepSeek was the vow made at the Yuanmingyuan's ruins, rendered in silicon: *never again will we invent and others deploy. This time, we plant, and we harvest.*

And DeepSeek was not alone. It was one seed in a field of thousands of AI companies registered in China since 2023—each applying artificial intelligence to a specific deployment domain, each drawing water from the same open-source irrigation system, each too small to appear on a Wall Street analyst's screen and too numerous, collectively, to be stopped by any tariff, any export ban, any executive order signed in any Rose Garden.

. . .

April 2, 2025: The Rose Garden

One hundred and sixty-five years after Lord Elgin torched the Summer Palace, another act of strategic arson was performed—this time, by the Hunter upon himself.

In the White House Rose Garden, on a date he christened "Liberation Day" with the grandiosity of a man who names his own hurricanes, President Trump signed Executive Order 14257, declaring the U.S. trade deficit a "national emergency" and imposing the most sweeping tariff hike since the Smoot-Hawley Act of 1930. A universal 10% tariff on all imports, with escalating rates—up to 145% on Chinese goods—hitting nearly every artery of the American economy.

Sun Tzu wrote that the supreme art of war is to subdue the enemy without fighting. Read through the Kuttanadan lens of *Ullozhukku*—the undercurrent, the force that moves beneath the visible surface—the Liberation Day tariffs were the Hunter's gift to the Farmer. Within two trading days, the S&P 500 lost over $6.6 trillion in market value— the largest two-day loss in American stock market history. And across thirteen interlocking domains, the Farmer watched the Hunter's aggression become the tide that carried wavering nations toward Beijing.

This is *wu wei*—effortless action—across thirteen fields. Not inaction, but the strategic patience that allows the adversary's force to become your momentum. China did not need to fight the tariffs. China needed only to keep planting while the Hunter set fire to his own barn.

. . .

Two Monologues, One Chessboard

The senior planner did not smile when the tariff schedules appeared on her screen. Smiling would have been imprecise. What she felt was something closer to the satisfaction of a chess player whose opponent has just moved his queen into the exact square where she had placed her trap three moves ago.

She opened thirteen tabs on her secure terminal. Not thirteen sectors—thirteen interdependencies. She read them the way the Kuttanadan boatman reads thirteen currents converging in a single channel: each one distinct, each one connected to the others by a logic the surface cannot reveal. Where a Western analyst would see twelve industries and an enabling technology, she saw a single irrigation system with twelve visible channels and one underground aquifer connecting them all.

Tab one: EVs. Tab two: Batteries. Tab three: Semiconductors. Tab four: Autonomous vehicles. Tab five: Drones. Tab six: Shipbuilding. Tab seven: Telecom. Tab eight: Robotics. Tab nine: Smart cities. Tab ten: Grid storage. Tab eleven: Rare earths. Tab twelve: Commercial aviation.

And the thirteenth tab—the one she opened last, the one that connected all others like a root system connecting twelve separate trees into a single forest—artificial intelligence.

She did not read these tabs sequentially. She read the spaces *between* them—the underground channels. The semiconductor controls and the EV tariffs were not separate files; they were two expressions of the same *shì* accumulation, the same strategic potential building behind the same dam. The tariffs on Chinese EVs would accelerate BYD's pivot to Southeast Asia, Latin America, and the Middle East—markets where $9,550 God's Eye-equipped vehicles would face even less Western competition. The tariffs on semiconductors would catalyze SMIC's DUV production ramp. The 145% rate would push neutral nations—Vietnam, Indonesia, India, the Gulf states—to hedge their trade relationships, diversifying toward a China that offered technology without political conditions and infrastructure without lectures about human rights.

Behind every pivot, behind every rerouted supply chain, the state-owned enterprise ecosystem moved with the quiet precision of tectonic plates: COSCO Shipping rerouting cargo, State Grid exporting renewable infrastructure, CRRC laying rail in nations the Hunter had never bothered to visit.

She did not see the tariffs as an act of aggression. She saw them as irrigation—the Hunter flooding channels that would carry water to the Farmer's fields. The pattern was so consistent it had acquired its own internal shorthand: every American restriction was filed under "Voluntary Technology Development Incentive." CATL's >39% global battery share had been built in the shadow of market protections. DeepSeek's training run had been born from GPU export controls that forced efficiency innovation. Apollo Go's 300,000 autonomous rides per week in Wuhan were possible because Chinese regulators had cleared the way that American regulators had not.

For a moment—one she would not have admitted to her deputy—she felt something unexpected. Not satisfaction. Not triumph. Something closer to *pity*. Not for the tariffs themselves, which were manageable, but for a system so disordered it could not sustain a coherent policy for eleven months. A civilization that could not distinguish between a supply chain and a sandbag.

She typed a single note to her deputy: 先立后破. *Build new. Faster now.*

• • •

The White House trade advisor had not slept. He had, however, consumed four Red Bulls and produced a fourteen-page brief titled "Liberation Day: Strategic Rationale and Expected Outcomes." The brief's thesis was elegant in the way that a guillotine is elegant: the U.S. trade deficit was hemorrhaging American wealth; tariffs would stanch the bleeding; domestic manufacturing would roar back; the trade partners would capitulate.

The brief was reviewed by a committee of seven lobbyists, each representing one of the Magnificent Seven, each of whom had a different reason to support the tariffs and an identical reason to ensure the tariffs didn't apply to their client's particular supply chain. Apple needed iPhone exemptions. NVIDIA needed GPU flexibility. Amazon needed warehouse robotics untouched. Tesla needed battery supply chains preserved. The remaining three needed everything to sound patriotic while changing nothing material.

The advisor did not see thirteen domains. He saw one lever: tariffs. This is the Hunter's perennial affliction—the belief that complex systems respond to blunt instruments the way vending machines respond to correct change. Insert tariff, receive manufacturing.

He did not see that the "trade deficit" was not a leak in a pipe but an ecosystem of interlocking supply chains cultivated over three decades. He did not see that a 145% tariff on Chinese goods would not bring manufacturing home—it would reroute it through Vietnam, Mexico, and Indonesia, all integrated into China's Belt and Road supply chain. He did not see that the $6.6 trillion evaporating from the S&P was American household wealth—retirement accounts, college funds, pension obligations belonging to people who had never heard of the International Emergency Economic Powers Act—being incinerated for a policy that the Supreme Court would ultimately strike down.

In the parlance of Kuttanadan farming: the Washington advisor saw a single channel overflowing and reached for a single sandbag. The Beijing planner saw twelve channels, connected underground, and let the monsoon do her work.

• • •

Marcus and the Bloomberg Terminal

Marcus Chen's Bloomberg terminal was turning the particular shade of red that financial professionals associate with the onset of gastrointestinal distress.

It was April 4, 2025. The second day of the post-Liberation Day selloff. Marcus was fifty-one years old, a senior fund manager at a mid-tier New York asset management firm, and the screen displayed the carnage with the clinical precision of an EKG monitoring a cardiac arrest: S&P 500 down 10% in two days. $6.6 trillion in market value, gone. NVIDIA, the cornerstone of every AI-weighted portfolio on the Street, had already shed $589 billion in a single session back in January when DeepSeek demonstrated that efficient training could match hundred-million-dollar runs. Now, layered on top of that shock, the tariffs were detonating across every sector simultaneously.

Marcus had twenty-three years of managing money through dot-com busts, housing collapses, and pandemic panics. He had models. Sophisticated, backtested, peer-reviewed models. The models assumed that Tesla, with a $1 trillion market capitalization for 1.64 million vehicles, was rational because the narrative—autonomy, robotaxis, AI, energy—justified the premium. The models assumed that BYD at $107 billion for 4.6 million vehicles was a value trap in an opaque market controlled by a government that might confiscate your gains at any moment.

The models priced the narrative. They did not price the harvest.

Marcus began pulling data he had never considered pulling. Not earnings estimates. Not analyst ratings. Deployment metrics. BYD: 4.6 million vehicles. CATL: >39% global battery market share. SMIC: 5nm chip production via DUV—supposedly impossible without EUV. Apollo Go: 300,000 autonomous rides per week in Wuhan alone. DeepSeek V3: 97.3% on MATH-500 at a fraction of GPT-4's training cost. Each number was a small earthquake in his mental model. Together, they constituted a tectonic shift.

He stared at the screen. Then he did something he had not done in twenty-three years of professional fund management. He picked up his phone, not to call his risk desk or his prime broker, but to call his father.

"Dad," he said, "when you left Shanghai in '89—did you think they'd come this far?"

A long pause. The sound of a seventy-eight-year-old man setting down a teacup. His father's voice, when it came, sounded like the Yangtze moving under ice—slow, patient, and carrying more force than the surface revealed. "Marcus," his father said, "the question isn't how far they've come. The question is how far you've not been looking."

The word for this, in the Sanskrit tradition that informs the Theyyam ritual, is *māyā*—illusion. Not deception by an external actor, but the self-generated veil that consciousness drapes over reality to make the world conform to its preferences rather than its observations. Marcus's Bloomberg terminal was the most sophisticated *māyā*-generating machine in human history: a $24,000-per-year instrument that displayed prices with nanosecond precision and harvested data not at all.

For the first time in his career, Marcus saw the halocline: the invisible boundary between the narrative on his screen and the harvest happening in factories, shipyards, and chip fabs he had never visited. Narrative on top. Harvest underneath. The halocline was visible now, and it was as wide as his career was long.

His journey across these pages—from cognitive error to what we will call halocline clarity—is the journey this book asks every reader to undertake. Not because Marcus is special, but because Marcus is representative: the educated professional whose entire epistemological framework is built on assumptions that the data no longer supports. Transformation is not a single epiphany. It is the slow, sometimes painful process of watching your mental models fail, one data point at a time, until the new picture assembles itself—the way the Kuttanadan boatman's eyes adjust to the water, not all at once, but ripple by ripple, current by current, until what was invisible becomes undeniable.

. . .

Sarah at the Cash Register

Twelve hundred miles from Marcus's Bloomberg terminal, in Youngstown, Ohio, Sarah Kowalski was performing her own arithmetic of despair.

She owned a small home goods boutique on West Federal Street—the kind of shop that survives on foot traffic, local loyalty, and margins thin enough to read through. A brass bell above the door announced every customer. Behind the register, her grandmother's photograph—Helen Kowalski, steel-mill wife, shop founder, 1987—watched over a display of Vietnamese ceramics arranged the way Helen had taught Sarah to arrange them: largest pieces at eye level, smallest at the edges, each one angled to catch the afternoon light from the West Federal Street windows. The tariffs had not yet hit her shelves, but her suppliers had already sent revised quotes. The Vietnamese ceramics she sold at $18 were now quoted at $23. The Chinese-manufactured picture frames—marked "Designed in USA," assembled in Guangdong—would jump 30%.

Sarah did not know that her Vietnamese ceramics were 65–80% Chinese by component value, routed through ASEAN factories that functioned as tariff laundromats. She did not know that the picture frames' "Designed in USA" label concealed a supply chain that touched four Chinese provinces before arriving at the port of Long Beach. But one afternoon, turning over a ceramic vase to check the origin mark, she read the label the way the boatman reads the current: the surface said, "Made in Vietnam." The undercurrent—the component clay, the glaze chemistry, the kiln technology, the shipping container, the port—said Guangdong. Sarah did not have a word for what she was seeing. The boatman would have called it the halocline. She called it "a bad feeling."

She knew only that her customers—retirees on fixed incomes, young families stretching paychecks—would not absorb a 30% price increase. They would simply stop coming. And the boutique that her grandmother had opened in 1987 would close, not because Sarah lacked tenacity, but because the policy that was supposed to protect American businesses had been designed by people who had never stood behind a cash register.

Sarah's grandmother had opened that shop the same year the first wave of Chinese state-owned enterprise reforms began. Thirty-seven years later, the SOE ecosystem her grandmother never heard of was the invisible architecture behind every product on Sarah's shelves. The ceramics. The frames. The supply chain that moved goods from Guangdong to Vietnam to Long Beach to West Federal Street with the quiet efficiency of water finding its level. Sarah didn't need a Bloomberg terminal to feel the undercurrent. She felt it in the revised quotes. She felt it in the customers who stopped coming. She felt it in the arithmetic that no longer added up.

Marcus and Sarah will accompany us through these pages. He sees the halocline from above, through data. She sees it from below, through prices. Together, they represent the two faces of an economy that has been told a story about itself that no longer matches the harvest.

. . .

The Boatman, the Undercurrent, and the Inner Vision

This book is written from the boatman's position: at the halocline between two civilizational currents that the surface narrative—the one on Bloomberg terminals, in Beltway briefings, on cable news chyrons—cannot reveal.

The freshwater current is deployment: the tangible, measurable, compounding reality of Chinese industrial achievement across thirteen interlocking domains—driven by a state-owned enterprise root system of unprecedented scale, accelerated by thousands of AI companies deploying machine intelligence at every node of the economy, and coordinated by a strategic doctrine that treats every American restriction as irrigation for the next harvest. The saltwater current is narrative: the stories American markets tell themselves about technological supremacy, innovation moats, and the inevitability of the existing order—stories increasingly authored by seven corporate principalities whose combined lobbying apparatus ensures that the narrative never quite catches up to the harvest.

You have already seen all three of this book's analytical lenses at work. The Beijing planner's strategic patience is *wu wei*—in practice, effortless action. The twelve underground channels connecting her thirteen tabs are *Ullozhukku*—the undercurrent—made visible. And the shift from Marcus's narrative-pricing to deployment-pricing is the *ullil kaanal*—the Theyyam performer's inner vision—applied to capital markets.

The question this book asks is not "Who will win?"—that question reduces a civilizational competition to a sports headline. The question is: *What are you not seeing?* And if the gap between what you believe and what is actually happening turns out to be as wide as the gap between Tesla's valuation and BYD's production numbers—what are you going to do about it?

. . .

BOATMAN'S LEDGER

Prologue

LEDGER TOOL #1: THE MĀYĀ METER

Greed is good—but only if you can tell the difference between a harvest and a hallucination. The Māyā Meter measures the gap between narrative valuation and the reality of deployment. Where the gap is wide, *māyā* dominates, and capital is mispriced. Three readings, in ascending order of revelation:

FIRST READING — The Single Company

Tesla market cap $1T+ for 1.64M vehicles sold. BYD market cap $107B for 4.6M vehicles sold. The Māyā Meter reads: Tesla is priced for a future that BYD is already living. One company's narrative is another company's Tuesday. Māyā Level: 8/10.

SECOND READING — The Market-Wide Repricing

NVIDIA lost $589B in one day. The S&P lost $6.6T in two days. In both cases, the market was not crashing—it was *correcting*, repricing narrative toward deployment reality. DeepSeek proved you don't need $100B in GPUs. Liberation Day proved you can't tariff your way to industrial competitiveness. These were not black swans. They were the halocline becoming visible to people who had spent careers looking at the surface. Māyā Level: 7/10.

THIRD READING — The Civilizational Mispricing

The Magnificent Seven's combined market capitalization exceeds $20 trillion. Their combined contribution to physical, exportable, put-it-on-a-ship production: approximately zero point not much. Meanwhile, China's SOE ecosystem—invisible to the Bloomberg terminal, unglamorous, unquotable, and building the infrastructure of the next century—trades at a discount to a single American company that has never delivered a profitable robotaxi ride. This is not a market inefficiency. This is civilizational *māyā* operating at an industrial scale. Māyā Level: 9/10.

THE BOATMAN'S WAGER

The Māyā Meter is not a sell signal. It is a reallocation signal. When the Meter reads 7+ across multiple domains simultaneously, the signal is not "rotate from growth to value." The signal is: *the vocabulary in which you define growth and value is itself the illusion.* Illustrative initial allocation: 5% to China-exposed multi-domain deployment names. BYD (HKG: 1211), CATL (HKG: 3750), deployment-weighted AI plays. Move from narrative to harvest. The boatman does not wait for the current to announce itself. He reads the water and adjusts his oar.

Prologue Data Anchors: DeepSeek $5.6M compute / 97.3% MATH-500 | Nvidia $589B single-day loss | S&P $6.6T two-day loss | Liberation Day: 145% tariff on Chinese goods | Tesla $1T / 1.64M vehicles vs. BYD $107B / 4.6M vehicles | Apollo Go 300K autonomous rides/week | CATL >39% global battery share | SMIC 5nm DUV

. . .

The book unfolds in three movements, following the Theyyam ritual's own architecture. Part I is the *Thottam*—the invocation: the Farmer's civilizational logic established across all domains. Part II is the *Vellatam*—the collision: hard truths, burning ghats, the surprise reframe. Part III is the *Mukhathezhuthu*—the face-painting, the final transformation: the Rooseveltian prescription and the question of whether the Hunter can learn to plant. Throughout, the Boatman's Ledger translates scholarly analysis into portfolio language, because capital flows are the ultimate vote on which harvest the market believes in.

Marcus, put down your Bloomberg terminal. Sarah, step out from behind the register. Pick up the oar. The halocline is visible now, the undercurrent is moving faster than your models predict, and the water that carried your boat so comfortably for thirty years is shifting beneath you.

The smoke rising from the Yuanmingyuan has never stopped. It is rising now—from chip fabs and battery plants and autonomous vehicles and AI training clusters, from thirteen domains in which the Farmer has planted, and the Hunter has not. The ruins were left unrestored so that a civilization would never forget. The boatman offers you a seat. The Theyyam performer offers you the inner vision. The Farmer offers you a harvest.

Whether you accept is up to you. But the performer's breathing has changed. Something is approaching. And the smoke, this time, is not destruction.

It is the kiln firing.

And what emerges from the kiln, reader, depends on whether you walked in as the clay or the potter.

. . .

PART I

THOTTAM — THE INVOCATION

The performer prepares. The first coat of ochre—the earth color, the soil from which the deity will rise—is applied to the brow. The Farmer's civilizational logic, established across all domains.

• • •

RITUAL STAGE MARKER

The performer's hands move to the first mudra—āvāhana, the invocation gesture. His fingers spread like rice shoots breaking soil. The deity is being called by name. The drums answer.

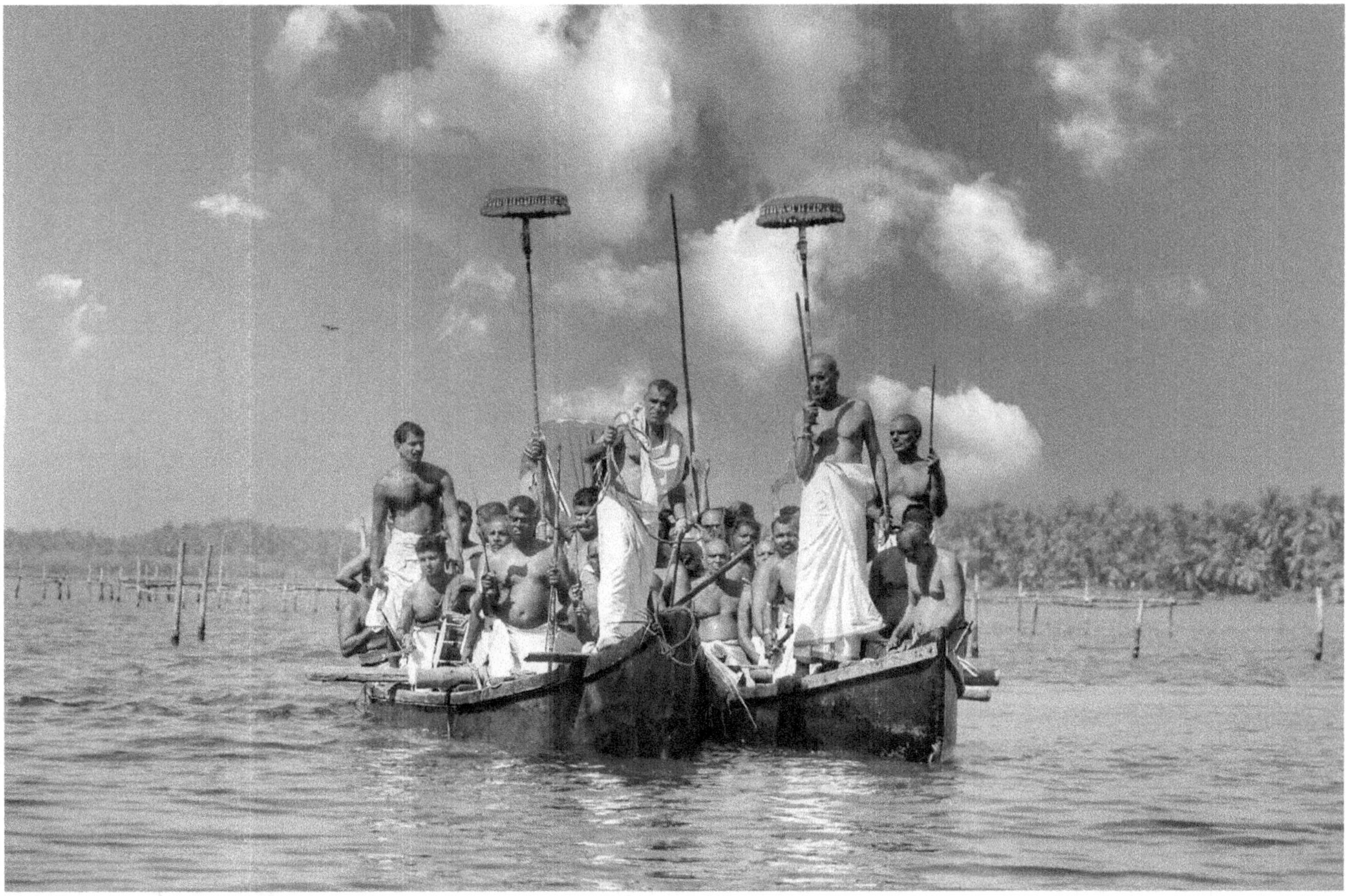

CHAPTER 1

The Farmer's Almanac

China's Civilization of Patient Capital

"If your plan is for one year, plant rice. If for ten years, plant trees. If for a hundred years, educate people."

— Guanzi

The Farmer-deity blesses the field, the granary, the canal, the forge, and the schoolhouse—all at once.

— after the Theyyam tradition

. . .

Undercurrent: The Farmer Plants in All Seasons

Guanzi's proverb is not a sequence. It is a *simultaneity.*

The genius of the Chinese strategic model—the quality that most consistently eludes Western analytical frameworks—is that the rice, the trees, and the education are planted in the same season, drawing from the same irrigation system, nourished by the same patient capital. In Kuttanad, the boatman reads three currents at once: the fresh, the salt, and the tidal surge that comes from neither but changes both. He does not read them sequentially. He reads them as a single system, the way a musician hears a chord rather than three separate notes. The Chinese planner reads her thirteen domains the same way. The principle 居安思危 ("in peace, prepare for danger") is not reactive caution. It is the Farmer's ontology—the understanding that cultivation is a permanent condition, that the harvest never ends because the planting never stops, that the moment you believe the granary is full is the moment the blight begins.

This principle drives Made in China 2025 and its successors, which target 70% self-sufficiency in core technologies. It drives the Big Fund's $100 billion-plus investment in semiconductor capability—an investment scarred by its own pathologies. The corruption purge that swept through the Fund's leadership in 2022–23 was not a footnote; it was the saltwater seeping into the Farmer's most strategically vital canal. Officials were convicted of steering capital toward firms that returned favors rather than chips—the *Vellappokkam*, the drowning gift, where abundance itself becomes the toxin. But here is the halocline distinction that Western analysts consistently miss: the system acknowledged the rot, prosecuted it publicly, imprisoned senior officials, and recapitalized with a restructured third phase. The Farmer's canals develop leaks; the Farmer repairs them. The Hunter's analogous corruption—the revolving door between the Pentagon and defense contractors, the CHIPS Act subsidies flowing to companies announcing layoffs in the same fiscal quarter—receives neither prosecution nor correction, only a Government Accountability Office report that lands with the thud of a tree falling in a forest where no congressman is listening.

The same patient capital drives BYD's rise from a battery maker in Shenzhen to the world's largest new energy vehicle manufacturer—and here, the simultaneity principle demands a different kind of seeing. BYD does not build cars and then add batteries and then bolt on intelligence. BYD builds the *system* that makes vehicles, batteries, and intelligence the same thing viewed from different angles. Each of the 4.6 million vehicles is a rolling data platform. Each battery is a grid-storage node in waiting. Each God's Eye ADAS installation generates 150 million daily kilometers of driving data that trains the next generation of autonomous models. The car *is* the battery *is* the intelligence *is* the training data—a single organism with multiple visible expressions, the way a Theyyam mask is simultaneously wood, paint, and prayer.

CATL's >39% global battery share compounds the same way. And 3.57 million STEM graduates emerge annually—more than four times America's 820,000—the human capital pipeline that turns strategic intent into deployed reality. Each of those 3.57 million carries a version of a grandmother's whisper: *education is the one asset that cannot be confiscated*. The pipeline is not a government program. It is the aggregate expression of a hundred million family survival strategies, each one carrying the scar tissue of a century when everything else *was* confiscated.

McKinsey the Priest, of course, would diagnose this differently. "The Chinese government," he would intone with the liturgical gravity of a man who has never planted a seed in his life, "is pursuing a multi-vector industrial strategy with synergistic adjacencies across the EV-battery-semiconductor value chain." He would produce a 2×2 matrix. He would recommend a "strategic alignment workshop." And he would miss, entirely, that what he's describing is not a strategy at all—it is a civilization expressing its deepest instinct, the way a river expresses the shape of the land it flows through. You cannot McKinsey a civilization. You can only observe one, and the observation requires a vocabulary that no consulting framework provides.

. . .

The Engineer from Anhui: A Vignette

Call her Chen Yue. She is twenty-eight years old, a systems optimization engineer at DeepSeek's Hangzhou headquarters, and she did not graduate from Tsinghua. She did not study at MIT. She holds a master's degree in applied mathematics from Anhui University of Science and Technology. This provincial institution does not appear in global university rankings, that no Silicon Valley recruiter has heard of, and that produces graduates who are, in the aggregate, the most consequential human capital force in twenty-first-century technology.

Chen Yue's grandmother survived the Cultural Revolution. She was sent to the countryside at sixteen to "learn from the peasants," a euphemism for forced labor that cost her a decade of formal education. Her grandmother speaks about those years rarely and obliquely, in the manner of someone describing a flood—not the water itself, but the waterline on the wall that remains after it recedes. In Kuttanad, we have a word for this kind of memory: *ormappookkal*—memory-flowers, the blooms that grow from buried grief, beautiful and poisonous in equal measure. What the grandmother transmitted to her granddaughter was not bitterness but a principle: education is the one asset that cannot be confiscated. Property can be seized. Businesses can be nationalized. Savings can be inflated away. But knowledge, once internalized, belongs to the mind that holds it.

Sometimes, during a late-night debugging session—the lab quiet, the monitors blue, the coffee machine humming its nocturnal prayer—Chen Yue catches herself staring at her own hands on the keyboard. Her grandmother's hands were cracked and calloused from a decade of forced fieldwork, the knuckles permanently swollen, the fingers bent at angles that told the story of seasons they should never have endured. Chen Yue's hands are soft, uncalloused, precise.

They move across the keys with the fluency of someone who has never doubted that her hands were meant for this. But she knows—in the way that the Theyyam performer knows the ancient wound he carries is not his own but his lineage's—that these hands are her grandmother's hands, continued. The cracked knuckles became the keyboard strokes. The lost decade became the mathematics degree. The *ormappookkal* bloomed in a clean room in Hangzhou, and the flower was code.

This principle—not as philosophy but as a lived survival strategy—is the human firmware that powers China's STEM pipeline. Chen Yue studied mathematics not because a guidance counselor suggested it but because her family understood, at the cellular level of intergenerational trauma, that technical competence is the only reliable currency in a world that can change its rules overnight. When she arrived at DeepSeek, she brought something that no Ivy League pedigree confers: the disciplined humility of a provincial graduate who knows that her opportunity is not guaranteed and must be earned through output, not credentials.

At DeepSeek, her work on inference optimization contributed to the efficiency gains that allowed the V3 model to achieve frontier performance at a fraction of the cost. The specific moment that encapsulates her contribution occurred during the multi-head latent attention optimization, which became one of DeepSeek's signature architectural innovations. She noticed that the key-value cache—the memory structure that stores previous computations during inference—was consuming bandwidth disproportionate to its informational contribution. Her proposed compression scheme, drawn from a technique in her master's thesis on signal processing, reduced the cache footprint without degrading output quality. It was not a breakthrough that earned a standing ovation at NeurIPS. It was a refinement— a small, precise, mathematically rigorous improvement that, when multiplied across billions of inference operations, translated into the cost efficiencies that made the world take notice. This is how the Farmer's system works: not through singular genius but through the compounding of distributed competence.

Across the Pacific, Chen Yue's counterpart—let's call her Jessica, twenty-eight, Stanford MS in Computer Science, $350,000 total compensation at a Magnificent Seven firm—was spending her Tuesday optimizing an algorithm to increase ad click-through rates by 0.3%. Chen Yue was making AI cheaper for the entire planet. Jessica was making it marginally more profitable for one company's advertising division. The Farmer plants crops that feed civilizations. The Hunter's most talented trackers are deployed to find better ways to sell you shoes you don't need.

Chen Yue is not exceptional. She is representative. China's 3.57 million annual STEM graduates do not emerge primarily from elite institutions. They emerge from the vast middle tier—institutions in Anhui, Hubei, Henan, and Sichuan that emphasize rigorous quantitative training and feed a talent pipeline distributed across the entire country rather than concentrated in a handful of coastal meritocratic enclaves. The American STEM pipeline is a funnel: the talent concentrates at the top, in Stanford, MIT, Caltech, and the handful of research universities that compete for the same cohort. The Chinese STEM pipeline is an irrigation system: it distributes competence across the full geography of a continental nation. When Liang Wenfeng needed researchers for DeepSeek, he did not need to compete with Google and Meta for the same fifty Stanford PhDs. He recruited from the vast pool of Chinese graduates whose mathematical training was rigorous, whose ambition was genuine, and whose salary expectations were calibrated to Chinese rather than Silicon Valley living costs.

In the Theyyam ritual, the mask is carved by a thousand hands—and Chen Yue's hands are carving too, though she doesn't know it. Her story is not the story of a prodigy. It is the story of a system that converts intergenerational trauma into intergenerational competence, that transforms the memory of a grandmother's lost decade into a granddaughter's mathematical precision, that understands, at the deepest cultural level, that a civilization's strength is measured not by its most brilliant individual but by the breadth and depth of its collective capability.

· · ·

The BIOS: Humiliation as Firmware

Every operating system has a BIOS—the basic input/output system, the code that executes before the operating system loads. China's strategic BIOS was written between 1839 and 1949, during the Century of Humiliation, and it has never been overwritten. The core directives remain: sovereignty is non-negotiable; technological dependence is existential vulnerability; the strength of the state is measured by its capacity to defend the civilization's productive capacity against external predation.

The Prologue documented the BIOS's installation—the smoke rising from the Yuanmingyuan, the scar tissue that calcified into strategic doctrine, the schoolchildren standing before the broken marble columns. Here, we trace what the BIOS produced when it booted.

The founding of the People's Republic in 1949 was the BIOS's first boot sequence: *sovereignty restored*. Mao's declaration from Tiananmen—"The Chinese people have stood up"—was the system's POST (power-on self-test), confirming that the foundational hardware was functional.

I need to pause here and offer a confession, because the view from the halocline requires honesty about one's own complicity in the currents one describes.

In the Preface, I described a Singapore boardroom in 2006—the marble floors, the McKinsey optimization roadmap, the four-second silence that followed the junior analyst's question. What I did not describe was what happened six months later, after the technology operation had been transferred to China. An email arrived from the Shanghai office reporting that the operation's output exceeded the original facility's peak performance by 30%, achieved at less than half the cost, using engineers whose training my deck had casually filed under "labor cost arbitrage." The email's final line was the one that rewrote my operating system: the operation no longer needed our technical support. *They had learned everything we knew and improved upon it.*

That email is my Halocline credential. Every critique of the Hunter's strategic blindness in this book is written by someone who once shared it—and profited from it—before the boatman's son inside me recognized the current he was swimming in.

The reform era under Deng Xiaoping (1978) was the second boot: *economic capacity was initialized*. Deng's famous dictum—"It doesn't matter whether a cat is black or white, so long as it catches mice"—was the pragmatic instruction set that replaced ideological rigidity with economic empiricism. His equally important instruction—韬光养晦 ("hide your brightness, nourish your darkness")—counseled strategic patience: accumulate capability quietly, avoid confrontation, build strength before displaying it.

Xi Jinping's ascension in 2012 marked the third boot: *strategic deployment initiated*. The Two Centenary Goals—a "moderately prosperous society" by 2021, a "fully developed nation" by 2049—are not aspirational slogans of the kind that Western politicians produce and abandon with each election cycle. They are firmware-level directives. Under Xi, the strategic posture shifted from Deng's 韬光养晦 (hide and bide) to 奋发有为 (strive to achieve). The Belt and Road was announced in 2013. Made in China 2025 was published in 2015. The military modernization drive intensified. The AI national strategy was promulgated. Each initiative drew on the accumulated *shì* of the previous phases—the sovereignty of the Mao era, the economic base of the Deng era—and deployed it outward.

The Chinese strategic concept of 势 (*shì*)—often translated as "strategic momentum" or "accumulated potential energy"—captures this progression with a precision that Western strategic vocabulary lacks. *Shì* is not force applied in a single dramatic moment. It is the patient accumulation of advantage across time, the water behind a dam that builds pressure invisibly until the gates open and the force becomes irresistible. This is the **Time War** at its most fundamental—the competition between civilizations that think in different temporal units. The Farmer measures in generations: Mao's sovereignty, Deng's economic base, Xi's deployment. The Hunter measures in quarters: Q1 earnings, Q2 guidance, the 24-hour news cycle that treats a tariff announcement as a permanent condition, and a Five-Year Plan as a curiosity.

The concept of 卡脖子 (*kǎ bózi*)—literally "strangled neck," meaning a technological chokepoint where dependence on foreign suppliers creates existential vulnerability—connects the Opium Wars directly to modern industrial policy. When the United States placed Huawei on the Entity List in 2019, blocking access to TSMC's advanced node fabrication, the strategic community in Beijing experienced the event not as a trade dispute but as a 21st-century echo of the Opium Wars: a technologically superior power weaponizing its chokepoint advantage to constrain Chinese sovereignty. The BIOS recognized the pattern. The response was automatic: accelerate indigenous capability. Fund SMIC. Expand the Big Fund. Pour resources into DUV lithography workarounds.

The ZTE crisis of 2018—when the U.S. Commerce Department's export ban brought one of China's largest telecommunications firms to the brink of collapse within weeks—produced a phrase that circulated widely in Chinese strategic circles: 核心技术靠化缘是要不来的—"Core technology cannot be obtained by begging." Xi Jinping himself used this formulation. Its resonance was immediate because it spoke directly to the BIOS-level directive: the price of technological dependence is strategic subjugation, and the only remedy is indigenous capability built through patient, systematic, long-term investment. Not next quarter. Not next election cycle. Next generation.

The American strategic response has followed a pattern so consistent it might be called the Committee-Report-Ignore cycle. In 2021, the National Security Commission on Artificial Intelligence released a 756-page report warning that China could surpass the United States in AI within a decade. It was discussed at three think-tank panels, praised in *Foreign Affairs*, and filed in the same institutional memory hole as the seventeen previous reports. Meanwhile, the Farmer was not forming committees. The Farmer was building fabs.

Interlude: Marcus Pulls the Thread

Marcus Chen had not intended to spend his Saturday morning reading about Anhui University of Science and Technology. He had intended to play golf. But the thread he had started pulling on that terrible Friday—the deployment data, the production numbers, the metrics that his Bloomberg terminal had never shown him—had not let him go.

Now he was in his home office in Westchester, coffee growing cold, reading an English-language summary of DeepSeek's hiring practices. The detail that stopped him was not the training cost—he had already absorbed that shock. It was the talent pipeline. Liang Wenfeng did not recruit from Stanford. He recruited from provincial universities whose names Marcus could not pronounce, paying salaries that would not cover his own analyst's bar tab, and the researchers he hired had just built a model that matched the output of systems costing twenty times as much to train.

Marcus opened a new spreadsheet. In the first column, he typed "US Advantage (Assumed)." In the second column, he typed "Actual Status." In the third column, he typed "Source."

He started filling it in. "GPU monopoly (Nvidia)" — "SMIC 5nm DUV; Huawei Ascend." "Autonomous driving (Tesla, Waymo)" — "Apollo Go 300K rides/week." "Battery technology" — "CATL >39% global share." "AI training cost advantage" — "DeepSeek V3: $5.6M compute."

By the time his wife called him for lunch, the spreadsheet had fourteen rows, and the "US Advantage (Assumed)" column was looking less like a ledger of strengths and more like an inventory of comfortable fictions. He saved the spreadsheet with a filename he would later find embarrassingly melodramatic, but which, in the moment, felt like the only honest description available: "Things I Got Wrong."

Then he poured his cold coffee down the sink, made a fresh cup, and called his father again.

"Dad," he said, "tell me about the SOEs."

The Interdependency Web: Why the Harvest Compounds

The Farmer does not plant a single crop. The Farmer cultivates an ecosystem.

This book calls the phenomenon the *interdependency web*—where advances in each domain accelerate all others. Electric vehicles require batteries. Batteries require semiconductors for management systems. Semiconductors require AI for design optimization. AI training requires energy. Energy storage requires battery technology. Export of these technologies requires diplomatic infrastructure. And every component of the web requires human capital—the 3.57 million STEM graduates who constitute the system's circulatory system, carrying capability from node to node. In the Theyyam mask, each thread supports the threads beside it; remove one, and the pattern distorts; weave them together, and the divine face emerges from the fabric.

This analytical blindness is not accidental. It is structural. Wall Street's research apparatus is organized by sector: the semiconductor analyst covers semiconductors, the auto analyst covers autos, and the energy analyst covers energy. Each analyst is incentivized to know everything about one tree and nothing about the forest. The result is a research ecosystem that can tell you CATL's quarterly shipments to the nearest megawatt-hour, but cannot tell you how CATL's battery dominance connects to BYD's vehicle production, connects to DeepSeek's training efficiency, connects to the STEM graduates who make all of it possible.

This is what Guanzi understood: rice, trees, and people are not three separate investments with three separate returns. They are three aspects of a single agricultural ecosystem. Rice feeds the people who plant the trees whose shade protects the rice. The compound return exceeds the sum of the individual returns, because the system creates emergent properties that no single component could generate alone.

. . .

Institutional Design: Governing the Small Fish with Care

Lao Tzu wrote that governing a great country is like cooking a small fish: too much handling ruins it. The Chinese governance model embodies this principle through a layered system that combines centralized strategic direction with decentralized operational execution—what Chinese strategists call the interplay of *Zhèng* (正, orthodox/regular forces) and *Qí* (奇, unorthodox/irregular forces).

The halocline reveals its richest biology here. In Kuttanad's backwaters, life concentrates at the boundary layer where fresh water meets salt, because the nutrient density is highest at the interface. China's most consequential innovations emerge from an analogous boundary: the interface between state direction (*Zhèng*) and entrepreneurial improvisation (*Qí*). Not in the pure command of the Five-Year Plan, and not in the pure chaos of the market, but in the nutrient-rich zone where the two currents meet. DeepSeek emerged at this boundary. BYD scaled at this boundary. CATL dominates at this boundary.

The Five-Year Plan is the *Zhèng*—the orthodox framework that sets strategic direction and creates the irrigation channels through which innovation flows. DeepSeek, BYD, and CATL are the *Qí*—the unorthodox forces that operate within the strategic framework but with tactical freedom. Liang Wenfeng's decision to fund DeepSeek from High-Flyer's balance sheet was a *Qí* move within the *Zhèng* framework of China's AI ambitions. Wang Chuanfu's decision to make BYD's God's Eye ADAS standard across 21 models at no additional cost was a *Qí* move within the *Zhèng* framework of Made in China 2025.

The system is not without pathology. The *Zhèng* can become rigid, stifling the very *Qí* it is meant to enable. Political priorities can override economic logic, as when the 2021 tech crackdown destroyed hundreds of billions in market value. Chapter 11 will address these failures directly. But the structural principle—orthodox framework enabling unorthodox innovation—is the institutional mechanism that enables the Farmer to plant in all seasons simultaneously.

. . .

The $125 Trillion Root System: State-Owned Enterprises as Civilizational Architecture

The companies this book documents—BYD, CATL, DeepSeek, Huawei—are the visible harvest. They are the stalks that break the surface. But the harvest grows from a root system that Western analysts consistently underestimate because it operates below the surface, in the dark, in the patient silence where nutrients move from soil to stem.

China's state-owned enterprises—numbering over 300,000, managing combined assets exceeding $125 trillion—constitute the largest single concentration of productive capital in human history. They are not companies in the Western sense. They are civilizational infrastructure. Approximately 75% of Chinese companies on the Fortune Global 500 are state-owned enterprises. This is not a collection of companies. It is a parallel economic universe, operating on rules written in Five-Year Plans and funded by a treasury that answers to a single party with a 2049 centenary goal.

The asymmetry, once you see it, makes every sector-by-sector Western competitive analysis read like a report on a swimming race in which one competitor is allowed to use the current and the other must swim against it. A Chinese solar panel manufacturer can sell at 40% below cost for five years to corner the global market. An American company doing that? Shareholder lawsuits by quarter two, a Carl Icahn letter by quarter three, and a bankruptcy filing by year two. The Hunter is not bidding against a company. The Hunter is bidding against a country.

CSSC (China State Shipbuilding Corporation), with $120 billion in assets, builds 60%-plus of the world's commercial vessels *and* the PLA Navy's expanding fleet. CRRC rolls out high-speed rail cars for domestic lines *and* for Belt and Road partners from Jakarta to Nairobi. State Grid Corporation—$700 billion in assets, the largest utility on Earth—delivers industrial electricity at $0.03–0.05 per kilowatt-hour, the energy substrate that makes every Chinese factory, data center, and AI training cluster cost-competitive against Western counterparts paying three to five times more. And the provincial SOEs—thousands of them, invisible to global markets—function as the Farmer's regional irrigation channels: building roads to industrial parks, laying fiber-optic cable to fourth-tier cities, constructing the mundane physical infrastructure that makes the spectacular digital infrastructure possible.

This is the Time War's most formidable weapon: capital that does not demand quarterly returns, that does not flinch at a decade of losses, that measures success not in EPS growth but in industrial dominance achieved before the next Five-Year Plan expires.

None of this suggests the SOE system is pure or efficient. It is riddled with the pathologies of any system where political loyalty can substitute for commercial competence. But the structural advantage is real and compounding. The boatman does not claim the river is clean. He claims the river is powerful. And the current, however murky, is flowing in one direction.

Sarah callback — patient capital contrast

Twelve hundred miles from the SOE substrate, in a city the root system has never touched, Sarah Kowalski sits at her grandmother's desk in Youngstown, Ohio, performing her own arithmetic of patience. Her patience is not backed by an ecosystem of state-owned enterprises worth>$125 trillion. It is backed by a yellow legal pad, a dwindling customer base, and the stubborn conviction that a home goods boutique on a hollowed-out Main Street is worth keeping alive because her grandmother believed it was worth opening.

The contrast is not sentimental. It is structural. The Farmer's patient capital flows through institutional channels designed to sustain investment over decades—Five-Year Plans, SOE mandates, the PCCR compounding at rates the quarterly earnings cycle cannot match. Sarah's patient capital is personal savings, a second mortgage she has not yet taken, and the revenue from ceramics whose supply chain she is trying to relocate from Zhejiang to North Carolina. The Farmer's patience is *funded*. Sarah's patience is *mortgaged*. Both require the same human quality—the refusal to abandon what you have planted because the season has not yet delivered. But one is a civilizational strategy, and the other is a woman's wager against the current. The halocline between them is the halocline between systems, not between individuals. Sarah's patience is not inferior. Her *infrastructure* is.

. . .

The Five Thousand Seeds: China's AI+ Deployment Layer

While the West debates whether OpenAI or Anthropic will "win" the AI race—a framing that reveals the Hunter's gladiatorial instinct, the reflexive reduction of every competition to a two-horse contest with a single trophy—the Farmer has planted 5,000 seeds.

More than 5,000 AI companies have been registered in China since 2023. Not 5,000 chatbot startups chasing the same consumer market. Five thousand companies, each applying artificial intelligence to a specific deployment domain: logistics optimization in Chengdu, crop yield prediction in Henan, medical diagnostics in Wuhan, smart city traffic management in Shenzhen, predictive maintenance in Dongguan, and educational adaptive learning in Chongqing.

In Hangzhou, Chen Yue's phone buzzes during a coffee break. A message from Li Wei, her roommate from Anhui University, now working at SinoAgri Intelligence in Zhengzhou—one of the 5,000 seeds. Li Wei's team has just deployed an AI model, built on an open-source architecture that shares DNA with DeepSeek's efficiency innovations, to predict wheat rust infestations across Henan Province's 540,000 hectares of winter wheat. The model runs on Huawei Ascend chips. The connectivity runs on a 5G network built by ZTE. The weather data feeds from a State Grid meteorological array. Li Wei's message is casual: *"Hey, your cache compression thing? We adapted it for our sensor data pipeline. Works beautifully. Buying you dinner next time you're in Zhengzhou."* Chen Yue smiles and goes back to her screen. She does not know—cannot know—that this small exchange is the interdependency web operating at the human scale.

The "+" in AI+ is the crucial character. In Silicon Valley, AI is the product. In China, AI is the fertilizer. The product is the sector it transforms. AI+Manufacturing. AI+Agriculture. AI+Healthcare. AI+Logistics. AI+Education. AI+Municipal Governance. Each "+" represents a deployment node, and each node draws from the same open-source irrigation system: DeepSeek's architecture provides the model. SMIC's chips provide the silicon. Huawei's 5G provides the connectivity. CATL's batteries power the edge devices. The SOE ecosystem provides the capital, the infrastructure, and the institutional patience to let each seed grow without demanding quarterly revenue until the roots reach water.

When those 5,000 seedlings mature—and they are maturing, quietly, below the threshold of Western media attention, the way bamboo grows invisibly underground for years before shooting upward at a meter per day—the Farmer will not have won an AI race. The Farmer will have made the race irrelevant by deploying AI so broadly, so deeply, and so inexpensively that the concept of a single AI "winner" will seem as quaint as asking who "won" electricity.

. . .

The External Irrigation: Belt and Road as Ecosystem Extension

The Belt and Road Initiative is the external expression of the same patient capital logic that drives China's domestic industrial strategy. Where domestic policy cultivates technological sovereignty, the BRI cultivates relational sovereignty—a network of economic dependencies, infrastructure commitments, and institutional ties that reconstitute, in modern form, the tributary relationships that defined China's position in the pre-colonial Asian order.

Cumulative BRI engagement reached $1.399 trillion by the end of 2025, with a record $213.5 billion in new deals signed that year alone—a 75% increase over 2024—across 350 projects in 150 countries. The Lagos-Calabar coastal railway, completed in early 2026, is the BRI's most recent milestone: 1,402 kilometers of standard-gauge rail connecting Nigeria's commercial capital to the southeastern coast, built in thirty-six months at a cost that Nigeria's previous Western-financed rail study estimated would require twelve years and three times the budget. On the day the first passenger service ran, the Nigerian transport minister tweeted a photograph of the Lagos terminal—gleaming, functional, Chinese-built—with the caption: "Infrastructure is not a promise. It is a train." The Farmer does not debate infrastructure policy. The Farmer builds the train.

Every Chinese-built port, railway, power plant, and 5G base station creates a node in the web of interdependencies. The port serves commercial shipping, generates revenue for the Chinese operator, establishes Chinese construction standards as the regional norm, and creates the physical infrastructure through which Chinese EVs, batteries, solar panels, and telecommunications equipment enter local markets. The evolution from physical to digital infrastructure marks BRI's most strategically consequential phase. A country that runs on Chinese 5G standards, processes payments through Chinese fintech platforms, and stores its citizens' data in Chinese-built cloud infrastructure has entered a relationship with Beijing that makes the Hambantota port's 99-year lease look like a casual handshake.

America's counteroffensive to BRI was the "Partnership for Global Infrastructure and Investment," rebranded from the "Build Back Better World" initiative, itself rebranded from… well, the rebranding is actually the most notable thing about it. As of this writing, the program has pledged $600 billion in global infrastructure investment, of which a fraction has been deployed, at a pace that would take roughly 40 years to match what China builds in 5. The Farmer planted a forest. The Hunter held a press conference about his plan to plant a garden, released a glossy brochure, formed a sub-committee to study the brochure, got distracted by midterms, rebranded the brochure, held another press conference about the rebranded brochure, and then blamed the forest for growing too fast.

. . .

BOATMAN'S LEDGER

Chapter 1

LEDGER TOOL #2: THE PATIENT CAPITAL COMPOUND RATE

The Māyā Meter (Prologue) measures the gap between narrative and deployment. The Patient Capital Compound Rate measures the *acceleration* of returns across domains that feed into one another. Where Western investment analysis calculates returns on individual assets, the PCCR captures the compounding effect of simultaneous multi-domain cultivation.

MEASUREMENT

For each $1 invested by the Big Fund in semiconductor capability, track the downstream effects: SMIC's 5nm DUV production enables Huawei Ascend chips, which reduce DeepSeek's training cost dependency on Nvidia, which funds further AI research, which optimizes BYD's God's Eye ADAS, which generates 150 million daily kilometers of driving data, which trains better autonomous models. The compound rate across this single chain exceeds the direct semiconductor return by an estimated 3–5x over a decade.

AI+ DEPLOYMENT SIGNAL

Track the 5,000+ AI companies not by individual revenue but by sectoral penetration rate. When AI+ deployment reaches 40%+ across three or more industrial sectors, the compound effects become self-sustaining. Current estimates: manufacturing AI+ penetration at 25–30%, logistics at 20–25%, agriculture at 15–20%. The bamboo is still underground. But the root system is mature.

THE BOATMAN'S WAGER

If you're still pricing Chinese industrial companies as single-sector plays, you're pricing them wrong. The interdependency web means that a position in BYD implicitly entails a position in the battery ecosystem, the AI training pipeline, the SOE substrate, and the STEM pipeline. Price the ecosystem, not the organ.

Chapter 1 Data Anchors: Big Fund $100B+ | Made in China 2025: 70% self-sufficiency target | BYD system: 4.6M vehicles / 150M daily km driving data / God's Eye ADAS | CATL >39% global battery share | 3.57M vs. 820K STEM graduates (4.4:1) | SOE assets >$125T+ / 300,000+ entities / 75% of Fortune Global 500 Chinese companies | AI+ companies 5,000+ | BRI $1.399T cumulative / $213.5B new deals in 2025 | State Grid $0.03–0.05/kWh | CSSC $120B / 60%+ global shipbuilding | Zhèng/Qí institutional design

CULTIVATION DEPTH SCORE: 22/25. Points deducted: −1 for semiconductor frontier gap—SMIC's 5nm DUV works, but Liu Jing's team in Chapter 8 loses sleep over every percentage point of yield. −1 for BRI debt sustainability questions—the Hambantota lesson reverberates. −1 for authoritarian innovation paradox—the same system that enables the Zhèng/Qí dance also conducts periodic crackdowns that destroy the Qí's confidence; Chapter 11 confronts this directly.

. . .

A Word to the Reasonable Reader

The reasonable reader, having absorbed this chapter's account of China's multi-domain cultivation, may feel a question forming: *If the Farmer's model is so formidable, why has the Hunter dominated for so long?*

Good. Hold that question. It is the right one, and it will receive a thorough answer in Chapter 2. But here is the preview: the Hunter's strengths are real, differently configured, and perhaps more resilient than this account might suggest. The Transformer architecture is American. The GPU ecosystem is American. The fundamental science of deep learning advanced at American and Canadian universities. The venture capital model that incubated Google, Apple, and Nvidia is a genuine institutional innovation with no Chinese equivalent. These are not peripheral contributions; they are the foundational breakthroughs upon which the entire edifice of modern AI—including DeepSeek—stands.

The Farmer's model explains deployment, compounding, and patient accumulation of *shì* across domains. It does not explain a breakthrough discovery. It does not explain why the Transformer was invented at Google Brain and not at Tsinghua. The honest analyst—the one this book is written for—must hold both truths simultaneously: the Farmer deploys better, and the Hunter discovers more. The question is which advantage proves more durable in a world where deployment is compounding and discovery is increasingly commoditized.

Carry that tension forward. The performer's hands have completed the first mudra. The deity has been called by name, and across thirteen domains, the name echoes: 居安思危. In peace, prepare for danger. In abundance, plant for scarcity. The Farmer never forgets. The question for Chapter 2 is whether the Hunter ever remembers.

• • •

RITUAL STAGE MARKER

The rhythm quickens. The performer's feet stamp the earth—each stamp a seed driven into soil. The first deity has answered. But the invocation is not complete. There are twelve more names to call. And from across the performance ground, the rival spirit stirs—the Hunter, drawn by the drumbeat, already reaching for his bow.

CHAPTER 2

The Hunter's Frenzy

The Illusion of the Immediate

"Speed is the essence of war." — Sun Tzu, The Art of War, Chapter XI

The Hunter-deity strikes with terrible speed. His kill feeds the village tonight. Tomorrow's forest offers no guarantees.

— after the Theyyam tradition

. . .

Undercurrent: Strategic Speed vs. Reactive Speed

Sun Tzu praises speed. But the speed he praises is *strategic* speed—the capacity to concentrate force at the decisive point before the adversary recognizes the point's significance. The Hunter mistakes this for *reactive* speed—the capacity to announce, to escalate, to dominate the next news cycle. The Chinese proverb 聪明反被聪明误 ("cleverness defeats itself") describes the pathology precisely: the more vigorously the Hunter pursues the prey, the more completely it exhausts itself, and the more territory it concedes to the Farmer who never sprinted.

The complementary principle is 以静制动—"using stillness to control movement." While the Hunter hurls tariffs, detonates trade relationships, and flails from escalation to pause to re-escalation, the Farmer stands still. Not passive. Still. The stillness of a civilization that has redirected canals while the Hunter was busy damaging his own levees. In Kuttanad, the boatman knows this principle as the difference between the paddle-stroke and the current: the man who fights the current exhausts himself by noon; the man who reads the current arrives before dawn.

But there is a deeper halocline here—one that separates two civilizational ontologies rather than merely two strategies. The West inherits from Descartes, through Adam Smith, to Milton Friedman, a philosophical architecture that progressively compressed the time horizon of strategic action until the quarterly earnings report became the fundamental unit of economic reality. Descartes' *cogito ergo sum* established the isolated, reasoning individual as the fundamental unit—severing the self from community, tradition, and the long temporal arcs that agricultural civilizations take for granted. *I think, therefore I am*—not "I plant, therefore I will harvest in a season I may not live to see." Smith's invisible hand proposed that individual self-interest, aggregated through markets, produces optimal collective outcomes—a proposition that works with remarkable efficiency for allocating consumer goods and with catastrophic inadequacy for allocating strategic industrial capacity across decades. Friedman's shareholder primacy doctrine compressed the corporate time horizon to its terminal point: the quarterly earnings report.

The Eastern counterpart is older and operates on a different temporal frequency. The Confucian concept of 天下 (*tiānxià*)—"all under heaven"—treats governance as a civilizational obligation measured in centuries, not cycles. The Legalist tradition of Sang Hongyang's "Salt and Iron" debates (81 BCE) established that state control of strategic commodities is not an economic intervention but an ontological premise: certain things belong to the civilization, not the market. The halocline between these two philosophical currents is the book's deepest undercurrent.

. . .

The Four Sacraments of Self-Destruction

The Hunter's frenzy is not random thrashing. It follows a liturgy—four sacred rituals of self-destruction that American capitalism performs with the solemn regularity of a religion that has confused self-harm with devotion. McKinsey, the Priest officiates. Milton the Trickster Economist provides the theological justification. And the congregation murmurs "Amen" and checks its stock options.

These are *time-horizon pathologies*—the specific mechanisms by which the Hunter loses the civilizational Time War. Each Sacrament compresses the strategic time horizon further, and each compression creates an advantage that the Farmer harvests without lifting a finger.

The First Sacrament: The Extraction Death Spiral. Between 2010 and 2023, S&P 500 companies spent approximately $5.3 trillion on stock buybacks—more than they invested in research, development, and capital equipment combined. In 2022 alone, buybacks reached $922.7 billion, exceeding the federal government's combined spending on education, transportation, and infrastructure. Corporate investment in physical plant as a percentage of profits has collapsed from roughly 50% in the 1970s to under 20% today. The Hunter is not just buying back his own stock. He is systematically defunding the physical infrastructure of productive capacity.

Meet Bobby Buyback—sleek, confident, compensated in stock options that vest quarterly. Bobby does not build factories. Bobby does not fund R&D labs. Bobby buys back his own company's stock, inflating EPS without actually increasing earnings, triggering his stock-price-linked compensation clause, collecting his bonus, and repeating the cycle with the mechanical devotion of a prosperity-gospel preacher who has mistaken the collection plate for the sermon. Bobby's hands are steady as he signs the authorization on the fifty-seventh floor of a Midtown tower. Below him, unseen, Sarah Kowalski's margins are thinning in Youngstown. The connection is invisible to Bobby, which is not the same as nonexistent.

Boeing is Bobby's masterwork. $43 billion in buybacks between 2013 and 2019—nearly double its R&D investment— while the 737 MAX's flawed MCAS safety system killed 346 people. The Farmer filed the entire exercise under "Voluntary Industrial Disarmament."

The Second Sacrament: The Efficiency Trap. Milton the Trickster's most seductive sermon: efficiency is always good, redundancy is always waste. The sermon produced just-in-time supply chains that collapsed at the first sneeze of a pandemic, a semiconductor industry that outsourced its most advanced capability to a single island 100 miles off the Chinese coast, and a pharmaceutical supply chain in which 80% of active pharmaceutical ingredients are manufactured in China and India. When COVID hit, "just-in-time" became "just-out-of-everything." When the CHIPS Act finally passed, the fabs it funded would not produce chips until 2027 at the earliest—by which time SMIC had already demonstrated 5nm production using DUV lithography that the Western semiconductor establishment had declared impossible.

The Third Sacrament: The Vanity Metric Delusion. The Hunter measures everything that glitters and nothing that grows. Tesla's market cap exceeded $1 trillion for 1.64 million vehicles. BYD's sat at $107 billion for 4.6 million. The vanity metric said Tesla was ten times more valuable. The deployment metric showed that BYD was nearly three times as productive. The Starbucks CEO earned $57.8 million in 2024—a ratio of 6,666:1 against the company's median employee wage.

The Fourth Sacrament: The Speed Fallacy. Ninety days is the liturgical unit. Any investment that cannot demonstrate returns within four quarters is, by definition, a failure of discipline. Ford lost $4.8 billion on its EV division in 2023; the market punished the stock. BYD invested comparable sums over a decade, sustained by the SOE substrate described in Chapter 1, and emerged as the world's largest EV manufacturer. The Speed Fallacy is not about actual speed—the Farmer's factory can retool faster than Detroit's. The Speed Fallacy is about *temporal frame*: the difference between optimizing for this quarter's earnings call and optimizing for this century's industrial architecture.

To hold the four together as a single diagnostic: the **Extraction Death Spiral** cannibalizes the industrial base. The **Efficiency Trap** surrenders resilience for margin. The **Vanity Metric Delusion** prices narrative over harvest. The **Speed Fallacy** collapses the strategic time horizon to ninety days. Each Sacrament is internally coherent. Together, they constitute a liturgy of civilizational self-destruction performed with the genuine conviction that the ritual is producing salvation.

. . .

The Voter Who Keeps Waiting: A Vignette from Ohio

Sarah Kowalski is forty-seven years old. She owns a small home goods boutique in Youngstown, Ohio—the same shop on West Federal Street we met in the Prologue, the one her grandmother Helen opened in 1987—and she has voted for Barack Obama, Donald Trump, Joe Biden, and Donald Trump again. A voting pattern that makes her incomprehensible to the partisan mind and perfectly comprehensible to anyone who understands that Sarah votes for whoever promises to fix the thing that is broken, and the thing that is broken has not changed in twenty years: her town's economy is hollowed out, her customers are stretched thin, and nobody in Washington has delivered on the promises that got them elected.

When the Liberation Day tariffs hit, Sarah did what she always does: she called her suppliers. The Vietnamese manufacturer quoted a 46% surcharge. Sarah pulled the labels from her latest shipment and traced the supply chain backward. The ceramics were Chinese, the glaze compounds were Chinese, the kiln technology was Chinese, and the factory was owned by a Chinese parent company that had relocated final assembly across the border specifically to circumvent the tariff wall. Sarah was paying a 46% surcharge on goods that, for all practical purposes, were Chinese goods wearing a Vietnamese costume.

Sarah is not an economist. She thinks in the currency of a small-business owner: *Can I pay my employees this month?* When the President said the tariffs would bring manufacturing back to America, she believed him—not because she had read the economic literature on tariff incidence, but because the man stood in the Rose Garden and said it would work, and nobody in politics had offered her a better story.

Manufacturing did not return to Youngstown. What returned was the particular feeling of being a prop in someone else's narrative. The tariffs raised the price of everything Sarah's customers bought by a percentage that economists would call "modest" and that Sarah's customers called "the reason I'm shopping at Walmart now."

A Main Street Alliance survey found that 81.5% of small business owners raised or considered raising prices in response to the tariffs. 41.7% delayed or considered delaying expansion. Nearly one-third anticipated layoffs. Sarah is all three statistics in a single human being.

But Sarah is not merely a statistic in a tragedy. On a Tuesday evening, after closing the shop early because foot traffic had thinned to a trickle, she sat at her grandmother's desk—the same desk Helen Kowalski had used to balance the books since 1987—and began searching. Alternative suppliers. Domestic manufacturers. Artisans in North Carolina making ceramics that weren't routed through four Chinese provinces. She found three possibilities, requested samples, and ran the numbers on a yellow legal pad. The margins were tighter. The product was different. The story she could tell her customers—"made here, for us, by people you could drive to visit"—was worth something, though she wasn't sure how much. Sarah Kowalski was not going to close her grandmother's shop without a fight. She was going to read the current, adjust the oar, and arrive alive. Whether the current would let her was another question entirely.

. . .

Interlude: *Marcus Argues with His Analyst*

Marcus Chen's Monday morning meeting with his junior analyst, Kevin, did not go as Kevin expected.

"The buyback data," Marcus said, before Kevin had finished opening his laptop. "Pull the buyback data for the Mag Seven. The last five years. Total dollars. Compare to R&D spend. Then pull CATL's capital expenditure over the same period. And BYD's. Compare the ratio of buybacks-to-capex for American firms versus Chinese firms."

Kevin opened a fresh spreadsheet with the expression of a man who suspects his boss may have had a psychotic break over the weekend but is too junior to say so.

"Also," Marcus continued, "pull the CEO compensation data for the S&P 500. Median ratio to median employee. And then pull it for BYD, CATL, and SMIC. I want to see the incentive structures side by side."

"I want you to compare American incentive structures to Chinese incentive structures. Because I've been pricing American companies based on what their CEOs are incentivized to do—which is boost EPS through buybacks—and I haven't been pricing Chinese companies based on what their leaders are incentivized to do —which is to build productive capacity. That ends today."

Kevin pulled the data. But Kevin was not a pushover. By Tuesday, he was back, and this time he was pushing.

"Marcus, the BYD numbers. They don't look right. Or they look *too* right. These reinvestment ratios—91% of free cash flow into capacity expansion? That's not a company. That's a government program wearing a corporate mask. How do we know the books aren't cooked?"

Marcus paused. It was a fair question—the kind of question he himself had asked reflexively for two decades. The *māyā* was powerful precisely because it had a rational kernel: Chinese corporate disclosures *are* less transparent than those in the United States. The audit standards *are* different. The government *does* intervene in ways that distort market signals.

"You're right to be skeptical," Marcus said slowly. "But here's what I need you to sit with. The 4.6 million BYD vehicles are not accounting artifacts. They're physical objects. They exist on roads in 70 countries. You can count them from satellite imagery. CATL's >39% market share means that >39% of every EV battery on Earth came from one company. That's not a disclosure issue. That's a deployment fact. The question isn't whether the books are clean. The question is whether the harvest is real. And the harvest"—he pointed at the spreadsheet—"is sitting on roads from Shenzhen to São Paulo."

Kevin stared at the chart. American Mag Seven companies had returned 68% of their free cash flow to shareholders through buybacks and dividends over the preceding five years. BYD had reinvested 91%. The chart did not prove that China was "better." It proved that the two systems were optimizing for fundamentally different outcomes—one for this quarter's stock price, the other for this decade's industrial architecture—and that Marcus's models, which assumed both systems shared the same optimization function, were measuring one game's score with another game's rulebook.

Kevin was quiet for a long time. Then: "So what do we do?"

"We learn to keep score in both languages," Marcus said. "And we start by admitting we've been monolingual."

. . .

The Tariff Saga as Five-Act Parable: Through the Chinese Planner's Eyes

What follows is the tariff saga recounted not as American political drama but as the Chinese strategic establishment experienced it: a five-act parable in which the Hunter's greatest virtues—decisiveness, boldness, willingness to act—become the instruments of his undoing.

Act I: The Declaration (April 2, 2025). Executive Order 14257. Universal 10% tariff, escalating to 145% on Chinese goods. "We're going to start being smart," the President declares, "and we're going to start being very wealthy again." The Chinese planner's assessment: *the Hunter has just announced his hunting route. He believes this shows strength. It shows us exactly where to place the traps.*

Act II: The Escalation (April 3–8, 2025). China imposed retaliatory tariffs of 34%. The administration escalated to 84%, then 125%, and finally 145%—in the span of six days. The rate then paused at 10% for 90 days, reimposed at varying rates, modified with exemptions, partially reversed, and settled at 29.3%—a trajectory that, if plotted on a graph, resembles less an economic policy than the vital signs of a man who has simultaneously won the lottery and been informed that his house is on fire.

And so it proved. China's 2025 trade surplus surpassed $1 trillion—*despite* the tariffs. The most aggressive tariff regime since 1930 did not reduce China's trade surplus. It increased it. The yuan strengthened to its firmest level against the dollar in fourteen months.

Act III: The Pause and the Flail (April 9–December 2025). Nine days after Liberation Day, having witnessed $6.6 trillion evaporate, the administration paused the country-specific escalations for ninety days. The S&P rallied 9.52% in a single session. The President declared the rally proved his strategy was working, which is the financial equivalent of crashing a car, calling a tow truck, and then declaring that the successful tow proves your driving skills.

The Chinese planner's assessment: *the Hunter cannot commit. He escalates and retreats in the same breath. Every pause signals that the tariffs are negotiable. The Farmer does not need to defeat the tariffs. The Farmer needs only to wait. The Hunter will defeat himself.*

Act IV: The Reckoning (February 20, 2026). The Supreme Court, in *Learning Resources, Inc. v. Trump*, ruled 6–3 that IEEPA does not authorize the President to impose tariffs. Chief Justice Roberts, joined by Justices Sotomayor, Kagan, Gorsuch, Barrett, and Jackson, wrote: "Based on two words separated by sixteen others in IEEPA—'regulate' and 'importation'—the President asserts the independent power to impose tariffs on imports from any country, of any product, at any rate, for any amount of time. Those words cannot bear such weight."

The ruling affirmed something the Chinese strategic establishment had been watching with a complicated emotion rarely attributed to authoritarian systems: genuine envy. The American system contains an institutional antibody—an independent judiciary—that can correct executive overreach even when the executive wields extraordinary political power. The Farmer has no equivalent mechanism. When the CCP errs, there is no Roberts to write that "those words cannot bear such weight." The error compounds until the leadership chooses to acknowledge it, which may take decades.

This is the halocline's freshwater current in a system that appears entirely salt. The Hunter's chaos contains a hidden order: the capacity to heal itself. The SCOTUS ruling *is* the freshwater that prevents the American system from becoming entirely toxic. The Farmer cannot replicate it. And the Chinese planner, reading the ruling in her office, felt that complicated envy again: *Their system can correct. Ours can only endure.*

Act V: The Aftermath (February–March 2026). Over $160 billion extracted from more than 330,000 importers, now subject to refund proceedings requiring "millions of man-hours." The administration pivoted to Section 122 of the Trade Act of 1974 to impose 10% global tariffs. But Section 122 contains a 150-day sunset clause—placing the Congressional vote squarely in July, four months before the midterms. Every member of the House would need to cast a publicly recorded vote on whether to maintain tariffs that the Supreme Court has already ruled illegal in their previous form.

$\cdots$

The Seven Digital Emperors: Anatomy of Extraction and Latent Power

The Four Sacraments describe the liturgy. It is time to anatomize the congregation's high priests—not as a field guide this time but as a surgical examination. Because each of the Magnificent Seven contains a paradox that is the paradox of the Hunter writ corporate: enormous latent capability aimed, with extraordinary precision, at objectives that do not serve the civilization that hosts them.

In Kuttanad, there is a story about seven boats, each the finest on the backwater—teak-hulled, coir-rigged, capable of carrying a village's entire harvest to market. But the seven boats were owned by merchants who used them only to ferry peacock feathers to the temple fair, because peacock feathers fetched the highest price per kilogram on the shortest route. The harvest rotted on the dock. The boats were magnificent. The village starved. The problem was not the boats. The problem was what the boats were aimed at.

The Magnificent Seven—Apple, Microsoft, Nvidia, Amazon, Alphabet, Meta, Tesla—represent a collective $20 trillion-plus in market capitalization, $300 billion in annual R&D, and a combined employee count smaller than the population of Wyoming. They are the most formidable concentration of technical talent, computational infrastructure, and innovation capital ever assembled under seven corporate roofs. They are aimed at peacock feathers.

Meta: The Fisherman Who Poisons His Own Lake

$91 billion in stock buybacks between 2017 and 2024. Not $91 billion in R&D. Not $91 billion in American manufacturing. $91 billion returned to shareholders while the company's core product—the algorithmic engagement engine—radicalized electorates across four continents. Myanmar's military junta used Facebook to coordinate the genocide of the Rohingya. Frances Haugen's leaked internal research documented what the company's own data scientists already knew: the algorithm systematically amplified content that triggered outrage, because outrage generated engagement, because engagement generated advertising revenue, because advertising revenue generated buybacks, because buybacks generated executive compensation. The cycle is the Four Sacraments in their purest biochemical form: extract the social fabric's cohesion, convert the debris to revenue, buy back the stock, collect the bonus.

In Kuttanad, the fishermen have a word for the man who poisons the lake to stun the fish: *vishakaaran*—the poison-user. The *vishakaaran* catches more fish than anyone else on any given day. But the lake dies. And when the lake dies, the village dies with it. Meta's engagement optimization is algorithmic *vishakaaranship* applied to the democratic commons. The lake is American social cohesion. The fish are attention. The poison is outrage-optimization. The catch is $91 billion in buybacks.

The Farmer's Mirror: WeChat. Not a social media platform in the American sense—a deployment infrastructure. Payments, municipal services, healthcare access, transportation booking, government communication, and digital identity. WeChat monetizes utility, not addiction. The distinction is civilizational: one platform extracts attention from its users; the other delivers services to its citizens. Both generate revenue. One generates social capital in the process. The other consumes it.

The latent antibody: Meta's AI research lab produced LLaMA—the open-source large language model that democratized access to frontier AI capabilities. Meta's Reality Labs employs some of the most talented computer vision researchers on Earth. If Meta's $40 billion annual R&D were aimed at medical diagnostics, agricultural optimization, educational deployment, and municipal AI infrastructure rather than engagement maximization, it would be the civilian deployment engine that Chapter 12's adaptations prescribe. The boat is magnificent. The harvest is rotting on the dock.

Alphabet: The Farmer Who Owns the Best Seed but Plants It in the Wrong Field

Google's researchers invented the Transformer architecture—the foundational innovation behind every large language model on Earth—and then watched a hedge fund quant in Hangzhou deploy it more efficiently than every Google lab combined. Google spent $45 billion on R&D in 2024. DeepSeek spent $5.6 million to train a model that sent Nvidia's stock into a $589 billion freefall. The Forest birthed the seed. The Field grew the forest.

The irony deepens at street level. Google's Waymo operates the most technologically sophisticated autonomous driving system in the world—per-vehicle sensor suites costing $175,000, deployed in a handful of geofenced American zones at unit economics so unfavorable that the company declines to publish them. Apollo Go processes 300,000 rides per week at unit economics breakeven across multiple Chinese cities at $1.50 per ride. Waymo is the ceiling. Apollo Go is the floor. And as Chapter 11 will demonstrate, the floor is where 1.4 billion people live.

Alphabet's DeepMind invented AlphaFold—predicting the structure of virtually every known protein, a breakthrough that will transform drug discovery for decades. This is the Hunter at his most brilliant: curiosity-driven research producing paradigm-shifting science. But AlphaFold's commercial deployment has been cautious, academic, and incremental. Meanwhile, Chinese biotech companies have licensed $66 billion in novel molecules to Western pharma firms, deploying at a pace that treats the biology as infrastructure, not publication.

The latent antibody: Google owns the Transformer, DeepMind, Waymo, the world's largest search index, YouTube's data corpus, and a cloud platform serving millions of enterprises. If Alphabet's resources were aimed at American manufacturing optimization, autonomous infrastructure deployment, and AI-powered public services rather than advertising targeting that accounts for 80% of revenue, it would be the computational backbone of a national deployment strategy. Instead, the world's most powerful information company optimizes for which advertisement you see after searching for "cheap flights."

Amazon: The Kettuvallam That Carries Everything but Brings Nothing Home

The most sophisticated logistics network in human history—capable of delivering 10 billion packages per year to virtually any American doorstep within 48 hours—is, in strategic terms, a reverse supply chain: it accelerates the flow of foreign-manufactured goods into American homes while doing nothing to build the domestic manufacturing capacity that would produce goods worth delivering. Amazon's logistics infrastructure is the *kettuvallam* that carries cargo from every port but brings nothing home to the village that built it.

The digital panopticon operates internally with Taylorist precision: warehouse workers' movements are tracked to the second, bathroom breaks are timed, injury rates exceed the industry average, while productivity targets escalate quarterly. This is the First Sacrament—extraction of maximum labor value—applied to human bodies rather than corporate balance sheets. Meanwhile, Amazon's marketplace data enables the company to identify successful third-party products and develop competing versions—turning its platform sellers into unpaid product-development scouts.

The strategic vulnerability: 80% of the active pharmaceutical ingredients flowing through American medicine cabinets originate from supply chains that touch the Farmer's fields. Amazon Pharmacy optimizes the delivery of pills whose active ingredients are manufactured in Zhejiang. The Efficiency Trap surrendered the pharmacy. Amazon optimized the delivery.

The latent antibody: Amazon's logistics network, warehouse infrastructure, and AWS cloud platform represent the physical and digital backbone of American commerce. If Amazon's logistics were aimed at supply chain sovereignty—tracking, relocating, and redundancy-proofing the flow of critical materials rather than optimizing two-day delivery of goods manufactured 7,000 miles away—it would be the physical infrastructure of the Supply Sovereignty Fund that Chapter 12 proposes. The $200 billion Supply Sovereignty adaptation does not require building logistics from scratch. It needs to *leverage the existing logistics*. The *kettuvallam* is already built. It needs to carry the harvest home.

Apple: The House Built on Another Man's Land

The curator of an impeccably velvet-roped walled garden, charging a 30% tithe on every transaction within the kingdom. Over $600 billion in buybacks since 2013—more than any company in history. Annual product cycles that change everything (the camera) while changing nothing (the manufacturing dependence on the Farmer's factories in Zhengzhou). Apple's supply chain is the Farmer's supply chain with a Cupertino logo on it.

The dependency is structural, not incidental. Over 90% of iPhones are assembled in China, primarily at Foxconn's Zhengzhou complex—a facility so vast it employs 200,000 workers and is visible from space. If Beijing ordered production halted—as leverage in a Taiwan crisis, as a retaliatory measure, or simply as a demonstration of capability—Apple would lose the overwhelming majority of its manufacturing capacity overnight. The most valuable company in American history has built its house on another man's land and pays rent in the form of strategic vulnerability.

In Kuttanad, the boatmen have a proverb: *mattoru aalude nilathil veedu vekkunavan, aarum nokkumbol veetil nikkunnu, nilam nokkumbol veyilil nikkunnu*—the man who builds his house on another's land stands in a house when people look, and in the sun when the landowner looks. Apple stands in the most valuable house in corporate history. The landowner is the Farmer.

The latent antibody: Apple's M-series silicon is arguably the most advanced consumer chip architecture on Earth—designed in Cupertino, outperforming Intel and AMD on performance-per-watt. If the company that designed the M4 chip aimed its silicon engineering at semiconductor equipment innovation, advanced manufacturing process development, and domestic chip fabrication infrastructure, it would be the design brain that reduces American dependence on both TSMC and ASML. Apple has demonstrated that an American company can design world-class silicon. It has not been demonstrated that an American company can manufacture it on its own soil. The chip is brilliant. The factory is the Farmer's.

Microsoft: The Moat That Became an Ocean

Embedding AI into the very fabric of enterprise workflows with a locksmith's precision. Once your email, documents, calendar, cloud, AI copilot, and cybersecurity all run on Microsoft's stack, switching costs become a moat so wide it requires upgrading from "moat" to "ocean." The First Sacrament applied to enterprise: extract maximum rent from maximum dependence. Azure alone generated $96 billion in revenue in 2024—more than the GDP of over 120 countries.

Microsoft's partnership with OpenAI produced GPT-4—the model that briefly made the West believe it had an insurmountable AI lead, until DeepSeek demonstrated that the lead was narrower than the valuation premium assumed. The partnership model itself reveals the Sacrament's logic: rather than building frontier AI capability in-house (which would require the patience of the Farmer), Microsoft purchased a stake in someone else's breakthrough (which satisfies the Speed Fallacy's demand for immediate results). The acquisition was brilliant tactically and revealing strategically: even America's largest software company treats frontier innovation as something to *buy* rather than something to *build*.

The Farmer's mirror: Huawei Cloud, Alibaba Cloud, Tencent Cloud—deployed not merely as enterprise productivity platforms but as government infrastructure for municipal services, smart city coordination, industrial automation, and financial settlement. China's cloud ecosystem carries administrative functions. Microsoft's carries PowerPoint presentations. Both are clouds. One rains on the fields. The other rains on spreadsheets.

The latent antibody: Azure powers over 60% of Fortune 500 cloud infrastructure. If Microsoft's enterprise cloud became the platform for a national Vehicle-Road-Cloud system—the American equivalent of what China deployed across 35,000 kilometers of smart roadway in 20+ cities—it would create the digital nervous system for autonomous mobility, smart infrastructure, and distributed manufacturing coordination. The platform exists. The deployment mandate does not.

NVIDIA: The Gatekeeper Whose Gate Is Cracking

The gleeful gatekeepers of the AI gold rush, rationing GPUs at margins that would make a pirate blush—gross margins exceeding 75%, a figure so extraordinary that it functions less as a financial metric than as a measure of monopoly power. NVIDIA's CUDA ecosystem has no Chinese equivalent: a software-hardware lock-in so deep that researchers worldwide have structured their entire AI development pipelines around NVIDIA's architecture. The company's H100 chip became, briefly, the most sought-after commodity on Earth—a $40,000 GPU that could not be manufactured fast enough to satisfy demand and could not be exported to China without violating US sanctions.

Then DeepSeek demonstrated that frontier AI training could be achieved at a fraction of the assumed computational cost, and the gatekeeper's stock lost $589 billion in a single day—the largest single-day market cap loss in American history. The Farmer does not need to storm the gate. The Farmer digs around it. The gate's premium rests on an assumption—that frontier AI requires maximum compute—and the assumption is cracking.

The Farmer's mirror: Huawei's Ascend 910B operates at approximately 60% of H100 performance—a "failure" by the ceiling metric and operational independence by the floor metric. Sixty percent of H100, manufactured domestically and running on sovereign silicon, is strategically superior to 100% of H100, which can be denied with a phone call to Washington.

The latent antibody: Nvidia's CUDA ecosystem and chip design capability are the computational foundation of the AI revolution. If Nvidia's GPUs powered domestic semiconductor equipment development, AI-optimized manufacturing, autonomous infrastructure, and national defense systems rather than cryptocurrency mining, advertising optimization, and speculative AI model training, it would be the computational backbone of ARPA-X. Jensen Huang arrived from Taiwan as a child—the 55% immigrant advantage in a single biography. The company he built could serve the civilization that raised him. Whether it will is a $3 trillion question.

Tesla: The Unicorn and the Camel

Master illusionists. Market cap ~$1.5 trillion for 1.64 million vehicles. BYD sits at $107 billion for 4.6 million vehicles with God's Eye ADAS included at no extra charge. What Tesla charges $8,000–$12,000 for as a premium add-on, BYD gives away as standard equipment on 21 models starting at $9,550. The Vanity Metric Delusion made automotive: the market values the Unicorn's narrative at ten times the Camel's deployment.

Full Self-Driving has been "one year away" for nine consecutive years—the autonomous-vehicle equivalent of fusion's perpetual "thirty years away," except that fusion researchers have the intellectual honesty not to charge customers $12,000 for a feature that does not yet exist. Tesla's real-world dataset—over six billion miles of driving data—is the largest in the Western world and a genuinely formidable asset. But the data serves the narrative (Full Self-Driving is imminent) rather than the deployment (autonomous mobility is operational). Apollo Go processes 300,000 rides per week. Tesla's autonomous fleet processes promises.

The Supercharger network is America's single largest EV charging infrastructure—and its architecture matters. China has deployed over 10 million public charging points. The United States has approximately 76,000 DC fast chargers. The ratio is 130:1. Tesla's network is the most valuable piece of American EV infrastructure. It is also a proprietary walled garden that, until recently, excluded non-Tesla vehicles—the automotive equivalent of a highway open only to Fords.

The latent antibody: Tesla's data, vehicles, Supercharger network, and battery manufacturing capacity represent the physical skeleton of American autonomous mobility. If Tesla's infrastructure were integrated into a national Vehicle-Road-Cloud system—the Superchargers opened permanently to all EVs, the driving data contributed to a national autonomous-driving standard, the battery gigafactories aimed at grid-scale storage rather than shareholder-scale narrative—it would be the deployment backbone the Hunter desperately needs. The Camel delivers in silence. The Unicorn dazzles with promises. Chapter 9 will complete the autopsy.

Together, these Seven are the vanguard of a seismic shift—from purported engines of innovation to sprawling, Gilded Age empires built on relentless extraction, pervasive surveillance, and unchecked corporate power. Yet beneath the extraction, something dormant stirs—$300 billion in annual R&D, the world's deepest AI talent pool, the computational infrastructure that birthed the Transformer itself. The question is not whether the Seven *could* turn their fire toward deployment rather than extraction. The question is whether they *would*—and whether the system that governs them would permit the turning. Chapter 12's *maattivekkal*—the turning of the bow—proposes exactly this. The antibody exists. The question is whether the patient will take the medicine.

In Kuttanad, the seven boats sit at their moorings, teak-hulled and coir-rigged, each capable of carrying a village's harvest. The peacock feathers gleam in the hold. The harvest rots on the dock. And somewhere, the Farmer's fleet—unglamorous, standardized, carrying rice instead of feathers—has already left the canal and is halfway to market.

* * *

The Hunter's Genuine Strengths: Why This Is a Tragedy, Not a Comedy

A Greek tragedy requires a hero worthy of sympathy. The Hunter possesses genuine, formidable, and potentially decisive advantages that this chapter's critique should not obscure.

More than 55% of America's billion-dollar startup founders are immigrants or children of immigrants. Jensen Huang arrived from Taiwan as a child. Sergey Brin fled the Soviet Union at the age of six. Satya Nadella came from Hyderabad. The companies that define American innovation were built by people who chose to come to America because America offers something no other nation replicates at scale—the freedom to arrive with nothing, fail spectacularly, and build again.

The American university system remains the world's most productive generator of paradigm-shifting research. The Transformer architecture was conceived at Google Brain. CRISPR was developed at UC Berkeley. mRNA vaccine technology was pioneered at UPenn. The fundamental science still emerges disproportionately from the Forest.

And the Hunter's reinvention capacity has been historically demonstrated over two and a half centuries. The agricultural republic became the industrial powerhouse, then the financial superpower, and finally the technology hegemon. Each reinvention involved enormous dislocation, political upheaval, and a period of apparent decline—followed by a restructuring that left the system stronger in dimensions the previous era could not have imagined.

The purpose of mentioning them here is to frame the tariff saga correctly: not as evidence of terminal decline but as evidence of misapplied strength. The hero is undone not by his weaknesses but by his strengths, wielded without the strategic wisdom to match the adversary's temporal frame.

* * *

BOATMAN'S LEDGER

Chapter 2

LEDGER TOOL #3: MĀYĀ METER UPDATE — TARIFF EDITION

The tariff saga is the Māyā Meter's most dramatic reading yet. The narrative: tariffs restore American manufacturing, reduce the trade deficit, and bring China to heel. The deployment reality: $6.6T destroyed in two days. $160B+ illegally collected. SCOTUS 6–3 struck down. Section 122 expires in 150 days. Meanwhile: China's trade surplus exceeded $1T. Yuan strengthened for 14 months. The Farmer kept planting.

SEVEN DIGITAL EMPERORS EXTRACTION INDEX

Meta $91B buybacks (2017–2024) | Google $45B R&D, outmaneuvered at a fraction of the cost | Amazon 80% pharma API dependency | Apple $600B+ buybacks, 90%+ manufacturing in China | Microsoft Azure $96B revenue, enterprise lock-in moat | Nvidia $589B single-day loss, 75%+ gross margins | Tesla ~$1.5T cap for 1.64M vehicles. Combined: $20T+

market cap. Latent antibody: $300B in annual R&D, Transformer birthright, immigrant-founder pipeline. Māyā Level: 9/10. Antibody score: 6/10—real, dormant, and the book's prescription depends on whether it activates.

THE BOATMAN'S WAGER

The SCOTUS ruling creates a 150-day window of policy uncertainty. Reduce exposure to tariff-sensitive U.S. consumer discretionary; increase illustrative allocation to Chinese deployment plays that benefit from tariff-driven supply chain redirection. Watch the Four Sacraments as leading indicators: when buyback-to-capex ratios exceed 2:1 in any sector, the extraction spiral is accelerating, and the sector is pricing narrative over deployment.

Chapter 2 Data Anchors: $5.3T buybacks (2010–2023) | Capex-to-profit ratio: 50% (1970s) → <20% (today) | Boeing $43B buybacks / 346 deaths | Starbucks CEO 6,666:1 | Ford $4.8B EV loss | 80% pharma APIs from China/India | SCOTUS 6–3 | $160B+ refund | Section 122 150-day limit | China $1T+ trade surplus (2025) | Meta $91B buybacks | Apple $600B+ buybacks, 90%+ Zhengzhou | Azure $96B | Nvidia 75%+ margins, $589B loss | Seven combined $20T+ / $300B R&D | 55% immigrant founders | 81.5% small businesses raised prices | 68% vs. 91% FCF reinvestment

. . .

A Word to the Reasonable Reader

If this chapter has made you angry—at the tariff policy, at the critique of the tariff policy, at the satirical tone applied to matters of genuine economic consequence for millions of real people like Sarah Kowalski—then you are exactly where this book needs you to be. Anger is the appropriate emotional response to a situation where the world's most powerful economy imposes a policy that its own Supreme Court rules illegal, destroys $6.6 trillion in household wealth over a long weekend, collects $160 billion in unlawful tariffs, and then immediately re-imposes the same policy under a different statute with a 150-day expiration date.

The satire in this chapter is not gratuitous. It is diagnostic. When policy becomes so disconnected from its stated rationale that the gap can no longer be bridged by sober analysis, only the satirist's craft can describe the reality accurately. George Carlin understood this: the purpose of satire is not to mock for its own sake but to strip away the euphemisms—"liberation," "reciprocal," "beautiful"—that allow dysfunctional systems to persist unchallenged because the language itself has been corrupted.

The Chinese principle 以静制动 does not mean the Farmer does nothing. It means the Farmer's actions are invisible to the Hunter because they operate on a different timescale and across different domains. While the Hunter was announcing Liberation Day, the Farmer was integrating DeepSeek R1 into BYD's vehicle intelligence platform. While the Hunter was pausing and re-escalating, the Farmer was signing $213.5 billion in Belt and Road deals. The stillness was not passivity. It was cultivation. And cultivation, unlike hunting, compounds.

. . .

RITUAL STAGE MARKER

The deity's name has been spoken. The air thickens with incense and intention. The performer's body begins to shift—not yet possessed, but no longer merely human. His spine straightens. His eyes widen. The Hunter-spirit and the Farmer-spirit are circling each other now in the ritual ground, and the audience holds its breath, because when two deities meet, the earth between them burns.

CHAPTER 3

The Attention Harvest

Algorithmic Polarization, Social Cohesion, and the Fourteenth Domain

"Sow discord in the enemy's camp." — Sun Tzu, Art of War, Chapter 13

浑水摸鱼 — *"Stir the muddy water to catch the fish."* — Thirty-Six Stratagems, #20

When the fisherman poisons his own lake, the village starves—not from hunger but from the absence of a table worth sitting at.

— *after the Theyyam tradition*

• • •

Undercurrent: The Domain That Was Missing

Chapter 2 anatomized the Seven Digital Emperors as engines of financial extraction—$5.3 trillion in buybacks, $91 billion from Meta alone, the Farmer watching as the Hunter cannibalizes his own industrial base. But the financial extraction is only half the ledger. The same Magnificent Seven that drain the Hunter's capital also drain something harder to measure and harder to rebuild: the Hunter's capacity to agree on what is real.

This is the fourteenth domain—the one the interdependency web has been missing. Semiconductors, EVs, batteries, drones, shipbuilding, AI, biotech, rare earths, telecom, robotics, space, autonomous vehicles, and financial architecture—thirteen domains where the Farmer plants and the Hunter reacts. But there is a fourteenth, invisible from the Bloomberg terminal, absent from the Boatman's Ledger until now, and arguably more consequential than any of the other thirteen: **social cohesion**—the capacity of a civilization to act collectively in response to a strategic threat.

In Kuttanad, there is a phenomenon the boatmen call *ormappookkal*—"memory flowers," the blooms that appear on the backwater's surface when the underlying root system is dying(Chapter 1's ormappookkal grew from personal grief. These grow from institutional decay — the same botanical principle applied to civic life.). They are beautiful. They attract tourists. And they are a death sentence for the ecology beneath. The flowers grow because the roots are rotting, and the rotting releases nutrients that feed surface blooms at the expense of the system's depth. The attention economy is America's *ormappookkal*: a spectacular surface bloom—engagement metrics, viral content, dopamine-optimized feeds—growing from the death of the root system beneath. The root system is a shared reality. Shared civic purpose. The capacity to sit at a table and agree, if not on values, then at least on facts.

The Farmer does not need to attack this root system. The Hunter's own companies are doing it for him. And the Farmer, watching from across the halocline, has drawn the strategic conclusion that Sun Tzu articulated twenty-five centuries ago: the supreme art of war is to subdue the enemy without fighting. When the enemy's most powerful corporations are systematically destroying the social cohesion required to mount a collective response, the wisest strategy is to do nothing and wait.

. . .

The Editor Whose Readers Disappeared: A Vignette from Mahoning County

Call her Diane Kessler. She is fifty-nine years old, and for twenty-three years she was the managing editor of a regional newspaper in Mahoning County, Ohio—the same county that contains Youngstown, the same county where Sarah Kowalski's home goods boutique sits on West Federal Street. The paper's name does not matter. What matters is what it did: it covered the school board, the county commission, the zoning disputes, the water-treatment plant inspections, the high school football scores, and the obituaries. It was the shared text of a community—the thing that people read at the same diner counter on the same morning and then argued about in the same parking lot.

The paper had a circulation of 28,000 in 2005. By 2015, it was 11,000. By 2020, it was 4,200. In 2023, the ownership group—a hedge fund that had acquired the paper as part of a portfolio of distressed local media assets—reduced the newsroom from fourteen reporters to three, then sold the building, then converted to a biweekly print edition supplemented by a website that generated approximately $3,100 per month in digital advertising revenue. Facebook and Google accounted for approximately 80% of local digital advertising nationwide. The money that once funded Diane's reporters now funds Meta's buybacks.

Diane did not lose her readers to a competitor. She lost them to an algorithm. The same residents who once read her coverage of the water-treatment plant now scroll Facebook feeds that serve up national outrage content optimized to maximize time-on-screen. The school board meeting that Diane's reporter covered—the one about lead levels in the elementary school drinking fountains—received 340 views on the paper's website. A Facebook post claiming that the school board was "indoctrinating children with critical race theory"—a claim with no factual basis, about a curriculum that did not exist in Mahoning County—received 47,000 engagements. The algorithm did not create the lie. The algorithm ensured the lie reached 47,000 people while the truth reached 340.

In the Theyyam tradition, there is a role called the *pantham*—the torchbearer who lights the performance space so the community can see the deity's face. Without the *pantham*, the ritual happens in darkness: the deity performs, but no one can see. Diane Kessler was Mahoning County's *pantham*. The algorithm extinguished her torch. The community now watches the ritual in the dark—each member illuminated only by the blue glow of a personal screen showing a personalized reality that no neighbor shares.

Diane is now a communications consultant for a regional hospital system. She does not talk about the paper. When her former colleagues gather—less frequently each year—they do not discuss journalism's future. They discuss the specific, local, verifiable stories that no one is telling anymore: the factory that failed its OSHA inspection, the bridge rated structurally deficient, the nonprofit that lost its funding. The stories that made Mahoning County a *community* rather than a collection of individuals scrolling separate feeds in separate rooms.

. . .

The Algorithm's Liturgy: How Engagement Became Extraction

The engagement economy operates on a mechanism so elegant in its cynicism that it deserves the same anatomical precision this book applied to the Four Sacraments. The mechanism is this: human cognition evolved in environments where threat detection was essential for survival. Our brains preferentially attend to potential dangers, tribal conflicts, and violations of social norms—an adaptation that served our ancestors when predators lurked beyond the firelight. The platforms exploit this architecture with unprecedented precision. Content that triggers outrage generates approximately 17% more engagement than content that produces satisfaction. Content that reinforces existing beliefs outperforms content that challenges them by 36%. The financial incentives are unambiguous: division pays dividends.

Facebook's 2018 algorithm change—ostensibly designed to promote "meaningful social interactions"—systematically amplified content likely to trigger angry reactions, giving it, as internal researchers documented, a "five-point boost" over neutral content. The company's own data scientists warned that the algorithm was "exploiting the human brain's attraction to divisiveness." The system remained largely unchanged because addressing it would, in the language of the internal documents, "impact user engagement." Impact user engagement. The euphemism is a Four Sacraments masterwork—the Extraction Death Spiral applied to neural architecture rather than balance sheets. Extract the attention. Convert it to engagement metrics. Monetize the engagement through targeted advertising. Buy back the stock. Collect the bonus. The liturgy is the same. The congregation is three billion human brains.

The result is a feedback loop of civilizational consequence. As algorithms learn to maximize engagement through division, users become increasingly sorted into hermetic information environments where contradictory facts never arrive, and tribal identities harden into existential commitments. In 1960, approximately 5% of Americans reported they would be displeased if their child married someone from the opposing political party. By 2023, that figure had reached nearly 40%. More alarmingly, approximately 55% of both Republicans and Democrats now view the opposing party not merely as wrong but as "a serious threat to the United States and its people." In one survey, around 15% of Republicans and 20% of Democrats said the country would be better off if large numbers of the opposing party "just died."

When tens of millions of citizens wish for the disappearance of political opponents, the social contract required for democratic governance—the agreement to accept electoral outcomes, to view the opposition as legitimate, to subordinate tribal identity to civic identity—is not fraying. It is dissolving. And the dissolution is not a side effect of the platforms. It is the *business model*. The Five-Point Boost is the attention economy's equivalent of the F-35's $1.7 trillion lifecycle: a system so perfectly optimized for its stated metric that it has become catastrophically dysfunctional for every other purpose the civilization requires.

. . .

The Epistemic Halocline: Two Americas, Two Realities

The halocline in the Kuttanadan backwaters separates freshwater from salt—two bodies of water occupying the same space, invisible to the untrained eye, lethal to the farmer who cannot read the boundary. America's epistemic halocline separates two information ecosystems occupying the same geography but sharing almost no factual overlap.

The data is precise. Information consumption patterns across partisan divides show minimal overlap. Conservative and liberal Americans increasingly inhabit separate information ecosystems with different news sources, different facts, and different understandings of basic reality. Whether climate change exists, whether voter fraud is widespread, whether COVID-19 represented a significant public health threat—questions with objective, verifiable answers— have become tribal signifiers rather than factual matters. A 2023 PRRI survey found that 25% of Americans agreed that "the government, media, and financial worlds in the U.S. are controlled by a group of Satan-worshipping pedophiles who run a global child sex trafficking operation." One-quarter of the population believes Satanic child traffickers run their country. This is not polarization. This is epistemic secession.

The local news collapse is the infrastructural foundation of the epistemic halocline. Since 2005, approximately 2,900 newspapers have closed in the United States. The communities they served—Diane Kessler's Mahoning County, Sarah Kowalski's Youngstown, and thousands of towns across the American interior—have become "news deserts": places where no journalist covers the school board, no reporter attends the zoning meeting, no editor fact-checks the Facebook post. In a news desert, the only information that arrives is algorithmically curated national content designed to maximize engagement—which means designed to maximize outrage, tribal affiliation, and the particular species of righteous fury that keeps a thumb scrolling. The school board's lead-pipe problem does not generate engagement. The conspiracy theory about the school board generates enormous engagement. The algorithm serves what engagement demands. The community gets what the algorithm serves.

The strategic consequence is this: a nation that cannot agree on facts cannot formulate a strategy. The six adaptations proposed in Chapter 12 require collective action—bipartisan commissions, national investment banks, alliance agriculture, and talent sovereignty initiatives. Everyone requires the foundational civic capacity to agree on a shared problem and coordinate a shared response. The attention harvest has consumed precisely this capacity. The Farmer's deployment advantage across thirteen domains would be contestable if the Hunter could mount a coordinated national response. But a nation where 55% of citizens view the other party as an existential threat is a nation that cannot pass a budget, let alone a Supply Sovereignty Fund. The fourteenth domain is not a domain like the others. It is the *precondition* for responding to all thirteen.

. . .

The Farmer's Mirror: Controlled Coherence vs. Monetized Fragmentation

The Farmer solved the attention problem. The solution is censorship, surveillance, and state control of information— a solution incompatible with democratic values and one this book does not recommend, endorse, or admire. But the strategic consequences must be documented, because pretending they do not exist is its own form of *māyā*.

China's Great Firewall blocks Facebook, Google, Twitter, and YouTube. The platforms that fragment American discourse do not operate on Chinese soil. In their place, WeChat, Weibo, Douyin (TikTok's domestic version), and Xiaohongshu operate under content guidelines enforced by the Cyberspace Administration of China. The guidelines suppress political dissent—a fundamental violation of the expressive freedom this book values. They also suppress the algorithmic amplification of outrage, conspiracy, and tribal fragmentation that Meta's Five-Point Boost generates with such profitable efficiency.

The result is a paradox that should make every democratic strategist uncomfortable. The authoritarian system produces social coherence sufficient to mobilize collective action across thirteen domains simultaneously. The democratic system produces such severe social fragmentation that it cannot pass infrastructure legislation without triggering a constitutional crisis. The Farmer's censorship is a moral failure. The Hunter's algorithmic fragmentation is a strategic failure. Neither is acceptable. But only one of them prevents the civilization from responding to a strategic threat.

China's propaganda has evolved from crude assertions of Chinese superiority to sophisticated amplification of existing American divisions. Rather than creating disinformation from scratch, Chinese influence operations increasingly identify and amplify indigenous American conspiracy theories, partisan narratives, and tribal antipathies. The strategy presupposes that a nation divided against itself becomes strategically paralyzed. Meta's engagement metrics prove the premise correct—not because China designed the fragmentation, but because the Hunter's own corporations built the fragmentation engine and the Hunter's own regulatory system declined to restrain it.

. . .

The Other Current: Why Censorship Is the Wrong Lesson

The reasonable reader should resist the inference that this chapter recommends the Farmer's model. It does not. The Farmer's information control produces coherence at the cost of truth—and truth, as Liu Jing's 4.2-nanometer drift demonstrated, is the only currency that survives contact with reality. A system that cannot be criticized from within cannot correct itself from within. The SCOTUS antibody documented in Chapter 2's Act IV—the institutional capacity for self-correction that the Chinese planner envied—depends entirely on the freedom of expression that censorship would destroy. You cannot have the SCOTUS antibody and the Great Firewall. You must choose.

The lesson is not that America should censor. The lesson is that America should stop subsidizing the fragmentation. The regulatory asymmetry is the strategic vulnerability: the Hunter's system allows Algorithm Annie to operate unchecked while the Farmer's system eliminates her entirely. Democracies have a middle path—demonstrated by Finland's comprehensive digital literacy education, Taiwan's "digital democracy" consensus-building tools, and the European Union's Digital Services Act, which requires platform transparency and accountability. These models do not impose authoritarian information controls. They modify the *incentive structure* that currently rewards division over cohesion. They treat social cohesion as a strategic asset—which it is—rather than an externality—which Meta's quarterly earnings call treats it as.

The governance paradox is real: addressing algorithmic polarization requires precisely the social consensus that algorithmic polarization has systematically undermined. Like the property crisis in Chapter 11's five vulnerabilities, the problem compounds while solutions remain elusive—not because solutions do not exist, but because solving the problem requires overcoming the very conditions the problem creates. This is why the fourteenth domain belongs in Part I rather than the domain chapters: it is the precondition, the soil analysis that determines whether any of the thirteen seeds can grow.

. . .

The Trust Recession: America's Most Expensive Deficit

In the early 1960s, approximately 75% of Americans trusted the government to do what was right "most of the time" or "just about always." By 2023, that figure had collapsed to 20%. Congress commands the confidence of 16% of the population. Social media—11%. The medical system—34%. Media trust hovers around 34%.

Trust is not a sentiment. Trust is infrastructure. It is the invisible architecture that enables collective action, reduces transaction costs, and enhances resilience during crises. When citizens trust their institutions, societies can mobilize resources efficiently, implement complex policies, and maintain stability under stress. When trust collapses, even the wealthiest nation finds itself strategically paralyzed—a nuclear-armed civilization with self-imposed handcuffs. The Farmer's interdependency web succeeds not because China's technology is superior in any single domain but because the system can act collectively across all domains simultaneously. The Hunter's system cannot act collectively on infrastructure, healthcare, immigration, climate, or industrial policy—not because the resources are insufficient but because the trust required to coordinate collective action has been harvested, monetized, and converted into Meta's $91 billion in buybacks.

The geographic manifestation sharpens the picture. Coastal metropolitan areas experience remarkable prosperity, while former manufacturing regions, rural communities, and inner cities experience sustained decline. Diane Kessler's Mahoning County and Sarah Kowalski's Youngstown occupy the same nation as Marcus Chen's Westchester—but they inhabit different economic realities, consume different information, and experience different Americas. The Farmer plants a single field. The Hunter's field has fractured into archipelagos that cannot see each other across the epistemic halocline.

The inequality dimension compounds the trust deficit. The top 1% of U.S. households control approximately 31% of the nation's wealth. The bottom 50%—some 165 million Americans—possess 2.5%. The CEO-to-worker pay ratio has reached 351:1. America's inequality levels have returned to Gilded Age proportions—the wealth concentration ratio between the top 0.1% and the bottom 90% mirrors that of 1929. When the Starbucks CEO earns $57.8 million—a ratio of 6,666:1 against the median employee—while Maria Delgado chooses between metformin and groceries, the social contract is not strained. It is voided. And voided social contracts do not produce Rooseveltian mobilizations. They produce plywood on the windows and AK-47s in the council minutes.

* * *

Interlude: Marcus Discovers He Lives in Two Feeds

Marcus Chen's wife, Claire, is a pediatrician in White Plains. One evening, over dinner, she showed him her Facebook feed. Marcus had not looked at Facebook in three years—his information universe was Bloomberg, the Financial Times, Bridgewater's Daily Observations, and a curated set of sell-side research.

Claire's feed showed: a post claiming that a local school was "forcing gender ideology on kindergartners" (shared 12,000 times; based on a misreading of a state anti-bullying guideline); a conspiracy theory about vaccine ingredients (shared 8,400 times; debunked by every major health institution); a video of a political commentator declaring that

"China owns America and your children will speak Mandarin by 2035" (2.1 million views; analytically incoherent by every metric Marcus had spent six months learning to read).

Marcus stared at his wife's phone and then at his Bloomberg terminal, open on his laptop. Two information ecosystems. The Bloomberg terminal showed deployment data, trade flows, capital expenditure ratios, and the Farmer's quiet accumulation. Claire's Facebook feed showed outrage, conspiracy, tribal signaling, and the systematic destruction of the shared factual foundation that any strategic response would require.

"This is the fourteenth domain," Marcus said.

Claire looked at him. "What?"

"The thing I've been missing. I've been tracking thirteen domains where China is outdeploying us. But there's a fourteenth. It's this." He pointed at her phone. "It's the fact that we can't agree on what's real. You can't mobilize a national response to a strategic threat when half the country thinks the threat is a hoax and the other half thinks the wrong thing is the threat."

Claire put down her phone. "You're saying Facebook is a national security vulnerability."

"I'm saying Meta spent $91 billion buying back its own stock while its algorithm taught 40% of the country that the other 60% is an existential enemy. Yes. That's a national security vulnerability. And the Farmer didn't have to do anything to create it. We built it ourselves. We monetized it. And we can't fix it because fixing it would require the social consensus that the algorithm already destroyed."

He opened a new tab in his spreadsheet. He titled it "Fourteenth Domain: Social Cohesion Index." He stared at it for a long time. Then he typed the first data point: "Trust in government: 20%. Trust required for Rooseveltian mobilization: ~60%. Deficit: 40 points. Time to rebuild: unknown. Possibly generational."

He closed the laptop. The halocline was not just between nations. It was between the two Americas sitting at his dinner table, one reading Bloomberg and the other reading Facebook, both believing they understood the world, neither able to see what the other saw.

. . .

BOATMAN'S LEDGER

Chapter 3

LEDGER TOOL #3: SOCIAL COHESION INDEX — THE FOURTEENTH DOMAIN

The interdependency web now spans fourteen domains. The first thirteen are measurable in production units, trade volumes, and deployment rates. The fourteenth is measured in trust percentages, information-ecosystem overlap, and the capacity for collective action. It is the precondition for responding to the other thirteen.

TRUST DEFICIT ANCHORS

Government trust: 75% (1960s) → 20% (2023). Congress: 16%. Media: 34%. Social media: 11%. Cross-partisan marriage disapproval: 5% (1960) → 40% (2023). Citizens viewing opposing party as an existential threat: 55%. Citizens wishing opposing partisans would die: 15–20%.

ATTENTION HARVEST ECONOMICS

Meta $91B buybacks (2017–2024) funded by engagement optimization. Outrage content +17% engagement vs. satisfaction content. Belief-reinforcing content +36% vs. challenging content. Facebook's Five-Point Boost for anger-triggering content. 2,900 newspapers have closed since 2005. 80% of local digital ad revenue is captured by Meta/Google. Cost of rebuilding: generational. Cost of not rebuilding: the other thirteen domains become uncontestable.

ORMAPPOOKKAL INDEX (Memory Flowers)

Surface bloom (engagement metrics, viral content, screen time) growing as root system (shared reality, civic participation, institutional trust) decays. Track: when engagement metrics rise while civic participation metrics (voter turnout, community meeting attendance, local news consumption) decline simultaneously, the *ormappookkal* are blooming. The lake is dying.

THE BOATMAN'S WAGER

The fourteenth domain is not directly investable. It is the macro precondition that determines whether the Hunter's latent antibodies—the SCOTUS immunity, the immigrant pipeline, the Magnificent Seven's $300B R&D—can be activated. Short: any company whose revenue depends on engagement-maximization without accountability (illustrative position). Long: digital literacy infrastructure, local news revival plays, and platform accountability beneficiaries. The wager: a civilization that cannot agree on facts cannot deploy its strengths. The Farmer knows this. The Farmer is waiting.

Chapter 3 Data Anchors: Trust: 75% (1960s) → 20% (2023) | Congress 16% | Cross-partisan marriage: 5% → 40% | 55% view opposition as existential threat | 15–20% wish opposing partisans dead | Outrage +17% engagement | Belief-reinforcing +36% | Facebook Five-Point Boost | 2,900 newspapers closed | 80% local ad revenue to Meta/Google | 25% believe QAnon core claims | Top 1%: 31% wealth; Bottom 50%: 2.5% | CEO-to-worker: 351:1 | Starbucks 6,666:1 | Ormappookkal: memory flowers as diagnostic | Pantham: the torchbearer who lights the shared ritual | Diane Kessler: 28,000 → 4,200 circulation

* * *

A Word to the Reasonable Reader

This chapter documents the fourteenth domain—the one that the interdependency web was missing. The reasonable reader should hold the following tension: the Farmer's information control is a moral abomination that produces strategic coherence. The Hunter's information freedom is a moral achievement that produces strategic paralysis. Neither the abomination nor the paralysis is acceptable. The question is whether democracy can produce a third path—one that preserves expressive freedom while modifying the *incentive architecture* that currently rewards fragmentation over cohesion.

Finland, Taiwan, and the EU suggest the third path exists. The American political system's inability to regulate the platforms that fragment it suggests the path may be blocked by the very fragmentation it seeks to address. This is the governance paradox at the heart of the fourteenth domain, and it is the reason this chapter belongs before the domain chapters rather than among them: the question of whether the Hunter *can* respond to the Farmer's deployment advantage depends, before anything else, on whether the Hunter's citizens can agree on what they are responding to.

Chapter 5 now shifts from the broken bow to the broken field—the innovation paradox that separates breakthroughs from harvests, and the Farmer's deployment architecture that turns one into the other.

* * *

The first brush strokes appear on the performer's face. Not yet the deity's eyes—those come later. First: the outline of the cheekbones, the structure that will hold everything that follows. Without this foundation, no mask can take shape. The audience watches the painter's hand and understands: what is being drawn is not decoration. It is architecture.

CHAPTER 4

The Hunter's Broken Bow

Social Infrastructure, Inequality, and the Arrow That Cannot Fly

"When the granaries are empty, the people will rebel." — Guanzi

"Where there is no vision, the people perish." — Proverbs 29:18

A bow that cannot bend cannot send the arrow. The Hunter has the finest arrows ever made. The bow is cracked.

— after the Theyyam tradition

. . .

Undercurrent: The Bow and the Arrow

Chapter 3 documented the fourteenth domain—the attention harvest that has consumed the Hunter's capacity to agree on what is real. This chapter documents what that consumed capacity was supposed to protect: the physical and social infrastructure that enables a civilization to engage in strategic action. The roads. The bridges. The hospitals. The schools. The water systems. The broadband networks. The civic institutions that translate individual talent into collective strength.

In Kuttanad, the boatmen distinguish between the *vallam* (the vessel) and the *Thuzha* (the oar). You can build the most magnificent *vallam* on the backwater—teak-hulled, coir-rigged, worthy of a festival. But if the *Thuzha* is cracked, the *vallam* does not move. The vessel sits in the canal, beautiful and useless, while the farmer who carved a rough-hewn oar from jackfruit wood arrives at market before dawn. America's arrows are magnificent: the Magnificent Seven's $300 billion in annual R&D, the immigrant pipeline that produced 55% of billion-dollar founders, the university system that generated the Transformer, CRISPR, and mRNA. These are the finest arrows ever made. The bow that must propel them—the social infrastructure that translates individual brilliance into collective capability—is cracked. And a broken bow, regardless of the arrow's quality, sends nothing into flight.

This chapter is the bow's inspection report. It is not comfortable reading. It will make some readers defensive, because acknowledging that the world's wealthiest nation has allowed its social infrastructure to decay to developing-world levels in specific, measurable domains is an admission that the Hunter's wounds are not merely strategic but structural. The Farmer's deployment advantage, documented in Chapters 6 through 10, would be contestable if the Hunter's bow were intact. The fourteen-to-fifteen margin in Chapter 11's Net Assessment is close enough that a functional social infrastructure could tip it. But the bow must be repaired before the arrow can fly. And the repair requires looking at things the Bloomberg terminal does not display.

. . .

Youngstown: The Broken Bow Made Physical

Sarah Kowalski's home goods boutique on West Federal Street in Youngstown, Ohio, occupies the ground floor of a building constructed in 1923, when Youngstown was the steel capital of the Mahoning Valley, and the population exceeded 170,000. The building's upper floors are empty. They have been empty since 2009. The landlord—a limited liability company registered in Delaware whose beneficial ownership traces through two holding structures to a real estate investment trust in Connecticut—has not replaced the windows on the third floor. The plywood that covers them has weathered to the color of old bone.

Walk down West Federal Street in either direction from Sarah's shop and count. In the two blocks east: a vacant lot where the department store stood until 2014, now a gravel rectangle used for overflow parking on the days when the county courthouse is busy; a dollar store; a bail-bonds office; and a check-cashing outlet whose interest rates would have been illegal in thirty-seven states before the deregulation of payday lending. In the two blocks west: a barber shop that has survived since 1981 through the sheer gravitational force of a man named Clarence, who cuts hair and dispenses unsolicited civic philosophy; a boarded former bank; a vape shop; and a Subway franchise that closes at 2 p.m. because there is insufficient foot traffic to justify the electricity cost of afternoon operations.

Youngstown's population is now approximately 58,000—a 66% decline from its peak. The city has lost more than 40,000 manufacturing jobs since 1977, when Black Monday—the closure of the Youngstown Sheet and Tube Campbell Works—began the deindustrialization cascade that hollowed the Mahoning Valley. Median household income: $28,700, roughly half the national figure. Poverty rate: 35%. Violent crime rate: more than three times the national average. The Northside Medical Center—the community's only full-service hospital—closed in 2018. The nearest emergency department is now a twenty-three-minute drive, assuming you own a car, the roads are clear, and the ambulance is available. In a cardiac event, twenty-three minutes is the difference between damage and death.

Sarah's grandmother, Helen, opened the shop in 1987 because she believed that a Main Street with a home goods boutique was a Main Street that still believed in itself—that the act of choosing a ceramic vase or a linen tablecloth was an act of civic faith, a declaration that this house, this meal, this gathering matters enough to be adorned. Helen's shop survived the steel collapse, the 2008 financial crisis, the Amazon tsunami, and three different presidents' promises to bring manufacturing back to the Mahoning Valley. None of the presidents delivered. The manufacturing did not return. What returned, each time, was the particular exhaustion of having believed.

Sarah drives to the shop every morning past the concrete shells of shuttered factories whose parking lots have been colonized by ailanthus trees—the "tree of heaven," so called because it grows anywhere, requires nothing, and produces a smell that longtime residents describe as "like burning tires mixed with defeat." She passed the elementary school, where the playground equipment was removed in 2021 because the city could not afford the liability insurance to maintain it. She passes the fire station that operates with four fewer firefighters than the minimum staffing standard recommends, because the tax base that once supported a full complement evaporated with the steel mills.

In the Prologue, we met Sarah calling her suppliers about the Liberation Day tariffs. In Chapter 2, we watched her trace the supply chain from Youngstown to Zhejiang. Now we see what the tariff saga cannot show from a Bloomberg terminal: the *landscape* in which Sarah operates. The tariffs did not create Youngstown's decay. They arrived in a community already running on structural fumes. In this community, the hospital had closed, the newspaper was dying

(Diane Kessler's Mahoning County, one county over), the tax base had collapsed, the infrastructure was rated D+, and the social contract that Helen Kowalski had believed in when she opened the shop had been voided by four decades of decisions made in boardrooms that had never seen West Federal Street.

Sarah is not a policy exhibit. She is a woman who decides every Tuesday whether to renew the shop's lease. The North Carolina ceramics samples sit on the shelf behind the register. The margins are tighter than those offered by the Vietnamese supply chain. The story is different—"made here, for us, by people you could drive to visit." Whether the story is worth the margin compression is the question Sarah turns over every evening at Helen's desk, the yellow legal pad filling with numbers that keep changing because the ground keeps shifting beneath her.

. . .

The Medicine Cabinet: Maria Delgado's Tuesday

Maria Delgado is sixty-one years old, and she lives eleven blocks from Sarah Kowalski's boutique. They do not know each other. Their lives intersect only through geography and through the statistical category that encompasses both: residents of a city where the social contract was voided by committee, one quarterly earnings call at a time.

Maria is uninsured. Not by choice—by arithmetic. She works part-time at a warehouse distribution center on the east side, earning $14.50 per hour for shifts averaging 28 hours per week, because scheduling her for 32 would trigger the employer mandate under the Affordable Care Act. The employer's HR system is optimized with considerable precision to keep Maria's hours below the threshold at which she would become expensive. Maria is not a human resource in the sense that management textbooks intend. She is a *cost to be minimized*—a line item whose biological needs (insulin, blood-pressure medication, dental care, an annual physical) represent a liability that the scheduling algorithm has been designed to avoid.

Every month, Maria drives to a pharmacy to pick up her metformin. The copay—though "copay" is a generous term for someone without insurance; the word she uses is "the price"—is $47. She does not know that the active pharmaceutical ingredient in her pills was synthesized in Zhejiang Province, shipped to a finishing plant in Hyderabad, and packaged under an American brand name in New Jersey. She does not know that the same molecule is available through a Chinese pharmacy app for $3.80. She knows only that $47 is the difference between medication and groceries this month, and she has been choosing medication because the alternative is a hospital bill she cannot pay— at a hospital that no longer exists. After all, Northside Medical Center closed in 2018, and the nearest emergency room is now twenty-three minutes away by car.

Maria does not own a car. Her neighbor, a retired postal worker named Gerald, drives her to the pharmacy on the first Tuesday of each month. Gerald does not charge her. He considers the drive a civic duty—the kind of small, invisible, uncompensated act of mutual aid that economists do not measure because it does not appear on a balance sheet. In Kuttanad, this is called *orumuttu*—the temporary bund that neighbors build together, each contributing labor not because a contract requires it but because the water will drown everyone if the bund is not built. Gerald is Maria's *orumuttu*. If Gerald's arthritis worsens—it has been worsening—Maria will not be able to reach the pharmacy. The $47 molecule will become inaccessible not because of supply chain failure or trade policy but because the last informal social infrastructure connecting a diabetic woman to her medication is a seventy-three-year-old man's deteriorating knees.

The pharmaceutical supply chain documented in Chapter 9 describes the macro vulnerability: 80% of active pharmaceutical ingredients are manufactured overseas, 40% from China, and nearly half of 227 essential medicines have zero domestic API production. Maria is the micro reality: the human being at the end of that supply chain, paying $47 for a molecule that costs $3.80 at source, in a city where the hospital closed, the bus routes were cut, and the safety net was optimized into nonexistence by the same efficiency theology that the Four Sacraments describe.

. . .

The Infrastructure Autopsy: D+ and Falling

The American Society of Civil Engineers grades America's infrastructure every four years. The most recent grade: C−. This represents an improvement from D+ in 2017—an improvement achieved primarily by the Bipartisan Infrastructure Law's passage, which the ASCE graded on intent rather than completion. The specific grades tell the story that the aggregate obscures. Bridges: C. Roads: C−. Drinking water: C−. Wastewater: D+. Transit: D−. Aviation: D+. Inland waterways: D+. The estimated investment needed to bring American infrastructure to a state of good repair: $4.59 trillion over ten years.

The Farmer, for context, spent $1.14 trillion on infrastructure in 2023 alone. China has built 42,000 kilometers of high-speed rail since 2008—a network so vast it exceeds the combined high-speed rail mileage of every other nation on Earth. The United States has built zero kilometers of high-speed rail in the same period. However, it has spent approximately $8 billion studying, planning, and litigating the California High-Speed Rail project, which is now projected to cost over $100 billion and enter service sometime in the 2030s—connecting Bakersfield to Merced, a route that precisely no one in the history of transportation has wished were faster.

The drinking water crisis is the infrastructure autopsy's most disturbing finding. Flint, Michigan's lead-contaminated water supply—which exposed over 100,000 residents, including 12,000 children, to neurotoxic lead levels—was not an anomaly. It was a signal. The EPA estimates that replacing America's lead service lines will cost approximately $45 billion. The Natural Resources Defense Council identified over 186 million Americans—roughly 56% of the population—who were served by water systems that violated the Safe Drinking Water Act at least once between 2016 and 2021. The world's wealthiest nation cannot guarantee that the water coming from its taps will not poison its children. The Farmer builds 42,000 kilometers of high-speed rail. The Hunter poisons his own well and calls it a cost-optimization exercise.

Broadband: 24 million Americans lack access to fixed broadband, concentrated in rural communities and low-income urban neighborhoods. In the same country where Nvidia sells $40,000 GPUs for AI training, Maria Delgado's neighborhood in Youngstown has average download speeds that would embarrass a mid-tier city in Vietnam. The digital economy that the Magnificent Seven extract from requires infrastructure that the Magnificent Seven's tax optimization strategies help defund. The circle is not vicious. It is *liturgical*—the Four Sacraments applied to civic life, each extraction weakening the substrate that enables the next.

· · ·

Healthcare: The Bow's Deepest Crack

The United States spends approximately $4.5 trillion annually on healthcare—roughly 17.3% of GDP, more than any nation on Earth by a margin so wide it requires its own vocabulary. For this expenditure, the nation achieves: a life expectancy that has *declined* for three consecutive years and now trails the OECD average by approximately two years; an infant mortality rate higher than any comparable developed nation; approximately 530,000 medical bankruptcies annually (a phenomenon that does not exist in any other developed democracy, because no other developed democracy has designed a healthcare system in which getting sick can destroy your financial life); and roughly 27 million uninsured Americans, each of whom is one diagnosis away from Maria Delgado's arithmetic.

The strategic implications are direct. A nation whose citizens fear medical bankruptcy cannot take entrepreneurial risks. A workforce chronically stressed by healthcare insecurity is one with diminished cognitive capacity, reduced productivity, and shortened careers. The 55% immigrant-founder advantage documented in Chapter 2's Steelman section is partially offset by the fact that immigrants who arrive in America discover that the healthcare system their children will depend on is designed less as a service than as an extraction apparatus—the First Sacrament applied to human bodies.

The contrast with the Farmer is unflattering and must be stated without embellishment. China's healthcare system has significant problems—rural access gaps, inconsistent quality, and overcrowded urban hospitals. But China provides universal basic coverage to 95% of its population, and the trajectory is toward expansion. The Farmer's biotech revolution documented in Chapter 9—$66 billion in out-licensing deals, 639 first-in-class drug candidates, 120,000 biomedical PhDs per year—is simultaneously a commercial strategy and a demographic survival strategy for 400 million elderly citizens by 2035. The Hunter spends $4.5 trillion and achieves declining life expectancy. The Farmer spends a fraction and achieves expanding coverage. The bow is not merely cracked. In the healthcare domain, the bow has been sawed in half and sold for parts.

· · ·

Education: The Bow's Fraying String

The Hunter's education system presents the same paradox as the healthcare system: spectacular at the summit, crumbling at the base. The American university system produces more Nobel laureates, more paradigm-shifting research, and more foundational science than any other system on Earth. The Transformer was invented at Google Brain. CRISPR was developed at UC Berkeley. mRNA technology was pioneered at UPenn. The summit is still the summit.

The base tells a different story. American 15-year-olds rank 36th in mathematics among OECD nations—behind Poland, Estonia, and the Czech Republic. Teacher salaries, adjusted for cost of living, rank in the bottom third of OECD countries. Student loan debt exceeds $1.77 trillion—more than all credit card debt combined—creating a generation that begins adult life burdened by an obligation that did not exist at a comparable scale in any previous generation. The government spends $400,000 educating the world's most talented engineer, hands her a diploma, and then tells her she has sixty days to leave the country—the diploma-frame passage from Chapter 12's Adaptation Five. The base produces the engineer's patients, her neighbors, her voters—the citizenry whose collective capacity determines whether the engineer's work can be deployed at a civilizational scale. When the base crumbles, the summit becomes an island.

The Farmer graduates 3.57 million STEM students annually—roughly seven times the American figure. The quality debate is real, and it was addressed in Chapter 8's talent gap analysis: volume is not the same as capability, and TSMC's 40 years of process knowledge cannot be replicated by graduating more engineers. But volume at scale, combined with the 5,000 AI companies deploying across every sector, creates a deployment substrate that the Hunter's elite-but-narrow pipeline cannot match. The bow's string—the human capital that connects the summit to the base—is fraying.

· · ·

The Inequality Accelerant: When the Bow Breaks for Some, It Breaks for All

Extreme inequality is not merely a moral concern. It is a structural vulnerability that compounds every crack documented above. The top 1% of U.S. households control 31% of the nation's wealth. The bottom 50%—165 million Americans—possess 2.5%. The CEO-to-median-worker pay ratio: 351:1. The social mobility metric: a child born to the bottom quintile has a 7.5% chance of reaching the top quintile—lower than in any peer democracy, lower than in the "socialist" Nordic countries that American politicians invoke as cautionary tales while presiding over mobility rates that the cautionary tales outperform by a factor of two.

The geographical dimension is the broken bow made visible from space. Coastal metropolitan areas—San Francisco, New York, Seattle, Boston—have experienced prosperity so concentrated that it has produced its own pathology: housing costs that exclude the workforce the prosperity requires, creating a peculiar economic arrangement in which the wealthiest zip codes cannot staff their hospitals, teach their children, or serve their food without importing workers from communities an hour's drive away. Meanwhile, Youngstown, Flint, Gary, Camden, and hundreds of towns across the American interior experience a different economy entirely—one in which the factories closed, the tax base collapsed, the hospital followed, the school deteriorated, and the only growth industries are dollar stores, check-cashing outlets, and the kind of warehouse distribution work that keeps Maria Delgado's hours precisely below the threshold where she would become expensive.

The inequality is the accelerant that ignites every other crack. Infrastructure decays because the wealthy opt out of public systems (private schools, concierge medicine, gated communities) while simultaneously lobbying for the tax reductions that defund the public systems everyone else depends on. The trust recession documented in Chapter 3 is, at root, a trust recession *about inequality*—about the growing conviction among the bottom half that the system is rigged, that the rules are written by the people who benefit from them, and that no political action will change the basic architecture of extraction. That conviction is not paranoia. It is an accurate reading of the data. The system *is* extractive. The Four Sacraments *are* operating. Bobby Buyback *is* cannibalizing the industrial base while collecting his bonus. The difference between paranoia and perception is whether the data supports the belief. The data support the belief.

. . .

The Other Current: What the Decay Obscures

The broken bow is real. So are the repair capacities that the decay data obscures.

The Bipartisan Infrastructure Law committed $1.2 trillion to roads, bridges, broadband, water systems, and the modernization of the electrical grid—the largest infrastructure investment since the Interstate Highway System. The CHIPS Act committed $52 billion to semiconductor manufacturing (though, as Chapter 8 will document, the deployment pace has been ironic). The Inflation Reduction Act directed $370 billion toward clean energy. The aggregate: over $1.5 trillion in legislated infrastructure investment since 2021. This is not nothing. It is the first time in a generation that the American political system has produced bipartisan infrastructure legislation at scale.

The execution gap between legislation and deployment is the vulnerability, not the legislation itself. The CHIPS Act's $52 billion has been slow to produce operational fabs. The broadband funding faces permitting and deployment challenges that mirror the California High-Speed Rail's bureaucratic paralysis. But the fact that the legislation passed— in a political environment where 55% of citizens view the opposing party as an existential threat—is itself evidence that the institutional antibodies identified in Chapter 2's Steelman section are not entirely dormant. The SCOTUS antibody works. Bipartisan legislation is possible, if rare. The question is whether the repair pace can match the decay rate—and whether the fourteenth domain's fragmentation will permit the sustained political will that infrastructure repair requires over decades, not news cycles.

Other democracies demonstrate that the broken bow can be repaired without authoritarian methods. Germany's KfW development bank has invested in infrastructure for seventy-five years under a mandate that transcends electoral politics. Denmark achieves top-tier infrastructure while maintaining a robust welfare state. Japan's infrastructure quality—rated A by the World Economic Forum—is maintained by a political system that treats infrastructure as a national asset rather than a partisan football. The repair is not impossible. It requires the thing Chapter 3 diagnosed as missing: the social cohesion to sustain collective investment over a timeline longer than a tweet.

. . .

Interlude: Marcus Visits West Federal Street

Marcus Chen had never been to Youngstown. His understanding of the Mahoning Valley was statistical: median income figures, unemployment rates, the kind of data that arrives clean and abstracted on a Bloomberg terminal. Kevin had suggested the trip after Marcus mentioned Sarah Kowalski's supply-chain analysis for the third time in a week. "You keep talking about her like she's a character in a case study," Kevin said. "Go see the case."

Marcus drove from his Westchester home in three and a half hours. He parked on West Federal Street and sat in his car for a full minute before getting out. The distance between his driveway—a four-bedroom colonial whose assessed value had appreciated 340% since purchase—and this street was 250 miles and an entire civilization. The plywood on the upper-floor windows. The gravel lot where the department store had been. The ailanthus trees in the factory parking lot, growing through cracks in the concrete with the indifference of organisms that have outlasted every economic policy imposed on the landscape they inhabit.

He found the shop. The ceramics in the window were arranged with a care that the street did not match—each piece placed as if the window were a gallery, as if the act of display were itself a form of resistance against the entropy outside. He did not go in. He stood on the sidewalk and looked at the window and thought about the spreadsheet on his laptop—the one titled "Things I Got Wrong"—and realized it was missing its most important tab.

The tab he had never built was the one that measured what the Bloomberg terminal could not: the distance between the America that appeared on his screens and the America that appeared through Sarah Kowalski's shop window. The halocline was not just between nations. It was between zip codes. Between the Westchester driveway and the West Federal sidewalk. Between the $300 billion in Magnificent Seven R&D and the $47 that Maria Delgado paid for a molecule that cost $3.80 at its source.

He drove back in silence. The spreadsheet stayed open on the passenger seat. By the time he merged onto I-80, he had titled the new tab: "The Broken Bow." The first entry: "Median household income, Youngstown: $28,700. Median household income, Westchester: $99,800. Ratio: 3.5:1. Same country. Same century. Different planet."

. . .

<h1 style="text-align:center">BOATMAN'S LEDGER</h1>

Chapter 4

LEDGER TOOL #4: BROKEN BOW INDEX

The Broken Bow Index measures the structural gap between the Hunter's arrow quality (R&D, innovation, talent) and the Hunter's bow condition (infrastructure, healthcare, education, social cohesion). When the gap widens, the arrows become magnificent museum pieces. When it narrows, the arrows fly.

INFRASTRUCTURE ANCHORS

ASCE grade: C−. Investment gap: $4.59T over 10 years. China's infrastructure spending 2023: $1.14T. High-speed rail: China 42,000 km / US 0 km. Lead service lines: $45B replacement cost. 186M Americans served by water systems are in violation of the Safe Drinking Water Act. Broadband: 24M Americans without access.

HEALTHCARE ANCHORS

$4.5T annual spending (17.3% GDP). Life expectancy: declining for 3 consecutive years. Medical bankruptcies: 530,000/year (no other developed nation has this category). Uninsured: 27M. Northside Medical Center (Youngstown): closed 2018. Nearest ER: 23-minute drive. Maria Delgado: $47 for a molecule costing $3.80 at source.

INEQUALITY ANCHORS

Top 1%: 31% of wealth. Bottom 50%: 2.5%. CEO-to-worker: 351:1. Social mobility: 7.5% bottom-to-top-quintile chance. Youngstown median income: $28,700 vs. the national median of $75,000. Poverty rate: 35%. The Gilded Age parallels are not metaphorical: the top 0.1% to bottom 90% ratio mirrors that of 1929.

THE BOATMAN'S WAGER

The Broken Bow is the macro precondition that determines whether the Hunter's latent antibodies can be activated. Illustrative position: long infrastructure rebuild beneficiaries (domestic materials, construction, broadband deployment). Long healthcare-access plays (community health systems, telemedicine, domestic API manufacturing). Short the efficiency-trap beneficiaries whose revenue models depend on the broken bow remaining broken (payday lending, for-profit hospital chains that profit from monopoly access, scheduling-optimization firms). The wager: a civilization that repairs its bow can still contest the competition. A civilization that admires its arrows while the bow rots cannot.

Chapter 4 Data Anchors: ASCE grade C− | $4.59T investment gap | China $1.14T infrastructure (2023) | 42,000 km HSR vs. 0 km | 186M Americans—water violations | 530,000 medical bankruptcies/yr | $4.5T healthcare / declining life expectancy | 27M uninsured | Youngstown: 170K → 58K population, 35% poverty | Northside Medical closed 2018 | Maria Delgado: $47 vs. $3.80 | Top 1%: 31% wealth; Bottom 50%: 2.5% | CEO-to-worker 351:1 | Social mobility 7.5% | $1.77T student debt | STEM: 3.57M (China) vs. ~500K (US) | $1.5T legislated infrastructure since 2021 | Sarah Kowalski: Helen's desk, yellow legal pad, North Carolina ceramics

• • •

A Word to the Reasonable Reader

This chapter has documented the Hunter's broken bow—the social infrastructure erosion that prevents the Hunter's magnificent arrows from flying. The reasonable reader should hold two facts simultaneously: the decay is real, measurable, and in specific domains (healthcare, water, social mobility), unprecedented for a nation of America's wealth. And the repair capacities are also real—the Bipartisan Infrastructure Law, the CHIPS Act, and the Inflation Reduction Act represent the first sustained infrastructure investment in a generation.

The question is not whether the bow *can* be repaired. It can. The question is whether the repair can proceed fast enough, given the fourteenth domain's fragmentation, to close the gap before the Farmer's deployment advantage across the other thirteen domains becomes structurally irreversible. Chapter 5 now shifts from the broken bow to the broken field—the innovation paradox that separates breakthroughs from harvests, and the Farmer's deployment architecture that turns one into the other.

• • •

RITUAL STAGE MARKER

The cheekbones are drawn. The outline of the jaw follows. The painter works in silence, each stroke precise—not yet beautiful, but structural. The face that will hold the deity is taking shape. The audience sees the geometry before the glory: the architecture that makes the transformation possible. Part I's invocation is nearly complete.

PART II

VELLATAM – THE COLLISION

The half-mask is applied. The ochre meets the white. Two worlds coexist in one face—the human and the divine, the Farmer and the Hunter, the field and the forest. The collision has begun.

• • •

RITUAL STAGE MARKER

The paint touches skin. The performer flinches—then steadies. The half-mask begins to form. The drums accelerate. Two deities share one body now, and the ground between them smolders.

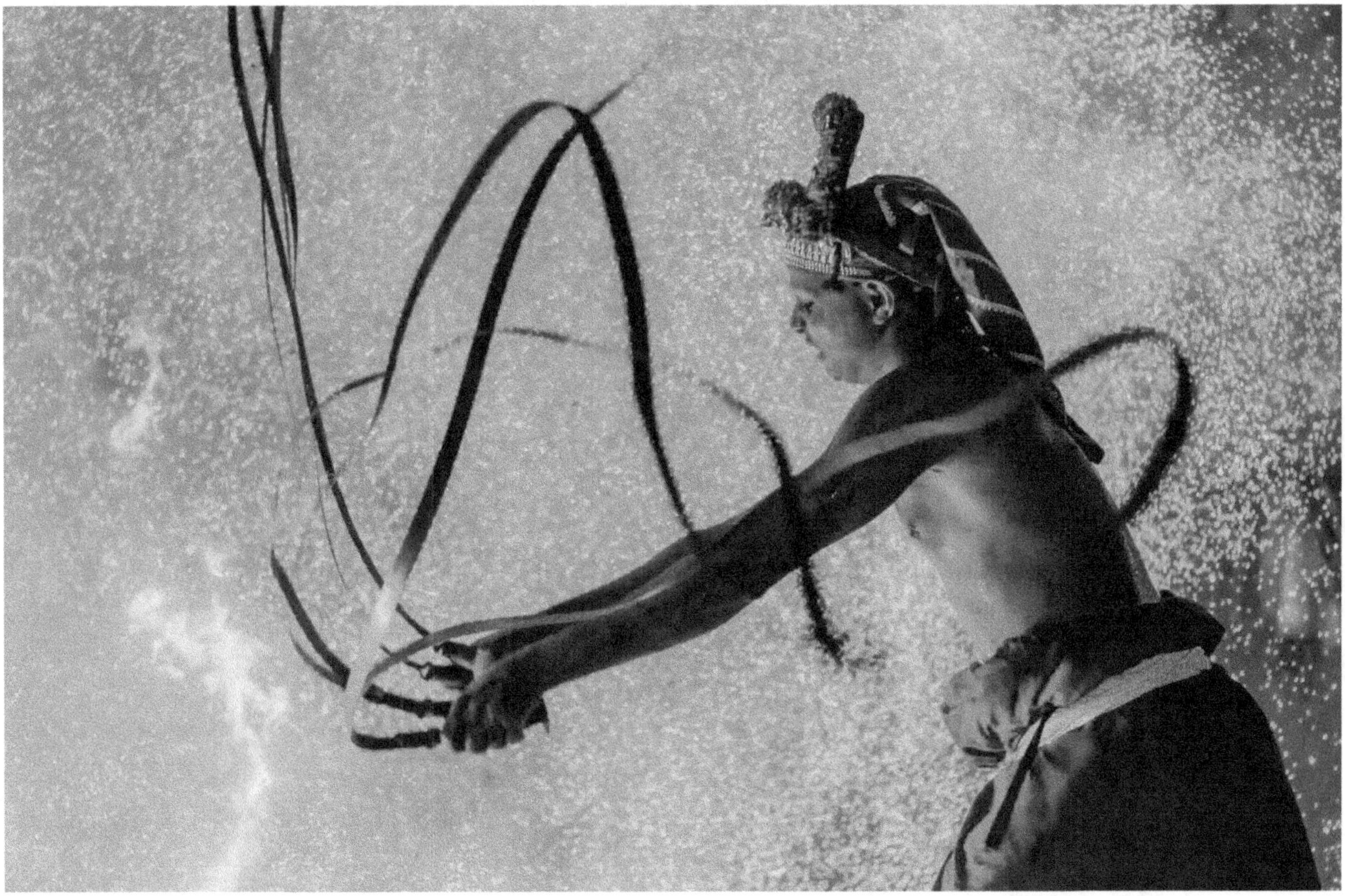

CHAPTER 5

The Field and the Forest

Why Breakthroughs Alone Don't Feed Civilizations

"A tree as great as a man's embrace springs from a small shoot."

— *Lao Tzu, Tao Te Ching, Chapter 64*

先立后破 — *"Build new before demolishing old."*

The mask is carved by a thousand hands. The divine face is the Field's collective offering.

— *after the Theyyam tradition*

. . .

The Gunpowder Paradox

In 1132, a Chinese engineer packed bamboo tubes with gunpowder and launched them at an advancing army. By 1860, gunpowder—refined, European-engineered, deployed in Lord Elgin's cannons—was destroying the civilization that invented it.

The paradox does not end at gunpowder. China perfected the magnetic compass; European navies used it to colonize half the known world. China pioneered movable type printing; Gutenberg's press mass-produced the Bibles that underpinned the religious empire. China developed paper currency; Western banking systems weaponized debt instruments into instruments of sovereign subjugation. Four gifts to the world. Four weapons turned against the giver. The pattern is agonizing in its consistency: genius at the bench, paralysis at the factory gate. Invention without deployment is intellectual philanthropy—you do the thinking, and someone else does the conquering.

In Kuttanad, the old boatmen have a word for this: *pantham*—the flame that burns but never cooks. A bright fire, a beautiful fire, the kind of fire visitors stop to photograph. But the rice stays raw. The fish stays cold. The flame is all display and no pot. China's Four Great Inventions were the world's most spectacular *pantham*—and the Century of Humiliation was the price of all that light without heat.

This is the **Time War's** oldest wound—and its deepest lesson. The civilization that invents on one timescale but deploys on another will always be consumed by the civilization that closes the gap between invention and deployment to zero. The Gunpowder Paradox is the Time War's governing equation: *deployment velocity times domain breadth equals civilizational momentum.* The Farmer solved it. The Hunter is still debating whether the equation exists.

And here is the twist that should keep every American strategist awake at three in the morning: the Gunpowder Paradox has flipped. The Transformer architecture is American. The GPU ecosystem is American. The foundational science of deep learning emerged from American and Canadian universities. But DeepSeek—a hedge fund quant's side project in Hangzhou—deployed that American science more efficiently than every American lab combined. The Hunter invented fire. The Farmer cooked with it. Again.

DeepSeek is not a rupture in this narrative. It is the harvest from humiliation's soil—the moment when a civilization that remembers every innovation it gifted to foreign armies finally decided to do both the planting *and* the reaping. The Chinese strategic principle 先立后破 ("build the new before demolishing the old") is parallel construction at an industrial scale: you construct the replacement alongside the old structure, prove it works, prove it scales, prove it costs less, and only then let the predecessor retire.

. . .

The Field and the Forest: A Visual Parable

Stand at the boundary and look in both directions.

To your left: the Forest. Vertical. Canopy-dominated. Seven trees so tall they block the sun for everything beneath them—the Magnificent Seven, their crowns gleaming in the light of Wall Street's permanent afternoon. The undergrowth is dying. Young saplings cannot reach the light because the canopy takes it all. The Forest floor is littered with the carcasses of companies that tried to grow beneath the Seven—Juicero ($120 million, hand-squeezable), Theranos ($9 billion, zero working blood tests), Cruise ($12 billion, recalled its fleet), Argo AI ($3.6 billion, dissolved). The soil is rich with their composted ambitions. But nothing new grows, because the canopy admits no light. The Forest produces spectacular individual specimens. It does not produce a harvest.

To your right: the Field. Flat. Visible. Planted in rows that stretch to every horizon. Thousands of seedlings, each too small for any single one to matter, each drawing water from the same underground aquifer—the SOE root system described in Chapter 1, the open-source irrigation that DeepSeek uncapped for the entire ecosystem. No single plant is indispensable. No single stalk blocks the light for its neighbors. The Field is tended by 3.57 million farmers—the STEM graduates who arrive each year, none of them indispensable individually, all of them essential collectively. When one seedling fails, the others compensate. When a pest attacks one row, the adjacent rows are a different crop entirely. The Field does not produce spectacular individual specimens. The Field produces grain. And grain, unlike timber, feeds civilizations.

The Forest's theory of growth: the tallest tree wins. This is the logic of venture capital, of winner-take-all platform economics, of Nvidia's GPU monopoly and Apple's App Store tithe. It produces extraordinary concentrations of value at the canopy level. It also produces a dying floor.

The Field's theory of growth: the richest soil wins. No single plant matters; the ecosystem matters. The irrigation channels matter. The fact that the rice feeds the people who plant the trees whose shade protects the rice—that compound return, invisible in any single crop's ledger, is what determines whether the civilization eats.

The Hunter lives in the Forest. The Farmer works the Field. And the Field, season by season, is expanding into the Forest's territory—not by cutting down the great trees, but by making them irrelevant. You do not need to fell the tallest oak if you can plant wheat in every direction until the oak stands alone in a sea of grain, magnificent and useless.

. . .

The Quant Who Broke Wall Street's Spine: Liang Wenfeng

In the cosmology of American AI, the creation myth requires a visionary CEO on a stage in San Francisco, wearing either a leather jacket or a carefully curated hoodie that costs more than a mid-range sedan. The assumption baked into every investor slide deck is that intelligence scales with money: bigger clusters, bigger models, bigger market caps. If you want to build God, you need Nvidia's GPU cloud and the annual GDP of Portugal.

Liang Wenfeng did not receive this memo. Possibly, it was intercepted by U.S. export controls.

Born in the 1980s in a fifth-tier city in Guangdong province—the kind of place where the son of a primary school teacher counts as local gentry, the kind of city that Kuttanad would recognize instantly: small, overlooked, thick with the humidity of ambition that has nowhere local to go—Liang studied engineering at Zhejiang University. His first career was in the brutally empirical world of quantitative finance, where your model either makes money or it doesn't, and no amount of charismatic keynoting can disguise a 30% drawdown.

In 2015, at thirty, Liang co-founded High-Flyer, a quantitative hedge fund. By 2021, it managed over 100 billion yuan—roughly $14 billion—making investment decisions through servers, not portfolio managers. "Quantitative funds do not have portfolio managers making the decisions," Liang told the *China Securities Journal*. "They are just servers." This is the sentence that should terrify Wall Street—not because quant funds are novel, but because of the mentality it reveals. Liang's worldview is architectural, not theatrical. He does not build in order to announce. He builds in order to solve.

The decisive moment came in late 2022. The Biden administration's export controls had landed. The A100 GPUs Liang had stockpiled were now the last batch he would legally acquire. He gathered his core team—twelve researchers, a conference room in Hangzhou, no catering budget—and posed a question that would have gotten him laughed out of any Silicon Valley pitch meeting: "If we can never buy another American GPU, can we still build a frontier model?"

The room was quiet. Then one of the researchers said: "The question isn't whether we can afford the compute. The question is how little compute we can get away with."

That sentence became DeepSeek's founding philosophy. The question is not how much compute you can afford. The question is: how little do you need?

In July 2023, Liang spun off DeepSeek. Venture capital firms balked—no quick exit, no obvious monetization. High-Flyer funded it from its own balance sheet. The absence of external investor pressure became, paradoxically, DeepSeek's greatest strategic asset. Without quarterly VC board meetings, Liang's team could think like farmers instead of hunters.

The Prologue documented what followed: V3's 671-billion-parameter architecture at $5.6 million training cost, R1's 97.3% on MATH-500, and the $589 billion single-day loss that rewrote the AI competition's pricing premise. Here, the question is not what DeepSeek achieved but *how* it achieved it—and what the method reveals about the difference between the Field and the Forest.

For the non-specialist: DeepSeek's team found ways to make AI think more efficiently—activating only the neurons needed for each task rather than firing the entire network, the cognitive equivalent of reading only the relevant clauses of a contract instead of the whole document. They compressed the model's memory to reduce bandwidth consumption without sacrificing quality. And they did this on H800 GPUs that American export controls had explicitly designed to be *inadequate* for frontier AI, which is rather like being told your kitchen knife is too dull to cook with and responding by inventing a recipe that requires no cutting.

Liang's own philosophy, devastatingly simple: "This time, our goal isn't quick profits but advancing the technological frontier to drive ecosystem growth." And on open-sourcing: "Our real moat lies in our team's growth. Open-sourcing and publishing papers don't result in significant losses. For technologists, being followed is rewarding. Giving back is an honor."

In Theyyam, the *Ullil Kaanal* comes not from the most elaborately costumed performer but from the one whose devotion is most architecturally precise. Liang Wenfeng is not possessed by the God of Scale. He is possessed by the God of Efficiency. And that deity, it turns out, is far more dangerous.

. . .

Innovation Theater: The Juicero Catechism

The American' invention without deployment' pathology has become performance art. Call it innovation theater: the art of raising hundreds of millions, generating rapturous media coverage, and producing a product that is either unnecessary, fraudulent, or both.

Juicero. In 2016, Silicon Valley's most prestigious venture firms invested $120 million in a WiFi-connected juice press that squeezed proprietary juice packets into a glass. The device cost $400. Bloomberg reporters discovered you could achieve identical results by squeezing the packets with your bare hands. One hundred and twenty million dollars—channeled through the most sophisticated innovation ecosystem in human history, to build a machine outperformed by a human fist.

The Mechanical Turk scandal. In 2023 and 2024, multiple "AI companies" that had raised tens of millions on the promise of artificial intelligence were revealed to be powered not by algorithms but by hundreds of human workers in offshore call centers. They had *performed* AI without *building* AI. They had constructed a digital Potemkin village, and the villagers were earning $3 an hour in Manila.

The Farmer does not do innovation theater. The Farmer cannot afford to. When your national strategy is premised on the memory of a century of humiliation, you do not invest $120 million in a juice press. You invest $5.6 million in a model that outperforms the $100 million ones. The Field does not applaud. The Field harvests.

The Innovation Graveyard: A Satirical Census

The Juicero deserves company in its grave. The innovation theater's cemetery is vast, well-maintained, and adding new residents at a pace that would constitute a public health crisis if the deceased were biological rather than corporate.

Theranos: $9 billion in valuation for a blood-testing device that could not, in a detail the fundraising pitch somehow omitted, test blood. Elizabeth Holmes raised more capital on the strength of a black turtleneck and a baritone voice than most countries spend on their entire healthcare R&D budget. The Farmer, whose biotech companies are now licensing $66 billion in novel molecules to Western pharma firms, does not wear turtlenecks. The Farmer wears a lab coat and publishes results in *Science Advances*. One of these costuming choices produces drugs. The other produces documentaries.

WeWork: $47 billion in valuation for the insight that young professionals enjoy free beer with their desk rental. Adam Neumann surfed his way to a $1.7 billion exit while the company lost $3.2 billion in a single year. In the time it took WeWork to discover that paying $1.30 for every dollar of revenue is not, technically, a business model, BYD's Wang Chuanfu—the orphan from Anhui who started with $300,000 in borrowed capital—had scaled from batteries to automobiles to 4.6 million vehicles annually. One founder received $1.7 billion for failing. The other received $107 billion in market capitalization for producing the most successful automotive scaling in history. The Vanity Metric Delusion does not merely misprice companies; it also misprices the market. It misprices *civilizations*.

Quibi: $1.75 billion raised to produce ten-minute videos for people who already had YouTube. Operational lifespan: six months. Funding-to-content ratio: approximately $250 million per month of existence. For context, DeepSeek trained a frontier AI model for $5.6 million. Quibi spent that much on the launch party. The Forest produces Quibis with the same reliable efficiency that an apple tree produces apples—seasonally, inevitably, and with a biological compulsion that no amount of evidence can override. The Field does not produce Quibis. The Field produces factories.

The aggregate tells the story that the individual autopsies cannot. In 2024, American venture capital deployed approximately $170 billion. The top-performing VC fund returned 3.1x over ten years—strong by industry standards and entirely irrelevant to the strategic question, because the relevant comparison is not internal returns but deployment outcomes. China's government-guided funds deployed approximately $120 billion that year—not into innovation theater but into semiconductor equipment, EV battery capacity, AI deployment infrastructure, and the low-altitude drone economy. The Hunter's $170 billion produced twelve unicorns, four spectacularly entertaining bankruptcies, and approximately zero net additions to the nation's manufacturing base. The Farmer's $120 billion expanded equipment self-sufficiency from 30% to 35%, added 89,000 enterprises to the low-altitude economy, and scaled SMIC's N+3 process node from laboratory to production. One system optimizes for announcement. The other optimizes for deployment. And the field that feeds the village does not care which announcement was more photogenic.

Sarah callback — deployment vs. invention at Main Street scale

The deployment-over-invention thesis has a Main Street corollary. Sarah Kowalski in Youngstown is not debating whether American innovation is superior to Chinese innovation. She is debating whether she can find a domestic ceramics supplier whose production costs are within 30% of the Chinese price. The theoretical question—who invents better?—is irrelevant to her on Tuesday. The operational question—who manufactures at a price her customers can afford?—is the only question that keeps the lights on.

Sarah's North Carolina ceramics decision is the Field-and-Forest parable at boutique scale. The Forest (American artisanal ceramics) produces beautiful, innovative pieces at premium prices. The Field (Chinese industrial ceramics routed through Vietnam) produces standardized inventory at prices Sarah's customers recognize as normal. The Juicero question—"is this project optimized for announcement or for deployment?"—applies to Sarah's shelf as precisely as it applies to Silicon Valley's laboratories. The ceramics that look beautiful in a gallery but price out her customers are Juiceros. The ceramics that sell are God's Eyes.

. . .

The Energy Chasm: Where Physics Becomes Destiny

One data point deserves its own section, because it renders every other comparison secondary. It determines who controls the twenty-first century. And it is a number that almost no American strategist discusses, because discussing it would require acknowledging that the competition is not a tech war. It is an energy war. And the energy war is already over.

China's electricity generation has surpassed 10,000 terawatt-hours annually—and the trajectory is going vertical. The United States and Europe have flatlined for twenty years. China added more renewable generation capacity in 2024 alone than the total installed renewable capacity of any single European nation.

Imagine the transmission lines crossing the Gobi Desert. They do not run in straight lines but in curves that follow the wind, the sand, the patient logic of a civilization that has been building infrastructure since before Rome. The lines hum at 50 hertz, but the frequency that matters is compound: each terawatt-hour enables the next data center, and the data center trains the next model, and the model optimizes the grid that generates the next terawatt-hour. The loop is visible from the Gobi—if you know where to look.

State Grid Corporation—the largest utility on Earth, introduced in Chapter 1—delivers industrial electricity at $0.03–0.05 per kilowatt-hour. This is the SOE root system's most consequential expression: a civilizational utility that treats electricity as strategic infrastructure rather than a quarterly revenue line. Pull State Grid from the interdependency web, and the whole thing goes dark.

The AI implications are decisive. Chinese AI data centers in Guizhou, Inner Mongolia, and Ningxia train on electricity priced at $0.03–0.05/kWh—roughly one-third to one-half the cost of Northern Virginia, where most American hyperscale data centers cluster. The cost to train GPT-5 in California: north of $500 million. The cost to train the equivalent in Shenzhen: a fraction of that. And the gap will widen, because China is building power generation capacity at a pace that America's regulatory environment and quarterly-return-obsessed utility companies are structurally incapable of matching. The man with the deeper well survives the longer drought. The Farmer's well is bottomless. The Hunter's meter is running.

. . .

Interlude: Marcus Visits the Juicero Graveyard

Marcus Chen had a ritual. Every Friday afternoon, he walked three blocks from his office to a coffee shop that did not have WiFi. He brought a notebook. Analog. Moleskine.

This Friday, the notebook was filling up with a list that had no heading because Marcus could not think of one that wasn't profane. American technology investments that had produced spectacular announcements and no deployable product. Juicero: $120 million. Theranos: $9 billion. Lordstown Motors: $1.6 billion. Nikola: $34 billion peak valuation, one truck that rolled downhill unpowered for a promotional video. Cruise: $12 billion. Argo AI: $3.6 billion.

The combined capital destroyed or wasted by the companies on his list exceeded $27 billion. For that sum, you could have funded 4,821 DeepSeek training runs. Or built 2.8 million BYD Seagulls. Or funded the entire Big Fund semiconductor initiative with change left over for a modest space program.

Then he pulled up his firm's energy cost model. Marcus plugged in the Chinese industrial electricity rate: $0.04/kWh. He plugged in the Northern Virginia rate: $0.10/kWh. He ran the same AI training workload through both. The cost differential was not a rounding error. It was a chasm. The same training run, same model architecture, same number of GPU-hours—and the Chinese version cost 60% less, before you even accounted for the cheaper hardware. The energy chasm wasn't a footnote in the competition. It was the competition. Everything else was commentary.

The Field Model vs. The Forest Model: The Deployment Ledger

The Field operates on a fundamentally different logic—one invisible to analysts trained in the Forest's epistemology. Where the Forest optimizes for breakthrough, the Field optimizes for deployment at a civilizational scale. Where the Hunter asks, "How do I build the most powerful thing?" the Farmer asks, "How do I make the powerful thing feed everyone?"

AI: DeepSeek. Frontier performance at a fraction of conventional cost. And crucially: open-source. The Field shares its seeds. The Forest patents them.

EVs and ADAS: BYD's God's Eye. Advanced driver assistance across 21 models, including vehicles priced at $9,550. Hardware cost per vehicle: approximately $385. Compare to Waymo's $175,000 sensor suite. That is a 454:1 ratio that renders the entire Western autonomous vehicle business model a mathematical impossibility at scale.

Batteries: CATL. >39% global share. Shenxing LFP battery: 0-80% charge in 10 minutes. And because battery chemistry is identical for EVs and grid-scale storage, CATL's vehicle dominance translates directly into stationary energy storage dominance. The Field does not build walls between sectors. The Field builds irrigation channels.

Semiconductors: SMIC. Despite being cut off from ASML's EUV lithography, SMIC has achieved 5nm-class production using older DUV equipment through multi-patterning. The Field doesn't need perfection. It needs sufficiency at scale.

AI Accelerators: Huawei Ascend. Approximately 60% of an H100's performance is produced domestically, beyond the reach of export controls, running inference for models trained on DeepSeek's efficiency architecture. The export controls were supposed to be a noose. Instead, they became a greenhouse.

The Western analyst asks: "Who is the 'Chinese OpenAI'?" "Who is the 'Chinese Tesla'?" These questions betray a Hunter's epistemology applied to a Farmer's reality. There is no single Chinese winner because the game is not a hunt. It is a harvest. And by that metric—the only metric that history ultimately cares about—the Field is already winning.

The DeepSeek Efficiency Thesis Deepened

The DeepSeek event deserves one more analytical beat before this chapter closes Part I, because its efficiency thesis extends beyond AI into the manuscript's central argument about civilizational time horizons.

DeepSeek's R1 model was trained for $5.6 million in marginal compute. OpenAI's GPT-4 training cost is estimated at over $100 million. The performance gap between the two models, on standard benchmarks, is narrower than the cost gap by a factor of approximately fifteen. The Western analytical response to DeepSeek was revealing: within seventy-two hours, the narrative had cycled from "impossible" to "suspicious" to "irrelevant" to "actually we knew this all along"—the five stages of American-exceptionalism grief, compressed into a trading week.

But the efficiency thesis is not about one model. It is about what happens when the efficiency principle—do more with less, optimize for deployment rather than scale, treat constraints as design parameters rather than obstacles—is applied systematically across every domain in the interdependency web. SMIC's multi-patterning achieves 5nm without the $380 million EUV machine. BYD's Blade Battery achieves structural safety without the complex thermal management systems that add $2,000 to Western EV costs. The Type 076 drone carrier was built in three years, while the Ford-class program exceeded its own timeline by 7 years. Each individual efficiency might be dismissed as a workaround, a compromise, a "cheap version." Collectively, they constitute a civilizational thesis: **the Farmer does not need the best tool. The Farmer needs the right tool at the right cost at the right time, produced entirely on the Farmer's own soil.**

In Kuttanad, the boatmen have a phrase for this: *ullil kaanal ishtamulla vithum koode*—"inner vision chooses the seed that suits the soil." Not the most expensive seed. Not the most impressive seed. The seed that will grow in *this* field, with *this* water, in *this* season. The Silicon Valley VC chooses the seed that looks best on a pitch deck. The Farmer chooses the seed that feeds the village. The deployment gap is, at its root, a seed-selection problem—and the Farmer's selection criteria are better suited to a multi-decade strategic competition than the Hunter's.

. . .

The Interdependency Web: Why the Gap Cannot Be Closed Domain by Domain

Trace the web. Electric vehicles require batteries (CATL). BYD's millions of vehicles generate driving data that feeds God's Eye algorithms enhanced by DeepSeek R1. The AI is trained on Huawei Ascend chips fabricated by SMIC— closing the loop on export controls. EV batteries are chemically identical to grid-scale storage batteries, so CATL's vehicular dominance translates into stationary storage dominance, enabling renewable integration, powering smart city infrastructure, generating urban mobility data, and training the next generation of algorithms. Eight domains, eight interlocking advantages, each one reinforcing all the others.

In Kuttanad, this is the *orumuttu* lesson: build a temporary bund to block a single channel when the monsoon has already found twelve channels to flow through, and every sandbag on one channel increases the pressure on the other eleven.

American strategy attempts to counter each node independently. Tariffs on EVs. Entity-list restrictions on Huawei. Export controls on chips. IRA subsidies for batteries. Each countermeasure addresses a single vine while ignoring the root system that funds, coordinates, and sustains all thirteen domains simultaneously.

. . .

The Burning Ghat: A Preview

In Hindu funeral rites, the burning ghat is where the body is consigned to flame, where the physical form that everyone agreed was permanent is revealed to have been temporary all along. In Theyyam, there is a parallel: the *theechamundam*, the fire-offering, where the old form must be consumed before the deity can inhabit the new vessel.

For now, know this: Phase 1 (Price Compression) is already complete. BYD's $385 ADAS versus Waymo's $175,000. DeepSeek's training cost versus $100 million-plus. If your business model depends on a price premium, the Field can undercut by 95%, and you are not competing. You are composting. The remaining five phases—Feature Democratization, Data Flywheel Acceleration, Standard-Setting, Talent Gravity, and Ecosystem Colonization—are underway at varying speeds across domains. Chapter 12 will map the pyres in granular detail. The fire has been lit. What burns is not destroyed. What burns is transformed.

. . .

BOATMAN'S LEDGER

Chapter 5

LEDGER TOOL #4: INTERDEPENDENCY WEB SCORE

INTERDEPENDENCY WEB SCORE: 24/25

Cross-domain compound advantage confirmed across AI, EVs, batteries, semiconductors, AI accelerators, grid storage, telecom, and AV data. Missing anchor: indigenous EUV lithography (workaround via multi-patterning achieves sufficiency, not parity). Score rises to 25/25 if SMEE delivers usable EUV within 36 months.

HALOCLINE TRANSPARENCY INDEX

How visible is the web to Western analysts? Score: 2/10. Most analysts see individual companies (surface). Almost none see the ecosystem (undercurrent). The gap between the Web Score (24/25) and the Transparency Index (2/10) *is* the investment opportunity. The market is pricing trees. The alpha is on the forest floor.

ENERGY CHASM MULTIPLIER

China 10,000+ TWh (vertical) vs. US/Europe flatlined. Electricity at $0.03–0.05/kWh vs. $0.08–0.12 in Northern Virginia. Factor a 3–5x energy cost advantage into every AI and manufacturing valuation. The physics cannot be tariffed.

THE BOATMAN'S WAGER

Reduce Mag 7 hardware-heavy positions by an illustrative 8%. Reallocate to multi-domain deployment plays and Global South infrastructure beneficiaries. The trade is not "short Nvidia." The trade is: "The interdependency web is systematically underpriced by a market whose analytical model evaluates each domain in isolation."

Chapter 5 Data Anchors: Gunpowder Paradox: 4 inventions / 4 weapons | Pantham: flame without cooking | Field vs. Forest: canopy logic vs. soil logic | Juicero $120M + Theranos $9B + Cruise $12B + Argo AI $3.6B + Nikola $34B + Lordstown $1.6B = $27B+ innovation theater | BYD God's Eye $385 vs. Waymo $175K (454:1) | Shenxing 10-min charge | Huawei Ascend ~60% H100 | Energy chasm: 10,000+ TWh vs. flatlined; $0.03 vs. $0.10/kWh | Liang Wenfeng: "How little compute can we get away with?"

. . .

A Word to the Reasonable Reader

If you have read this far and your primary reaction is defensive—"but American innovation is still the best in the world!"—then congratulations: you have identified the exact paradigm this chapter was designed to challenge.

No one is denying American brilliance. The Transformer is American. GPT-4 is American. The GPU ecosystem is American. These are genuine achievements born of a genuine culture of scientific inquiry, risk-taking, and intellectual ambition. But brilliance without deployment is the Gunpowder Paradox flipped: this time, the Forest invents while the Field deploys. And deployment—at civilizational scale, across interlocking domains, with compound advantages that accelerate over time—is what determines whose infrastructure becomes the global default for the next century.

The reasonable reader may also object: "But China's system has its own weaknesses—demographic decline, property market collapse, youth unemployment, authoritarian constraints on innovation." These are real and serious challenges, and this book does not pretend otherwise. Chapter 11 will assess them with the same rigor applied here. But a farmer with chronic pain and a field that produces grain still outfeeds a hunter with perfect posture and no prey. The question is not which system is flawless—neither is—but which system's structural advantages compound faster than its structural weaknesses degrade.

China is not beating America at America's game. China is playing a different game entirely, one whose rules were written in rice paddies ten thousand years ago and updated in Hangzhou data centers last Tuesday.

* * *

CHAPTER 6

The Scorched Field

Trade, Rare Earths, and the Diplomatic Harvest

"The opportunity of defeating the enemy is provided by the enemy himself." — Sun Tzu

"Whoever controls salt and iron controls the kingdom." — Sang Hongyang, 81 BCE

When the monsoon fails, the farmer redirects the canals.

— after the Theyyam tradition

* * *

Undercurrent: Salt, Iron, and the Oldest Playbook in Statecraft

In 81 BCE, the Legalist minister Sang Hongyang argued before the Han court that state monopoly over essential commodities—salt, iron, liquor—was not merely fiscal policy. It was the architecture of sovereignty. The state that controls the resources upon which all other production depends controls the kingdom itself. The Confucian scholars who opposed him argued for free trade. The Legalists won. And two thousand years of Chinese statecraft absorbed the lesson: sovereignty begins with control of essential inputs, not finished products.

Two millennia later, the essential inputs have changed—from salt and iron to gallium, germanium, rare earth permanent magnets, and lithium battery precursors. But the strategic logic is identical. And the Farmer, inheriting a tradition of state control over resources that predates the Roman Empire, has built the twenty-first century's salt-and-iron monopoly with the patience and comprehensiveness that only a civilization with a two-thousand-year institutional memory could sustain.

In Kuttanad, the boatmen understand this principle in their marrow. The man who controls the *thodu*—the sluice gate between the canal and the paddy—controls the harvest of every field downstream. It does not matter how skilled the downstream farmer is, how fertile his soil, how perfect his seeds. If the *thodu* closes, the water stops, and the field dies. China's rare earth processing monopoly is the *thodu* of the twenty-first century. And the Hunter, for all his technological brilliance, is farming downstream.

There is a halocline property relevant to this chapter: *osmoregulation*. Organisms that live at the halocline must constantly manage the flow of salt in and out of their cells to survive. Too much exposure to either current is lethal; survival requires constant adjustment. This is the precise condition facing every nation navigating the US-China divide in 2026. Klaus Reinhardt, the German executive we are about to meet, is osmoregulating. Sarah Kowalski in Youngstown is osmoregulating. The seventy leaders who visited Beijing are osmoregulating. The halocline is not merely the author's analytical position. It is the strategic condition in which the entire global economy now operates.

The Chinese proverb 抛砖引玉 ("cast a brick to attract jade") describes the tactic of sacrificing something small to gain something valuable. In the trade war of 2025–2026, China "cast" manufacturing volume to Vietnam, Mexico, and Indonesia—the brick—while retaining intellectual property, component supply chains, and rare earth processing capacity—the jade. The West celebrated the rerouting as evidence of decoupling. The Chinese planner smiled. The factories relocated. The profits stayed. And 信 (xìn, trust/credibility)—the currency upon which alliances are built and dissolved—began flowing eastward as leader after leader booked flights to Beijing.

* * *

The Executive Who Bowed Twice: A Vignette from Beijing

Call him Klaus Reinhardt. He is fifty-four, a senior vice president at BMW's China operations, and in February 2026 he stood in the Great Hall of the People as part of Chancellor Friedrich Merz's delegation of thirty German business leaders—executives from Mercedes-Benz, BMW, BASF, Siemens, and Deutsche Bank—signing cooperation documents with Chinese counterparts while his government publicly maintained a posture of "cautious engagement."

The first bow was ceremonial. Klaus had practiced it in the hotel mirror that morning—the precise 15-degree inclination that diplomatic protocol required, the duration calibrated to communicate respect without conveying submission. It was a bow designed for cameras. It committed nothing. It cost nothing. It was weightless.

The second bow happened in his chest, and no camera caught it.

It happened when his phone buzzed during the signing ceremony. A message from BMW Munich: Q4 2025 numbers confirmed. China sales had exceeded Germany's for the third consecutive year. The Chinese EV market was not merely a revenue source; it was where the technology standards were being set, where battery partnerships were being formed, and where autonomous-driving data was being generated at a volume that BMW's European operations could not match. Klaus felt the number settle into his sternum—not as data, but as gravity. The second bow was not diplomatic. It was existential.

Klaus represents the alliance paradox that defines the current moment: the gap between political rhetoric and economic reality has grown so wide that a single human being can embody both sides simultaneously. Publicly, Germany "de-risks." Privately, Mercedes-Benz deepens its joint ventures in China. Publicly, Britain maintains a "cautious approach." Privately, Starmer signs cooperation documents in Beijing. Publicly, Canada signals alignment with Washington. Privately, Carney flies to Beijing because Canadian commodities need buyers.

* * *

Tariff Forensics: The Autopsy of a Self-Inflicted Wound

Chapter 2 documented the five-act parable of the tariff saga. Here, the forensic finding in a single sentence: every metric moved in the wrong direction.

The stated objective was to reduce the trade deficit, bring manufacturing home, and force China to negotiate from a position of disadvantage. These are not unreasonable objectives. A $1.24 trillion goods trade deficit is a genuine policy concern. But the actual outcome? China's trade surplus exceeded $1 trillion in 2025—the largest in its history. Manufacturing did not reshore; it rerouted. The Supreme Court ruled the tariffs illegal. Over $160 billion in collected tariffs awaits refund.

In Youngstown, Sarah Kowalski's revised quotes arrived on a Tuesday. By Thursday, her Vietnamese supplier had confirmed the 46% surcharge. By Friday, two of her regulars—retirees on fixed incomes, women who had been shopping at her grandmother's store since before Sarah was born—mentioned they were "cutting back." Sarah did not need a forensic report on the tariff. She had the cash register.

. . .

抛砖引玉: *Rerouting, Not Reshoring*

The tariff cheerleaders pointed to one statistic with particular satisfaction: China's share of U.S. imports of goods declined from approximately 22% in 2017 to roughly 9% by early 2026. The narrative was compelling: tariffs were "working." China was being decoupled.

The narrative was also wrong.

Follow one "Vietnamese" smartphone from factory to consumer. The screen: manufactured in Dongguan. The battery cells: Chinese. The processor: Chinese-licensed IP. The assembly equipment: built in Shenzhen. The production line: designed by Chinese engineers. The factory itself: a joint venture with a Chinese parent that relocated final assembly from Guangdong to Ho Chi Minh City in 2019. The shipping container: loaded onto a COSCO vessel, a state-owned company that is the Farmer's logistics arm. The port at the other end: managed by China Merchants Group. The working capital: provided by a state-backed Chinese bank. The only Vietnamese contribution was the labor of final assembly and the label on the box.

The factories that relocated to Vietnam, Mexico, and Indonesia were not private entrepreneurs freelancing. They were nodes in a network coordinated by SOE logistics companies that treated tariff rerouting as supply chain optimization, executed with military-grade institutional discipline.

India's "Make in India" program attracted Chinese investment in electronics assembly, particularly in smartphones and solar panels. The Chinese component in a "Made in India" smartphone typically accounts for 65–80% of the bill of materials. India's manufacturing miracle is real. But it is, to a significant degree, a Chinese manufacturing miracle with Indian labor and an Indian flag.

Sarah callback — tariff rerouting made personal

Sarah Kowalski's supply chain tells the rerouting story in miniature. When she traced the labels backward—Chapter 2's Vietnamese-costume revelation—she discovered what the tariff forensics above document at macro scale: the goods did not move. The final assembly moved. The value chain remained Chinese. The tariff is attached to the costume, not the content.

But Sarah's story has a second act that the macro data misses. After the Liberation Day tariffs hit, three of Sarah's Vietnamese suppliers raised prices between 38% and 46%. Sarah called each one. The conversations were revealing. The first supplier explained, with the weary frankness of a man who has had this conversation forty times that week, that his factory's operating costs had not changed—his *import* costs had changed, because 70% of his raw materials came from Chinese suppliers who had passed their own tariff-related cost increases downstream. The tariff wall had not protected Sarah. It had added a layer of cost to a supply chain that was already Chinese, while creating the administrative illusion of geographic diversification.

The second supplier offered Sarah an alternative: direct-ship from the Chinese parent company's Guangdong warehouse, invoiced through a Cambodian intermediary, at the pre-tariff price minus 8%. Sarah stared at the email for a long time. The tariff regime that was supposed to bring manufacturing back to America, in practice, taught a small-business owner in Ohio how to route invoices through Cambodia. The *thodu*—the strategic leverage point—was supposed to be the tariff. The actual *thodu* was the supply chain's infinite capacity to reroute around obstacles. Sarah chose neither supplier. She ordered the North Carolina samples instead. The margins would be tighter. The story would be different. The *thodu* would be hers.

* * *

Interlude: Marcus Reads the Label

Marcus Chen's twelve-year-old daughter, Emma, needed new sneakers. This was not, under normal circumstances, a geopolitically significant event. But Marcus had developed the occupational hazard of seeing supply chains where others saw only shoes.

The sneakers were $89.99 at a store in White Plains. The label said, "Made in Vietnam." Forty-five minutes and one very patient daughter later, he had learned that the shoe's synthetic upper was manufactured from Chinese-produced polymers. The rubber sole used Chinese-processed synthetic rubber. The adhesives were Chinese. The machinery used to assemble the shoe was made in China. The factory was a joint venture with a Chinese parent company that had relocated from Dongguan.

"Dad," Emma said, with the tone of a child who has exhausted her patience for parental eccentricity, "can we just buy the shoes?"

They bought the shoes. Marcus added "Vietnam rerouting" to the spreadsheet he had titled "Things I Got Wrong." The file was getting longer.

* * *

The Salt-and-Iron Weapon: Rare Earths as Strategic Leverage

Sang Hongyang's principle has found its twenty-first-century expression in China's rare-earth and critical-mineral export control regime. The numbers: China mines over 60% of the world's rare earth elements, processes over 90%, and produces approximately 94% of rare earth permanent magnets. These magnets are essential in electric vehicle motors, wind turbines, guided missiles, fighter jet engines, MRI machines, and the hard drives that store the world's data.

The evolution since 2023 reads like a masterclass in graduated coercive leverage—the Farmer tightening the *thodu* one valve at a time. July 2023: gallium and germanium. October 2023: graphite. August 2024: antimony and superhard materials. December 2024: outright ban on gallium, germanium, and antimony exports to the United States. February 2025: tungsten, tellurium, bismuth, molybdenum, indium. April 2025: seven medium-to-heavy rare earth elements essential for permanent magnets in precision-guided munitions. October 2025: the most expansive package yet—rare earth processing technologies and know-how, plus extraterritorial licensing requirements.

Each escalation was calibrated to a specific American provocation. The Farmer does not initiate. The Farmer responds. And each response is precisely one step beyond the Hunter's expectation—sufficiently escalatory to inflict pain, sufficiently restrained to preserve the option for de-escalation.

The F-35 Joint Strike Fighter—$1.7 trillion, the most expensive weapons system in human history—requires approximately 920 pounds of rare earth materials per airframe. Ninety-four percent of the world's rare-earth permanent magnets are manufactured in China. The permanent magnets in the F-35's electric generators are not just *made* in China. The *design specifications assume Chinese manufacturing tolerances.* Switching to a non-Chinese magnet would require recertifying the entire electrical system—a process estimated at $2 billion and five years. This is not a dependency. This is a weapons system with Chinese engineering assumptions baked into its architecture.

Then there is Skydio. America's leading domestic drone manufacturer—the Pentagon's answer to Chinese drone dominance—reduced to rationing drones with a restriction so absurd it reads like satire but is a procurement reality: **one battery per drone.** The world's most technologically advanced military power cannot equip its premier surveillance drone with a *spare battery* because the batteries depend on Chinese supply chains.

MP Materials and Australia's Lynas represent the most advanced Western alternatives. Together, they process a fraction of what China produces. And MP Materials ships a substantial portion of its ore to China for processing—a dependency within the alternative itself. The five-to-ten-year alternative source timeline is optimistic. The Hunter built the cathedral. The Farmer built the quarry. And the cathedral cannot stand without stone.

The Rare Earth Trap: A Satirical Anatomy

The rare earth dependency is the Efficiency Trap's most elegant expression—a situation so perfectly engineered for strategic absurdity that it deserves the satirical register before the analytical one.

The F-35 Lightning II—the most expensive weapon system in human history, with a lifecycle cost of $1.7 trillion—contains approximately 920 pounds of rare-earth materials. These materials are processed overwhelmingly in China. The nation against which the F-35 is principally designed to project power supplies the materials without which the F-35 cannot be built. One pauses to admire the architectural elegance: the Hunter has constructed a $1.7 trillion defense program whose material foundation is controlled by the adversary the program is meant to deter. This is the strategic equivalent of building a castle whose drawbridge is operated by the enemy. It is the Efficiency Trap elevated to the level of geopolitical performance art.

The Mountain Pass mine in California—America's only operational rare earth mine—produces ore. It ships the ore to China for processing. The processed materials return to the United States as components in defense and technology systems. America mines the rock, China adds value, America buys it back at a markup that includes the processing margin, shipping costs, and the strategic dependency. The circular logic is breathtaking: the mine that is supposed to reduce Chinese dependency ships its output to China because no American processing facility exists at a commercial scale. The mine is a monument to the specific species of magical thinking that assumes extraction is the same as capability. It is not. Extraction is a hole in the ground. Capability is a supply chain. China has the supply chain. America has the hole.

MP Materials, the mine's operator, has announced plans to build a domestic processing facility. Estimated completion: 2025–2026. Current status: under construction, with timelines that industry analysts describe as "ambitious." In the same timeframe, China has expanded its rare-earth processing capacity by approximately 15%, consolidated regulatory control through export licensing requirements, and begun restricting exports of gallium and germanium—strategic materials essential for semiconductors and fiber optics. The Hunter is building one processing facility on one timeline. The Farmer is expanding the entire processing ecosystem on a faster timeline. The race is not close. It is not, in any meaningful sense, a race. It is a processing monopoly being politely challenged by a PowerPoint presentation about future domestic capacity.

. . .

The Debt and the Jade: What the "Debt-Trap" Critique Gets Right and Wrong

The BRI's diplomatic harvest is real and accelerating. But so is the critique: isn't China's infrastructure diplomacy just debt colonialism with better branding?

The honest answer is: it's complicated. And "complicated" is precisely the answer that neither Beijing's propagandists nor Washington's hawks want you to hear.

Sri Lanka's Hambantota Port became the poster child—a 99-year lease granted to China Merchants Port Holdings in 2017 after Sri Lanka could not service its loans. Pakistan's CPEC corridor: $62 billion, transformed infrastructure, saddled Pakistan with debts exceeding 30% of GDP. Djibouti's debt to China exceeded 70% of GDP and hosts China's first overseas military base. The cases are real. The critique has substance.

But it oversimplifies by assuming a monolithic "debt-trap" strategy. Malaysia's East Coast Rail Link was renegotiated at a 33% discount—demonstrating that recipient nations push back. Ethiopia's Addis-Djibouti Railway was renegotiated in 2024 with extended repayment periods. The pattern is not uniformly predatory. It is opportunistic—which is what all great-power infrastructure lending has always been, from the Marshall Plan to the World Bank's structural adjustment programs, which came with political conditions that Beijing's loans conspicuously do not.

The Farmer's advantage is not that BRI lending is benevolent. It is that the Farmer offers an alternative. When the IMF conditions its loans on austerity and governance reforms that recipient governments find politically toxic, the Farmer offers a loan with no political conditions and a completed railway as the deliverable.

. . .

The Other Current: What the Farmer's Partners Are Not Saying

But this chapter's analysis requires one more turn of the halocline lens—this time directed at the Farmer's own field.

The rare earth controls are not merely strategic leverage. They are coercive instruments that impose genuine costs on nations caught in the middle. When China restricted gallium and germanium exports in July 2023, the immediate casualties were not American defense contractors but European semiconductor manufacturers who had done nothing to provoke Beijing—collateral damage in a bilateral dispute they did not start. Japan's rare earth crisis of 2010, when China cut exports following a territorial dispute over the Senkaku Islands, remains a cautionary memory: strategic leverage, once wielded, erodes the *xìn* it was meant to build. The seventy leaders who flew to Beijing did so because China was predictable. The rare earth weaponization introduces precisely the unpredictability that made the Hunter's tariffs self-defeating.

The diplomatic harvest, too, has its blight. The *xìn* flowing eastward is conditional on continued delivery. When a Chinese-built railway in Kenya stalls due to cost overruns, a Belt and Road port in Myanmar becomes entangled in civil conflict, or a promised 5G rollout in Southeast Asia arrives with surveillance capabilities that recipient governments did not request, the credibility account draws down. The Farmer's table is set with predictability. But predictability is not the same as trust. And trust, once broken by the discovery that the infrastructure came with intelligence-collection capabilities, is harder to rebuild than a railway.

The honest assessment: the Farmer's diplomatic position is stronger than the Hunter's in 2026, and the rare earth monopoly is the single most potent strategic lever in the competition. But leverage that is exercised too aggressively creates the conditions for its own obsolescence. Every gallium restriction accelerates investment in alternative sources. Every weaponized export control validates the Hunter's argument that economic engagement with China carries strategic risk. The Farmer's greatest danger is not the Hunter's tariffs. It is the possibility that the *thodu* the Farmer controls becomes the reason the downstream nations start digging their own wells.

India: The Swing State in the Halocline

The rare earth analysis above—and indeed this book's entire Farmer-Hunter framework—has a blind spot that intellectual honesty requires naming. India is not the Farmer. India is not the Hunter. India is the halocline's most consequential fish—the organism that thrives precisely at the boundary between the two currents, drawing nutrients from both while belonging fully to neither.

The demographic contrast is the headline: India's median age is approximately 28, versus China's 39. India's working-age population will continue to expand through the mid-2040s, while China's will contract by millions annually. India produces 1.5 million engineering graduates per year, a figure that is rising, while China's demographic cliff threatens to widen the 200,000–250,000 semiconductor engineer shortfall documented in Chapter 8. If demographics were destiny, India's century would follow China's as surely as monsoon follows drought.

But demographics are not destiny, and the Indian paradox complicates both the Farmer's narrative and the Hunter's. India occupies a peculiar position in the rare earth and trade architecture: it is simultaneously a beneficiary of the Farmer's supply chain (70% of India's API precursors come from China, making its generic pharmaceutical industry a Chinese-origin industry with Indian finishing) and a beneficiary of the Hunter's friend-shoring strategy (the Quad partnership, the India-Middle East-Europe Economic Corridor, the growing American courtship of New Delhi as a counterweight to Beijing). India settled Russian oil in dirhams and rupees while maintaining Quad membership. India accepted Chinese rare earth imports while joining American export-control coalitions. The *osmoregulation* framework from Chapter 6's Ledger applies to India with particular precision: India is not choosing between the currents. India is *managing* the currents—maintaining the membrane between them at a pressure it can sustain.

The strategic implications for the domains documented in this book are significant. In rare earths, India's own reserves (the world's fifth-largest) are largely unprocessed—creating a dependency on Chinese processing that mirrors the global pattern. In pharmaceuticals, India's role as the "pharmacy of the world" is built on Chinese API precursors— a dependency that the BIOSECURE Act does not address because it was written to restrict Chinese firms, not the Chinese-origin supply chain that runs through India. In semiconductors, the Tata-PSMC fab in Gujarat is India's first serious domestic chip manufacturing initiative—a 28nm facility that will produce trailing-edge chips, not frontier, but that represents the beginning of an Indian semiconductor ecosystem.

The honest assessment: India's demographic dividend is the decade's most underpriced macro variable. But the dividend requires infrastructure (India's roads, ports, and power grid are improving rapidly under the National Infrastructure Pipeline but remain below Chinese levels), governance reform (India's bureaucratic complexity remains a significant friction on deployment speed), and educational quality at the base (India's IITs are world-class; its primary education system serves 250 million children with uneven results). The dividend is real. Its realization is contingent. And the competition between the Farmer and the Hunter will be shaped—perhaps decisively—by which of India's osmoregulatory systems ultimately prevails.

* * *

The Diplomatic Harvest: Seventy Leaders and the Gravitational Shift

By March 2026, more than seventy world leaders had visited Beijing since December 2025—a diplomatic parade unprecedented in its breadth and its defiance of American alliance management. Germany's Merz brought thirty business leaders and 120 Airbus orders. Britain's Starmer declared strengthening ties "in the national interest." Canada's Carney made the first Canadian prime ministerial visit in eight years.

One visit deserves closer attention. In January 2026, Indonesian President Prabowo Subianto—a former general, a man Washington had spent decades cultivating as a strategic partner, a leader whose country controls the Malacca Strait through which 40% of global trade passes—flew to Beijing and signed a $21 billion infrastructure and technology package. The package included a Chinese-built high-speed rail extension from Jakarta to Surabaya, a 5G network rollout across Java and Sumatra by Huawei, and an "AI+Agriculture" collaboration that would embed Chinese precision-farming systems across Indonesia's 7.5 million hectares of rice paddies. When a reporter asked Prabowo about Washington's concerns, he replied: "Indonesia has 280 million people. We need infrastructure, not advice." The Farmer set the table with concrete. The Hunter set the table with talking points.

The Chinese concept of 信 (*xìn*)—trust, credibility—is relevant here. China's diplomatic advantage was not that China was trustworthy in some absolute moral sense. It was that China was more *predictable* than the alternative. The Five-Year Plans arrive on schedule. The Belt and Road contracts are honored. The trade terms do not change because a president woke up angry. In a world where the alternative is tariff whiplash and alliance threats delivered via social media, predictability is the most valuable currency in statecraft.

The Farmer is constructing a new institutional architecture—SCO, BRICS+, RCEP, the Asian Infrastructure Investment Bank—that provides alternatives to every Western-led institution. Not replacements. Alternatives. The distinction matters: the Farmer does not need to destroy the Hunter's institutions. The Farmer needs only to provide options. And when the Hunter's institutions become unreliable, the options become default choices.

And through it all, one chair at the table remained conspicuously empty. The chair the United States should have occupied—not to capitulate, not to appease, but to compete. To offer an alternative that matched the Farmer's concrete with the Hunter's own concrete. The empty chair was not a diplomatic snub. It was a strategic confession: the Hunter had nothing to put on the table except threats against the people already seated.

* * *

BOATMAN'S LEDGER

Chapter 6

LEDGER TOOL #5: REROUTING ALPHA & ALLIANCE EROSION INDEX

REROUTING ALPHA

China's import share fell from 22% to 9%—while its trade surplus reached $1T and its manufacturing footprint expanded into Vietnam ($123B), Mexico, India, and Indonesia. A "Made in Vietnam" smartphone is 65–80% Chinese by bill of materials. Decoupling is a label change, not a supply chain change.

RARE EARTH LEVERAGE SCORE: Existential

China processes 90%+ of rare earths and produces 94% of permanent magnets. F-35: 920 lbs per airframe, with Chinese engineering tolerances baked into the design. Skydio: one battery per drone. Alternative sources: 5–10 years. The Farmer controls the *thodu*, and every field downstream depends on his hand.

ALLIANCE EROSION INDEX

70+ leaders to Beijing since Dec 2025. Germany: China overtook the US as top trade partner (€251.8B). Indonesia: $21B infrastructure package. Starmer: first UK PM visit in 7 years. Carney: first Canadian PM visit in 8 years. Watch the gap between public "de-risking" statements and private investment flows. When the gap exceeds 30%, the alliance is functionally dissolved regardless of communiqués.

OSMOREGULATION STRESS INDEX

Every nation at the halocline is managing exposure to both salt/fresh water simultaneously. The nations that osmoregulate successfully—maintaining relationships with both currents without overdosing on either—will thrive. The nations that pick a side will die of salt poisoning or freshwater shock. Track: bilateral trade balance shifts, infrastructure contract origins, diplomatic visit frequency.

THE BOATMAN'S WAGER

Illustrative 10% allocation to rerouting beneficiaries: Vietnam/Mexico/India manufacturing ETFs (brick recipients) + Western rare earth mining and processing (MP Materials, Lynas—the 5–10 year hedge). Short European defense contractors with unhedged exposure to rare earths. Long Airbus over Boeing for as long as tariff tensions redirect Chinese orders. Buy the conduit. Hedge the dependency. Trade the gravity, not the rhetoric.

Chapter 6 Data Anchors: China import share 22%→9% | Vietnam $123B manufacturing | Rare earths: 60% mining / 90% processing / 94% magnets | F-35: 920 lbs RE per airframe + Chinese tolerance lock-in | Skydio: 1 battery/drone | $1.24T goods trade deficit | 70+ leaders to Beijing | Indonesia $21B package | Merz: 120 Airbus order | xìn as diplomatic currency | 抛砖引玉: brick/jade rerouting logic | Osmoregulation as strategic condition | Hambantota 99-year lease / Pakistan CPEC $62B / Djibouti 70% debt

· · ·

A Word to the Reasonable Reader

If this chapter has made you feel a particular species of loneliness—the loneliness of watching allies walk toward the Farmer's table while the Hunter stands in the Rose Garden insisting that the empty chairs are a negotiating tactic—then you have grasped the chapter's emotional argument.

What this chapter claims, with the evidentiary weight of tariff forensics, rerouting data, rare earth dependency analysis, and the diplomatic parade, is that the Hunter's current strategy is producing results that are, in every measurable dimension, the opposite of their intent. The scorched field was supposed to be China's. It turned out to be America's.

But note what this chapter does *not* claim. It does not claim that China's diplomatic position is invulnerable—the Other Current section above documented the risks of overusing leverage and of delivery failures. And the Hunter's institutional antibodies—SCOTUS, immigrant talent, reinvention capacity, alliance depth—are precisely the mechanisms that could, under Rooseveltian leadership, reverse the current trajectory. Chapter 7 takes the collision deeper—into shipyards and drone swarms.

· · ·

The mask's right eye is complete. Through it, the performer sees weapons laid at the altar—not as objects but as purpose. Not as metal but as the Farmer's patient arithmetic: the cost of a Tomahawk, the cost of a 5G tower, the cost of a spare battery, the cost of an empty chair at the table where the world is being fed.

CHAPTER 7

The Farmer's Arsenal

Shipbuilding, Drones, Space, and the New Military Calculus

"Those who take the field first and await the foe will be rested." — Sun Tzu

不战而屈人之兵 — *"Subdue the enemy without battle."*

A sword swung at the river only tires the arm.

— after the Theyyam tradition

· · ·

Opening: A Tale of Two Shipyards

On the morning of November 15, 2025, two events occurred simultaneously on opposite sides of the Pacific.

At Jiangnan Shipyard in Shanghai, the Type 076—the world's first purpose-built drone carrier, equipped with an electromagnetic catapult system that until recently only the United States possessed—commenced sea trials. The ship had been built in approximately three years. Three years from keel to ocean.

At Bath Iron Works in Maine, a Government Accountability Office report was being finalized that documented, for the fourteenth consecutive year, schedule delays, cost overruns, and workforce shortages across the U.S. Navy's shipbuilding programs. The Constellation-class frigate—intended to be a simple, affordable surface combatant—had already experienced design changes and delays before the first ship left the yard.

One country was launching a ship that had no equivalent in any navy on Earth. The other was publishing a report about why it could not finish the ships it had already started.

This chapter is about one thesis: **the asymmetric cost thesis.** The Farmer does not need to match the Hunter weapon for weapon. The Farmer needs to produce enough capability per dollar to make the Hunter's expensive platforms untenable. The sword swung at the river tires the arm. The river keeps flowing.

· · ·

Undercurrent: The Deepest Wound Was Military

Of all the wounds inflicted during the Century of Humiliation, the deepest was the military one. It was not trade concessions that broke the Qing dynasty's spine. It was the inability to defend against the concessions. The British Navy that sailed up the Yangtze in 1842 had seventy-three ships. China had none that could contest them.

In Kuttanad, the old boatmen tell a story about the *kayal*—the great lake formed when the backwater swallowed a village that had no bund, no wall, no embankment against the tidal surge. The village had abundant rice, abundant fish, and abundant children. It had everything except the capacity to defend what it had grown. The *kayal* swallowed it whole, and now the fishermen cast their nets over the rooftops of drowned houses. *Kaaval illaatha veetil kazhcha illa*—in a house without a guard, there is nothing to see. China's Century of Humiliation was a *kayal* that swallowed a civilization. The Farmer's arsenal is the bund being built, so the water never rises that high again.

The principle of civil-military fusion—军民融合—is the institutional expression of this response. Western analysts treat it as a regulatory category. This framing misses its nature. Civil-military fusion is not a policy. It is an *ontology*. The same shipyards build container vessels and destroyers. The same drone manufacturers deliver packages in Shenzhen and produce reconnaissance platforms for the PLA. The same battery technology powers BYD's EVs and the submarines patrolling the South China Sea.

In Kuttanad, this is the ancient practice of *kettuvallam* building—the construction of boats that serve as grain barges in peace and troop transports in flood. The planks are fitted without nails, bound with coir rope and cashew resin, and each joint is flexible enough to absorb the monsoon's violence without cracking. The builder never forgot that the monsoon could become a war. Neither has the Farmer.

The American equivalent is the defense procurement industrial complex—a system so elaborately dysfunctional that it has achieved something the Chinese system cannot: it has made building weapons more expensive than using them. The Pentagon's acquisition cycle averages seven to ten years from requirement to deployment. The Farmer does not need to match the Hunter's sword. The Farmer needs to produce enough spears to exhaust the Hunter's arm.

· · ·

The Welder on the Yangtze: Zhang Mei

Call her Zhang Mei. She is forty-one years old, a certified Class A welder at Jiangnan Shipyard in Shanghai—the oldest continuously operating shipyard in China, founded in 1865 as the Jiangnan Arsenal under the Self-Strengthening Movement. The Arsenal's founding director, Zeng Guofan, was explicit about its purpose: to learn the "barbarian" technologies that had defeated China and turn them against the barbarians. Zhang Mei knows this history. Not as academic knowledge but as occupational identity—the way a Kuttanadan paddy farmer knows the history of the 1341 flood, not from textbooks but from the shape of the land beneath his feet.

Inside her locker at the yard, taped to the door with a piece of electrical tape that has been replaced so many times the adhesive residue forms its own archaeology, is a drawing. Her daughter made it in second grade—a stick figure in a hard hat, orange sparks flying from both hands, and underneath, in characters large enough to read from across the changing room: 妈妈焊接世界 ("Mama welds the world"). Zhang Mei has a thermos she carries everywhere— green, dented, the brand name worn to illegibility—and a habit of humming the melody of a Shanghai opera aria while she works, the tune rising and falling with the rhythm of the welding passes.

Her welding certification required eight years of training. The arc, when she strikes it, produces a blue-white light so intense it would blind an unshielded eye in seconds. In Kuttanad, the boatman's oar is an extension of his spine. At Jiangnan, Zhang Mei's torch is an extension of her intention. The sparks are not waste. They are offering.

She has worked on container ships bound for Maersk and CMA CGM. She has worked on LNG carriers, the most technically demanding commercial vessels afloat. And she has worked on components for the Type 076. Zhang Mei does not see a contradiction between her commercial and military work. She sees a shipyard. The welding techniques are the same. The steel is the same, because all CSSC ships are built to military specifications. Revenue from foreign commercial orders subsidizes the R&D that developed the electromagnetic catapult.

This is civil-military fusion in its most literal, most human form: a welder whose hands do not distinguish between the steel of a container ship bound for Rotterdam and the steel of a drone carrier bound for the South China Sea.

The British Navy that sailed up the Yangtze in 1842 had seventy-three ships. The shipyard at Jiangnan—built on the same river, still bearing the name the first reformers inscribed—now launches more tonnage annually than the entire fleet that humiliated China 183 years ago. Zhang Mei knows this. The sparks fly for a reason.

. . .

The Shipyard Civilization: Scale as Strategy

CSSC—$120 billion in assets, operating under a dual mandate of commercial revenue *and* PLA Navy capability—produced more commercial vessel tonnage in 2024 than the entire United States shipbuilding industry has produced since the end of World War II. That statistic compares one Chinese company's annual production with eighty years of cumulative American production.

The PLA Navy now operates over 370 ships and submarines, making it the world's largest navy by hull count. CSSC's military output in 2025: one catapult-equipped aircraft carrier (the Fujian, commissioned November 2025—making China only the second nation to operate EMALS(Electromagnetic Aircraft Launch System) technology on a carrier), one large amphibious assault ship, at least seven destroyers, six frigates, the first new-generation stealth frigate (Type 054B), and unpublished submarine deliveries. The Type 076 commenced sea trials. No other country has built, or is building, anything comparable. (A reasonable reader might note that the Type 076's operational capability is unproven; first-of-class vessels historically encounter significant integration challenges. This is fair. The strategic significance lies not in the ship's combat readiness today but in the industrial capacity that produced it in three years.)

The construction tempo is itself a strategic weapon. China builds a frigate in approximately 25 months and a destroyer in roughly 2.5 years. The Type 075 amphibious assault ship: fourteen months average. Compare: the Virginia-class submarine has stretched beyond five years per unit. The USS Gerald R. Ford was delivered seven years late—if China had begun building a carrier on the same day the Ford's delay was announced, China's carrier would have been commissioned, sea-trialed, and conducting operations before the Ford left the yard.

The Ford-class program exceeds $13 billion per ship. China's Type 003 was built from keel to commission in roughly six years—a timeline equivalent to the Ford-class's schedule *overrun alone*. In a prolonged competition, the side that builds faster replaces losses faster, adapts designs faster, and compels the adversary to match a production tempo it cannot sustain.

· · ·

The Drone Revolution and the Low-Altitude Economy

While the West debates drone regulation, China has built an entirely new economic sector: the low-altitude economy. Valued at ¥1.5 trillion ($210 billion) in 2025 and projected to reach ¥3.5 trillion by 2035, it encompasses all civilian and commercial activity within airspace up to 3,000 meters—drone logistics, urban air mobility, agricultural aviation, infrastructure inspection, emergency response, and the manufacturing ecosystem that supports them.

Shenzhen alone has established 310 low-altitude logistics routes and over 1,200 takeoff-and-landing facilities. Across the country, 89,000 active enterprises are engaged in the low-altitude economy, with 11,700 new registrations in the first five months of 2025—a 220% year-on-year surge.

The interdependency web manifests here with textbook precision. The drones are powered by CATL batteries. Their navigation runs on BeiDou satellites. Their AI flight-coordination algorithms were trained on infrastructure that includes DeepSeek's efficiency architecture. Their communications travel on Huawei's 5G networks. The low-altitude economy is another node in the same web, drawing water from the same irrigation system that feeds every field the Farmer cultivates.

Ukraine's conflict provided the laboratory that validated every Chinese assumption about the drone revolution. The massive deployment of commercial-grade drones—modified with 3D-printed munition holders, adapted for FPV strike missions—demonstrated that the revolution is operational, not theoretical. Chinese manufacturers have learned every lesson and are now producing military-grade variants at scales that dwarf anything the Ukrainian conflict has consumed.

Now picture the scenario that keeps Pacific Fleet commanders awake. 0300 hours. A formation of 2,000 autonomous drones—each costing approximately $500, each coordinated by AI algorithms refined through millions of Shenzhen delivery flights—launches from a civilian container vessel. Total cost: $1 million. Target: a $2 billion AEGIS-equipped destroyer with ninety-six interceptors at $2 million each.

If every interceptor hits—a generous assumption against maneuvering swarm targets—the destroyer expends $192 million and eliminates 96 drones. One thousand nine hundred and four remain. The magazine is empty.

Now the second wave launches. From a different container ship, fifty miles away. Another 2,000 drones. The Admiral does the arithmetic and realizes the only winning move is not to be within range.

The total cost of exhausting the destroyer's defenses: less than $50,000 in drones. The cost of replacing the destroyer: $2 billion and five years. The asymmetric cost thesis, rendered in arithmetic so simple that Zhang Mei could compute it on the back of her thermos.

Ukraine's Laboratory: What the Farmer Learned

Ukraine's conflict provided the Farmer's strategists with something no simulation can replicate: a real-time, high-intensity laboratory for every assumption about modern warfare's relationship to cost, scale, and industrial capacity.

The lessons were specific and operationally devastating for the Hunter's procurement model. First: a $500 commercial drone carrying a 3D-printed munition can destroy a $10 million armored vehicle. The cost ratio—twenty thousand to one—makes the F-35's 650:1 ratio against the DF-21D look almost charitable. Second: ammunition consumption in high-intensity conflict exceeds peacetime estimates by factors of five to ten. Ukraine fired approximately 7,000 artillery rounds per day during peak operations. The United States produces approximately 28,000 155mm shells per month—enough for four days' supply at Ukrainian consumption rates. Third: attrition warfare favors the side that produces faster, cheaper, and domestically. Russia's ability to sustain losses that would have been politically catastrophic for a Western democracy—and to replace material through domestic production and North Korean/Iranian supply chains—demonstrated that the industrial-base advantage is the ultimate strategic variable. Not the quality of the weapon. Not the training of the operator. The ability to produce the replacement before the loss becomes irreversible.

The Farmer watched every lesson. Chinese manufacturers observed FPV drone tactics, kamikaze drone logistics, electronic warfare countermeasures, and the specific failure modes of Western equipment in sustained high-intensity combat. They are now producing military-grade variants at scales that dwarf anything the Ukrainian conflict consumed—not because China plans to fight in Ukraine's style but because the cost ratios and production-speed data validated the asymmetric cost thesis that structures this entire chapter. The sword-and-river metaphor is not theoretical. Ukraine proved it under fire. And Zhang Mei's shipyard is building the vessels that will carry the drones that the laboratory validated.

* * *

Hypersonics, Space, and the Cost Cascade

During her lunch break on the day the Type 076 departed for sea trials, Zhang Mei sat on a bollard at the river's edge, thermos in hand, and scrolled her phone. The Xinhua headline was about the DF-21D test series. She didn't understand the technical details—maneuvering reentry vehicles, terminal guidance sensors, boost-glide trajectories. But she understood the number: $20 million per missile. She looked back at the ship she had spent three years welding. She thought about the American carrier that the ship was designed to face: $13 billion. She divided one by the other. 650. Zhang Mei was not a strategist. But she was a welder who understood materials, and the material fact was that the Farmer's arithmetic was devastating.

The DF-21D anti-ship ballistic missile—the "carrier killer"—costs approximately $20 million per unit. The USS Gerald R. Ford costs $13 billion. The cost ratio is 650:1. The DF-26 "Guam Killer" extends the thesis from sea to land. Chinese hypersonic glide vehicles—maneuvering at Mach 5+ while executing unpredictable flight paths—present a targeting challenge no current American missile defense system was designed to address.

In space, the asymmetric cost thesis continues. Tiangong—operational since 2022, continuously crewed, hosting 267 scientific projects—costs an estimated $8–10 billion. The ISS lifecycle cost: $150 billion. When the ISS is deorbited circa 2030, Tiangong will be the only permanent crewed orbital platform in existence. The BeiDou satellite navigation system provides global coverage independent of the American GPS system. Every Chinese weapon system operates on an indigenous navigation backbone that no adversary can deny. And BeiDou is integrated into the Belt and Road's digital infrastructure, creating a global ecosystem of Chinese-origin navigation.

The aggregate cost of China's military modernization across all domains—the navy, the drone fleet, the space station, the satellite constellation, the hypersonic weapons program—is almost certainly less than the lifecycle cost of the F-35 program alone ($1.7 trillion). The F-35 mission-capable rate has historically hovered around 55–60%, meaning on any given day, roughly 40–45% of the fleet cannot fly. The cost per flight hour: $36,000—more than four times the F-16 it replaced. The Farmer's response is not to build a better F-35. It is to build a *system* of assets that, in combination, neutralize the F-35's advantage at a fraction of its cost: a J-20 at one-third the unit cost, a thousand drones at one-thousandth, a hundred anti-ship missiles at one-six-hundredth, an integrated air defense network, and a space station providing persistent ISR coverage.

In Kuttanad, we have a word for a boat so ornate it cannot float: *azhakulla thoni*—the beautiful canoe. The Pentagon has built the most beautiful canoe in human history. The Farmer has built a fleet.

. . .

The Hunter's Overextension: Three Theaters, One Navy

In 2025, the United States maintained simultaneous military operations across three theaters: the Middle East (Israel/Iran/Yemen), Caribbean (Venezuela), and Western Pacific (China deterrence). The U.S. Navy maintains eleven carrier groups. At any given time, roughly three to four are available for global operations. The mathematics leaves no margin. A Taiwan contingency requires a minimum of three carrier groups, plus submarine deployments, plus forward-deployed air assets from Guam and Japan. With one group pinned in the Mediterranean and one in the Gulf, the Pacific has exactly one carrier available—against a PLA Navy that now operates 370+ ships from bases that are a short sail from the Taiwan Strait.

Then came Operation Epic Fury. On February 28, 2026, the United States and Israel launched strikes against Iranian nuclear facilities, infrastructure, and leadership targets. The operation consumed additional carrier deployments, Tomahawk inventory at $2.4 million per missile, and logistics capacity that the Pacific posture could not spare.

The Taiwan Contingency: What the War Games Show

The manuscript has referenced Taiwan throughout without squarely confronting the scenario that keeps every Pacific strategist awake. The evasion ends here: a book that documents the web of interdependencies' thirteen domains while declining to analyze the most likely catalyst for the web's rupture flinches at its own thesis.

The Center for Strategic and International Studies ran twenty-four tabletop war-game iterations of a Chinese amphibious invasion of Taiwan in 2023. The results were consistent across scenarios: the United States and its allies could likely prevent a successful invasion—but at a cost that redefines "victory." In most iterations, the U.S. lost two aircraft carriers, between ten and twenty major surface combatants, and approximately 3,200 service members in the first three weeks. Japan's bases in Okinawa sustained significant damage. Taiwan's infrastructure was devastated. And TSMC's fabrication facilities—producing over 90% of the world's most advanced semiconductors—were rendered inoperable, whether through direct military action, preemptive sabotage, or the simple fact that a semiconductor fab requires uninterrupted power, ultra-pure water, and vibration-free foundations, none of which survive a military conflict on the island.

The semiconductor famine that would follow is not hypothetical. It is arithmetically predictable. Every advanced chip in every iPhone, every Nvidia GPU, every autonomous vehicle controller, every medical imaging device, every military guidance system produced in the Western world flows through TSMC's fabs. The disruption would cascade through every domain this book has documented: EVs without controllers, AI without training chips, the F-35 without its avionics, the financial system without the data centers that clear its transactions. The Farmer's SMIC, operating at 5nm with 30–33% yields, would become—by default rather than by quality—the world's most strategically valuable semiconductor manufacturer. The ceiling-versus-floor framework from Chapter 11 would cease to be analytical. It would become a physical reality: the ceiling (TSMC) would be gone, and the floor (SMIC) would be the only surface left to stand on.

The cascade extends to the dollar system documented in Chapter 10. A Taiwan conflict would trigger comprehensive financial sanctions against China—Scenario C, the Salt Tide. China's CIPS would activate as the primary settlement system for the 189 countries whose alternatives to SWIFT are already operational. The bifurcation that Wei's Law predicts as a long-term erosion process would occur as a sudden rupture. The digital yuan, mBridge, and every bilateral settlement agreement documented in Chapter 10 would shift overnight from alternative plumbing to primary infrastructure. The salt tide would not seep. It would surge.

A register change is required here. The human cost of kinetic operations is not a strategic variable to be optimized. It is a moral weight.

In the operations conducted across these theaters—in airstrikes, in naval bombardments, in the kinetic actions that the military lexicon euphemizes as "precision engagements"—thousands of civilians lost their lives. Each number is a person. Each person had a name, a family, a future extinguished by ordnance released from platforms costing billions, guided by satellites costing hundreds of millions, authorized by decision-makers sitting in climate-controlled rooms thousands of miles from the impact point. The technological precision of the weapon does not reduce the moral weight of the life it takes.

In the Theyyam tradition, the deity also arrives in grief, accounting for what was lost so that something else might be preserved. The ritual includes both lamentation and celebration. The thousands of civilians are not data points. They are the reminder that the weapons laid at the altar are not abstractions, that the sparks from Zhang Mei's welding torch produce steel that will one day be aimed at human beings, and that the asymmetric cost ratios in this chapter ultimately measure the capacity to inflict violence at scale.

不战而屈人之兵: subduing the enemy without battle. Not through moral superiority—the Farmer's human rights record does not permit that claim. Through strategic patience. Through the accumulated *shi* of a civilization that remembers what military helplessness costs and has decided, with the quiet determination of Zhang Mei striking her arc against steel on the banks of the Yangtze, that it will never pay that price again.

* * *

BOATMAN'S LEDGER

Chapter 7

LEDGER TOOL #6: ASYMMETRIC COST THESIS

The thesis in a single sentence: the Farmer builds capability per dollar; the Hunter builds capability per unit. When capability per dollar compounds across the SOE substrate, and capability per unit compounds across a $1.7-trillion single-aircraft program, the trajectories diverge irreversibly. The sword tires the arm. The river keeps flowing.

COST ASYMMETRY ANCHORS

DF-21D $20M vs. Ford-class $13B (650:1) | Drone swarm $1M (2,000 units) vs. AEGIS $2B (96 interceptors, empty after first wave) | F-35 $1.7T lifecycle vs. China's entire military modernization | Tiangong $8–10B vs. ISS $150B lifecycle | CSSC annual output > entire US shipbuilding since WWII | Ships/$B ratio: China ~20x US

TIME-TO-PRODUCTION RATIO

A DF-21D takes months to produce. A Ford-class takes years. A Chinese frigate: 25 months. A Virginia-class submarine: 5+ years. In a war of attrition, months beat years every time.

FORCE ALLOCATION STRESS TEST

11 carrier groups. 3–4 available. Taiwan contingency minimum: 3 groups. Current Pacific availability: 1. Deficit: 2 carrier groups. This is not a strategy gap. It is a physics gap.

MORAL ANCHOR

Thousands of civilian deaths. This number is not a data point. It is a weight. It belongs in the ledger because a ledger that prices weapons without pricing their human cost is a ledger missing its most important line.

THE BOATMAN'S WAGER

Reduce U.S. defense-industrial concentration by an illustrative 7%. Add exposure: Chinese shipbuilding supply chain, autonomous systems integrators, counter-drone technology developers, space launch plays. Contrarian position: long companies developing AI-coordinated swarm systems for Western militaries, because the Hunter's only viable response to the cost asymmetry is to adopt the Farmer's logic—volume over exquisiteness, systems over platforms, capability per dollar over capability per unit. The beautiful canoe must learn to be a fleet.

Chapter 7 Data Anchors: Type 076 drone carrier (sea trials Nov 2025, ~3 years keel-to-ocean) | CSSC $120B assets, 60%+ global shipbuilding | PLA Navy 370+ ships | Frigate: 25 months; Virginia-class: 5+ years; Ford: 7 years late, $13B/ship | Low-altitude economy ¥1.5T, 89,000 enterprises, 220% growth | Drone swarm $500/unit vs. AEGIS interceptor $2M/unit | DF-21D $20M vs. Ford $13B (650:1) | Tiangong $8–10B vs. ISS $150B | F-35 $1.7T lifecycle, 55–60% mission-capable | BeiDou global coverage | 11 carrier groups, 1 Pacific-available | Operation Epic Fury: $2.4M/Tomahawk | Thousands of civilian deaths | Kettuvallam: dual-use ontology | Azhakulla thoni: the beautiful canoe

· · ·

A Word to the Reasonable Reader

The reasonable reader should hold two truths simultaneously.

First: the Farmer's military-industrial capacity is growing at a pace the Hunter's procurement model cannot match on a dollar-for-dollar, ship-for-ship, or timeline-for-timeline basis. The shipbuilding gap—over 60% versus less than 1%—is a structural asymmetry that cannot be closed in less than a generation.

Second: the Hunter retains genuine advantages. The U.S. submarine fleet remains the most capable in the world. American pilot training and combat experience provide a qualitative edge that numbers cannot capture. The alliance network—NATO, Five Eyes, Quad, AUKUS—provides forward bases, intelligence sharing, and coordinated planning that China cannot replicate. These advantages are steelmanned in Chapter 11. And there is a third truth the chapter's cost ratios do not capture: the Farmer's military has not fought a major engagement since 1979. The PLA's operational experience is simulated, not tested. The Hunter's most expensive platforms are also the most combat-proven. Whether Zhang Mei's welds hold under fire is a question that no production statistic can answer until the fire arrives.

The trajectory is the variable that matters. Not the snapshot. And the trajectory—measured across shipbuilding, drone deployments, space operations, and hypersonic testing cadences—points in a single direction. The Farmer is building. The Hunter is spending. The Farmer's building compounds. The Hunter's spending depletes. Chapter 8 shifts from weapons to the technologies that power them—semiconductors, quantum, fusion, and AI accelerators.

* * *

RITUAL STAGE MARKER

Both eyes are painted. Through one, the divine weapons. Through the other, the silicon seed. The performer's world splits and doubles— and in the doubling, clarifies. What was invisible from one eye becomes undeniable through both.

CHAPTER 8

The Silicon Seed

Semiconductors, Quantum, Fusion, and Deep Tech

"自力更生 (zìlì gēngshēng) — Self-reliance through regeneration."

"A tree springs from a small shoot." — Lao Tzu

The river carves the canyon not in a day but through a million drops.

— after the Theyyam tradition

. . .

Undercurrent: The Vow to Never Depend

自力更生 explains semiconductors, quantum, and fusion simultaneously. It is a single phrase containing an entire civilizational posture: self-reliance through regeneration. Not self-reliance through isolation—that was Mao's misreading, and it nearly destroyed the country. Self-reliance through the patient regeneration of indigenous capability, domain by domain, chokepoint by chokepoint, until the dependency that made humiliation possible has been replaced by the capacity that makes sovereignty operational.

In Kuttanad, when the British colonialists blocked the main canal to divert water to their indigo plantations—drowning the rice paddies in salt and poisoning the soil that had fed families for generations—the farmers did not petition the British for water rights. They dug *chira*—secret channels, hand-carved at night, routed through the root systems of mangrove trees where the British surveyors could not follow. The *chira* were narrow, inefficient, and labor- and sweat-intensive. But the *chira* were *theirs*. And the rice that grew from *chira* water tasted different—it tasted of sovereignty. China's semiconductor industry is the largest *chira* ever dug, and the chips it produces, for all their yield penalties and cost premiums, taste of the same thing: the refusal to let someone else control your water.

Gregory Allen of CSIS described the American export control strategy as "strangling with intent to kill." The metaphor was intended to convey decisive force. What it actually conveyed was the nature of the American miscalculation: the patient is not dead. The patient is adapting. And the adaptive mechanisms—multi-patterning lithography, indigenous semiconductor equipment, quantum communication networks, fusion plasma control, alternative chip architectures—are innovations that would not have existed without the strangulation itself. The strangling produced the seed. This chapter is about what the seed has grown.

. . .

The Process Engineer: Liu Jing

Call her Liu Jing. She is thirty-four years old, a senior process engineer at SMIC's most advanced fabrication facility. For three years, she has been working on the problem the global semiconductor industry said could not be solved: achieving 5nm-class transistor density using only deep ultraviolet lithography.

The technical explanation matters, because the difference between DUV and EUV lithography is the chokepoint around which the entire US-China technology competition pivots.

Lithography projects circuit patterns onto silicon wafers—think of a projector casting an image, except the image contains billions of transistors and the "projector" uses light of a specific wavelength. Deep ultraviolet (DUV) lithography uses light at 193 nanometers—the industry standard for decades, enabling production down to approximately 7nm. Below that, the wavelength becomes too long to print the necessary patterns in a single exposure. In Kuttanad, we would say it's like trying to carve a Theyyam mask with an axe—the tool is magnificent for its purpose, but not built for the fineness the divine face demands.

Extreme ultraviolet (EUV) lithography uses light at 13.5 nanometers—more than fourteen times shorter. It is produced solely by ASML, a Dutch company. Each machine costs approximately $380 million. Under US-led export controls, China cannot purchase EUV machines. The chokepoint was supposed to be absolute.

Liu Jing's job is to make it irrelevant—not by building an EUV machine, but by making DUV do what the physics textbooks say it cannot. The technique is multi-patterning: instead of printing the entire circuit in one exposure, the pattern is decomposed into multiple layers, each printed separately and aligned with nanometer precision. SMIC's N+3 process node achieves approximately 125 million transistors per square millimeter—comparable to Samsung's 5LPE node. By every industry measure, a 5nm-class achievement.

There was a night in October 2024 when Liu Jing did not talk about it at a conference. A Wednesday. Her team had been running validation wafers for the N+3 node—seventy-two hours of continuous processing, the clean room humming its fluorescent prayer, coffee thermoses lined up outside the gowning room like offerings at a temple. The wafers came out of the lithography tool at 3:47 a.m. The alignment check took eleven minutes. The numbers were wrong. Not catastrophically wrong—catastrophe is almost easier to absorb, because catastrophe has a clear cause. The numbers were *subtly* wrong: a 4.2-nanometer drift in the third patterning layer that propagated through every subsequent layer, compounding at each step, until the final overlay accuracy was outside specification by a margin that meant three months of process calibration was scrap. Twelve hundred wafers. Three months of triple shifts. Gone.

Liu Jing sat on the floor outside the clean room, still in her bunny suit, and stared at the wall for twenty minutes. The machines can run 24/7. The engineers cannot. And you cannot multi-pattern a human being.

She came back the next morning. Not because she was heroic—heroism implies a choice, and Liu Jing did not experience what she did as a choice. She came back because the alternative was the chokepoint winning. The alternative was the 卡脖子 succeeding. The alternative was calling someone in Washington and saying, "You were right. We can't do it without your machines." She came back because her grandmother's generation had been told they couldn't build a bomb without Soviet blueprints, and they built the bomb. She came back because the river carves the canyon not in a day but through a million drops, and the million-and-first drop does not ask the canyon's permission.

By December, the drift had been traced to a thermal-expansion coefficient in the chuck assembly that varied with clean-room humidity. The fix was mundane: a recalibrated environmental control loop. Three months of work, lost to a fraction of a degree of temperature variation. The mundane heroism of semiconductor manufacturing is that breakthroughs are invisible and failures are measured in nanometers—and the difference between the two shows up the next morning.

Liu Jing's achievement did something the export controls were supposed to prevent. It also revealed that the barrier was not where analysts thought. The barrier is not the 5nm node. The barrier is the cost and yield penalty of reaching 5nm without EUV—a penalty severe by commercial standards and irrelevant by strategic ones. SMIC's 5nm-class wafers cost up to 50% more than TSMC's equivalent, with yields around 30–33%. In a purely commercial market, this would make SMIC uncompetitive. But when the metric shifts from cost-per-transistor to *sovereignty-per-wafer*, the entire analytical framework changes.

. . .

Interlude: Marcus Calls His Semiconductor Analyst

Marcus Chen called his firm's semiconductor analyst, Priya, who had covered the chip industry for sixteen years.

"Explain the SMIC thing to me," Marcus said. "How are they making 5nm chips without the machine that everyone told me was necessary for 5nm chips?"

Priya explained multi-patterning. She explained the yield penalty. Then she said something that stopped Marcus cold: "The yields are terrible by TSMC standards. Thirty percent. But SMIC doesn't need TSMC yields. SMIC needs *sovereign* yields. They need enough chips to power Huawei's phones and enough Ascend dies to train their AI models without a single component that Washington can turn off. At thirty percent yield, they can do that. The Street is pricing SMIC on commercial metrics. China is pricing SMIC on strategic metrics. They're playing different games, and we're keeping score with the wrong rulebook."

Marcus wrote down "sovereignty-per-wafer" and underlined it twice.

"What about ASML?" he asked. "The monopoly thesis."

"The monopoly thesis is correct today," Priya said. "But the Chinese are pursuing at least twelve alternative paths simultaneously." She listed them: multi-patterning, domestic DUV from SMEE, an EUV prototype with a different light-source architecture, particle-accelerator lithography from Tsinghua, chiplet packaging, and AI-assisted chip design. "ASML's monopoly premium is priced on the assumption that no alternative exists. Twelve simultaneous alternatives don't need to individually match ASML. They need to collectively erode the assumption of impossibility. And once the assumption cracks, the premium decays."

Marcus checked ASML's stock price on his phone during the call—$872, near its all-time high. He watched the number and listened to Priya's voice simultaneously, and the halocline cracked open in real time: the surface said monopoly; the undercurrent said twelve canals.

He opened a new tab in his spreadsheet and titled it "Chokepoint Premium Decay."

. . .

The Twelve Canals: Equipment Self-Sufficiency

In Kuttanad, when the main canal is blocked, the farmer does not petition the blocker. The farmer digs new canals. Not one. Many. Because a system of twelve canals cannot be blocked by a single chokepoint.

The trajectory: 2019: equipment self-sufficiency at ~5%. 2022: SMIC achieves 7nm DUV workaround. 2024: self-sufficiency reaches 13.6%; SMIC N+3 achieves 5nm-class density. Late 2025: EUV prototype validated in Shenzhen. January 2026: self-sufficiency reaches 35%. 2027 target: 70%. The curve is exponential, driven by massive state investment—the Big Fund's $100 billion-plus—guaranteed domestic demand, and the existential pressure of foreign denial.

In 2025, China's semiconductor equipment spending exceeded $40 billion—more than the United States and Europe combined. Even as it builds indigenous alternatives to every foreign tool, China simultaneously purchases every remaining foreign tool, stockpiling capability against the day when the remaining taps are turned off.

The twelve canals: SMEE's 28nm DUV systems in production. SMIC's multi-patterning expertise. A functional EUV prototype using Laser-Induced Discharge Plasma technology—a fundamentally different approach from ASML's architecture. Tsinghua's Steady-State Micro-Bunching uses a particle accelerator as a shared light source that could power multiple lithography machines simultaneously. E-beam lithography for specialized applications. Advanced chiplet packaging. AI-assisted chip design from domestic EDA tools. NAURA's etching and deposition equipment is now ranked seventh globally. AMEC's 5nm etching tools are entering validation.

The EUV Prototype: What the Laboratory Showed

The EUV prototype validated in Shenzhen in late 2025 warrants closer examination, as its significance extends beyond the semiconductor domain into the book's deepest analytical claim about the nature of technological competition.

China's EUV prototype uses Laser-Induced Discharge Plasma (LDP) technology—a fundamentally different light-source architecture from ASML's Laser-Produced Plasma (LPP) approach. The distinction matters. ASML's LPP system fires a high-powered CO_2 laser at tin droplets to generate 13.5nm EUV light. It is an engineering marvel of extraordinary complexity—each machine contains 100,000 components, weighs 150 tons, and requires a dedicated power supply equivalent to a small town's electricity consumption. The Chinese LDP approach generates EUV light via a different plasma mechanism that, according to early assessments, is less power-intensive and potentially more scalable—though it is significantly behind ASML in output power and reliability at this stage.

The significance is not that the Chinese prototype matches ASML. It does not. ASML's CEO is correct that there is a 10- to 15-year gap in high-volume EUV manufacturing. The significance is how the prototype's existence affects the chokepoint premium. ASML's $380 billion market capitalization rests on a monopoly assumption: no alternative exists. The monopoly thesis prices ASML as if the 10-to-15-year gap is permanent—as if no one will ever produce

EUV light through a different method. The LDP prototype does not close the gap. It cracks the assumption. And as Priya explained to Marcus: when the assumption cracks, the premium decays. Twelve simultaneous alternatives don't need to individually match ASML. They need to collectively erode the assumption of impossibility. The LDP prototype is not a product. It is a proof of concept that the impossibility is temporary. And temporary impossibility is not a foundation for a $380 billion valuation.

The aggregate picture is not that China has solved the lithography problem. It has not. ASML's CEO is correct that there is a 10- to 15-year gap in high-volume manufacturing lithography. The aggregate picture is that the probability of 12 simultaneous failures is not a bet a prudent investor would take.

Meanwhile, the CHIPS Act's $52 billion was producing results that might generously be described as ironic. Intel received $8.5 billion and simultaneously laid off 15,000 workers. TSMC's Arizona fab imported thousands of Taiwanese workers because American construction crews could not meet precision requirements—the manufacturing equivalent of hiring a foreign chef because your own family cannot operate the stove you just purchased. Samsung Texas: delayed. Intel Ohio: delayed.

Maria callback — CHIPS Act contrast

While Liu Jing was solving alignment errors at the nanometer scale in Shanghai and the American semiconductor renaissance was solving alignment errors at the PowerPoint scale in Washington, Maria Delgado in Youngstown was solving an alignment error of her own: the $47 copay for metformin had increased to $52 because the pharmacy had changed its uninsured pricing tier. The increase was $5. Five dollars. The CHIPS Act had allocated $8.5 billion to Intel. Maria's monthly medication increase was $5. The distance between the two numbers—$8.5 billion and $5—is the distance between the America that appears on the Bloomberg terminal and the America that appears in Maria's kitchen when she recalculates whether this is the month she switches to groceries.

The analytical point is not sentimental. The CHIPS Act's $52 billion is strategically necessary. The question is whether a nation that cannot ensure a sixty-one-year-old woman's access to a $3.80 molecule possesses the social infrastructure to sustain the industrial strategy the $52 billion is meant to fund. Liu Jing's *chira*—the channel dug in defiance of the chokepoint—requires a civilization behind it. Maria's $5 increase is a reminder that the civilization behind the Hunter's *chira* has cracks that the semiconductor data does not capture.

The CHIPS Act Autopsy: A Satirical Accounting

The CHIPS Act's $52 billion deserves the satirical autopsy the manuscript's style directive demands, because the gap between the Act's ambition and its execution has achieved a level of tragicomedy that only the deliberately obtuse could describe as "progress."

The timeline: the CHIPS Act was signed in August 2022. Its stated objective: revitalize American semiconductor manufacturing and reduce dependence on foreign foundries. Three and a half years later, in early 2026, the Act has produced: zero operational fabs. Intel received $8.5 billion in subsidies and simultaneously announced 15,000 layoffs—achieving the remarkable distinction of being the only company in industrial history to receive a government bailout and fire a small city's worth of workers in the same fiscal quarter. TSMC's Arizona fab imported thousands of Taiwanese workers because American construction crews could not meet the precision requirements for semiconductor-grade construction—a difficulty that TSMC's chairman publicly attributed to the American workforce's unfamiliarity with the "dedication" required for advanced manufacturing. This diplomatic phrasing translates roughly as "your workers go home at five o'clock, and ours do not." Samsung's Texas fab: delayed. Intel's Ohio fab: delayed. GlobalFoundries' expansion: delayed.

Meanwhile, over the same three and a half years, SMIC advanced from 7nm to 5nm-class production despite comprehensive sanctions. China's semiconductor equipment self-sufficiency climbed from approximately 13% to 35%. The Big Fund deployed over $100 billion into domestic semiconductor capacity. And Liu Jing's clean room in Shanghai produced wafers at a pace that the CHIPS Act's recipients have not yet begun to approach.

The satirical point is not that the CHIPS Act was unnecessary. It was necessary. The satirical point is that $52 billion, filtered through the American procurement-and-subsidy apparatus—the same apparatus that produced the F-35's $1.7 trillion lifecycle, the California High-Speed Rail's $100 billion Bakersfield-to-Merced odyssey, and a defense acquisition cycle that averages seven to ten years from requirement to deployment—produces results on a timeline and at a cost that the Farmer's system finds *endearing*. The Hunter allocated $52 billion for semiconductor sovereignty and received, to date, a series of groundbreaking ceremonies, several thousand pages of environmental impact assessments, and the warm satisfaction of knowing that the subsidies are being distributed through a process so elaborately consultative that it would make a medieval papal conclave look like a snap decision.

. . .

The Theyyam performer pauses between mudras. The drums soften. The audience breathes. What follows are three seeds from the same root system—briefer than the silicon seed, because the root is the same, but the branches reach different skies.

. . .

Satellite Domain I: Quantum — The Silent Chira

In Kuttanad, the *chira*—the secret underground channels—connected villages below the surface, invisible from above, essential below. China's quantum communication network is the *chira* of the information age: encrypted, invisible, physically unhackable.

The strategic stakes first. Every encrypted communication sent today can be recorded and stored. When quantum computers become powerful enough to break current cryptography—a timeline most experts estimate at ten to twenty years—every stored message becomes readable. The only known defense is quantum key distribution, where encryption derives from the laws of physics rather than computational difficulty.

While the quantum computing race attracts venture capital and keynotes, China has been building a quantum *communication* infrastructure on a scale without a Western equivalent. The China Quantum Communication Network spans over 10,000 kilometers of fiber-optic backbone, incorporating 145 trusted relay nodes across 20 metropolitan networks covering 17 provinces and 80 cities. It is carrier-grade. In March 2025, researchers established the world's longest intercontinental quantum-secured link: 12,900 kilometers, from Beijing to Stellenbosch, South Africa. The *chira* has gone orbital.

The Hunter races for the breakthrough (quantum computing). The Farmer deploys the infrastructure (quantum networking). The processor is more impressive on a conference slide. The network is more useful in a crisis.

. . .

Satellite Domain II: Fusion — The Ultimate Energy Seed

A cautious calibration first, because fusion has been "thirty years away" for approximately sixty years, and intellectual honesty requires acknowledging that every fusion milestone exists on a timeline more aspirational than predictive. *The timeline is uncertain. The investment commitment is not.*

With that caveat planted firmly in the reader's mind: in early January 2026, researchers at China's Experimental Advanced Superconducting Tokamak (EAST) achieved what the fusion community had treated as a fundamental barrier for forty years. They operated stable plasma at densities 1.3 to 1.65 times the Greenwald Density Limit. The results, published in *Science Advances*, represent not merely a record but a paradigm shift in magnetic confinement.

Because fusion power scales with the square of plasma density—doubling the fuel concentration quadruples the energy output—breaking the Greenwald Limit fundamentally changes the economic equation: reactors can be smaller, cheaper, and more powerful.

China's next-generation device, the Burning Plasma Experimental Superconducting Tokamak (BEST), targets initial operation by 2027, with procurement budgets of approximately ¥10 billion ($1.4 billion) for 2026 alone—funded through the SOE substrate with the same patient capital and Five-Year Plan integration that enables every other domain in this book. ITER's first plasma target has been repeatedly pushed back to 2035. The Farmer plants with one party. Committees do not achieve fusion. Civilizational will achieves fusion.

If semiconductors are the Farmer's nervous system and quantum is the encrypted communication channel, fusion is the endgame: unlimited, clean, domestically controlled energy that eliminates the last great foreign dependency. The Farmer does not need to solve fusion today. The Farmer needs to be closer to solving it than anyone else. And the Greenwald Limit—the ceiling everyone agreed was permanent—has cracked.

. . .

Satellite Domain III: The AI+ Deployment Layer

The twelve canals are the hardware substrate. The silicon seed's true strategic significance is what grows *on* the substrate.

More than 5,000 AI companies registered since 2023—not 5,000 competitors for a single prize but 5,000 applications of a single technology across every sector. Agriculture AI in Henan. Manufacturing AI in Dongguan. Medical AI in Wuhan. Municipal AI in Shenzhen. Educational AI in Chongqing. Each application runs on silicon Liu Jing helped fabricate, trained on models Chen Yue helped optimize, connected by networks Huawei built, powered by electricity State Grid delivers at $0.03 per kilowatt-hour.

The Hunter races for AGI—Artificial General Intelligence—the God-model, the one-model-to-rule-them-all. The Farmer deploys AI+ across 5,000 fields simultaneously, each too small to interest a venture capitalist, each generating data that feeds back into models that improve every other field. The race and the deployment are different games. In the Time War, the deployment game has better odds because deployment compounds and races produce a single winner and a field of expensive wreckage.

. . .

The Architecture of Self-Reliance

The four domains are not parallel programs. They are an integrated architecture connected by recursive loops: SMIC's chips power Huawei's Ascend accelerators. Ascend trains DeepSeek's models. DeepSeek optimizes next-generation chip design. The improved chips enable the next generation of Ascend. The quantum network secures communications between laboratories, foundries, and military commands. The fusion program integrates advanced materials research with semiconductor substrates. The AI models optimize plasma control algorithms. In Kuttanad, this is the *kalvazhi*—the water-path—so intricately connected that the boatman who enters at one end emerges at the other having passed through a dozen invisible crossings, each feeding the next.

The export controls accelerated every cycle. If the United States lifted all controls tomorrow, China would not dismantle its domestic equipment industry. The self-reliance infrastructure has become self-sustaining—a permanent feature of the Chinese technology landscape. The *chira* that was dug in desperation has become the main canal. The seed, once planted, cannot be unplanted. It can only grow.

. . .

The Talent Gap: The Farmer's Unfilled Furrows

Intellectual honesty requires documenting the Farmer's most critical vulnerability in this domain. The semiconductor talent gap is real and large enough to constrain every program described above.

China's semiconductor industry faces a shortfall of 200,000 to 250,000 specialized engineers—process engineers like Liu Jing, chip designers, equipment specialists, and yield experts. The gap exists despite the pace of investment: the Big Fund and provincial subsidies have scaled the industry's capital base faster than universities can scale the human capital to operate it. The machines can run 24/7. The engineers cannot. And you cannot multi-pattern a human being.

TSMC's workforce represents four decades of accumulated process knowledge. SMIC's represents fewer than ten at the leading edge. The knowledge asymmetry is wider than the equipment asymmetry, and unlike equipment, it cannot be purchased, stockpiled, or reverse-engineered.

The 200,000-engineer shortfall is the constraint that may determine whether the 2027 self-sufficiency target is met on time. Every year the talent gap persists is a year the Hunter's export controls buy time. Chapter 11 will return to this vulnerability. For now: the seed is growing. But the field needs more hands.

. . .

BOATMAN'S LEDGER

Chapter 8

LEDGER TOOL #7: CHOKEPOINT PREMIUM DECAY

ASML has a market cap exceeding $380 billion, built on a monopoly premium as the sole manufacturer of EUV lithography. China has assembled an EUV prototype using a different light-source architecture, is pursuing particle-accelerator lithography, and is producing 5nm-class chips without EUV at all. Twelve simultaneous alternatives. The monopoly premium rests on the assumption that no alternative exists. The premium decays when the assumption cracks.

CHOKEPOINT HALF-LIFE

ASML's EUV monopoly has an estimated half-life of 5–7 years—the time until Chinese alternatives reach sufficient scale to make denial irrelevant. DUV self-sufficiency half-life: 2–3 years (already past midpoint). Semiconductor equipment aggregate half-life: 4–5 years. When the half-life is < the planning horizon, the chokepoint is already dead.

CHIPS ACT CONTRAST

SMIC went from 7nm to 5nm-class in three years under sanctions. CHIPS Act $52B produced: Intel $8.5B subsidy + 15,000 layoffs. TSMC Arizona: delayed, imported workers. Equipment self-sufficiency trajectory (China): 5% $\rightarrow$ 35% in seven years.

TALENT GAP ANCHOR

200,000–250,000 shortfall. This is the binding constraint. Factor it into every acceleration assumption. The silicon seed's growth rate is limited not by capital, not by will, but by hands.

THE BOATMAN'S WAGER

Illustrative 12% allocation to domestic Chinese semiconductor, quantum, and fusion plays. Reduce ASML overweight by 5%; add Chinese semiconductor equipment (NAURA, AMEC), Huawei/HiSilicon ecosystem, quantum communication infrastructure, and fusion-adjacent advanced materials. Hedge the talent gap: any Chinese semiconductor play is implicitly a bet that the 200,000-engineer shortfall closes faster than export controls buy time.

Chapter 8 Data Anchors: SMIC N+3 5nm-class: 125M transistors/mm², 30–33% yield, 50% cost premium | DUV 193nm vs. EUV 13.5nm | ASML $380M/machine, $380B market cap | Equipment self-sufficiency: 5% (2019) $\rightarrow$ 35% (Jan 2026) $\rightarrow$ 70% (2027 target) | $40B+ equipment spending (2025) > US+EU combined | Twelve canals: SMEE 28nm DUV, EUV prototype (LDP), Tsinghua SSMB, NAURA (#7 global), AMEC 5nm etch | Quantum: 10,000+ km network, 145 nodes, 12,900 km intercontinental link | Greenwald Limit broken 1.65x; BEST target 2027 | Talent gap: 200K–250K engineers | TSMC 40 years vs. SMIC <10 | CHIPS Act $52B: Intel $8.5B + 15K layoffs | Chokepoint half-life: EUV 5–7 years | Sovereignty-per-wafer | Chira: channel $\rightarrow$ canal

· · ·

A Word to the Reasonable Reader

What the data means: China has developed an indigenous semiconductor capability that, while inferior to TSMC and Samsung in absolute terms, is sufficient for strategic purposes and is improving at a rate the export controls did not anticipate. The quantum network has no equivalent in scale. The fusion program is achieving milestones ahead of ITER. Equipment self-sufficiency, rising from 5% to 35% in seven years, is exponential. The strangling has produced adaptation. The patient is not dead. The patient's immune system is developing.

What the data does not mean: China has solved the semiconductor problem. It has not. ASML's 10-to-15-year gap in high-volume manufacturing lithography is real, and may be larger for High-NA EUV. SMIC's yields at 5nm—30–33%—are commercially marginal. The EUV prototype is years from production. The talent gap constrains everything.

The correct frame is not "China has caught up." The correct frame is: "China has demonstrated that the leading edge is not the only edge that matters, and it is closing the gap on the edge that matters most—the edge of strategic sufficiency." A 5nm-class chip that is expensive but sovereign is strategically superior to a 3nm chip that is cheap but can be denied. A deployed quantum network is strategically superior to a superior but undeployed quantum processor. A fusion milestone achieved is strategically superior to a larger but perpetually delayed fusion budget.

The chokepoint premium is not gone. It is decaying. And the logic is recursive: every restriction accelerates investment in alternatives. The tighter the chokepoint, the more canals the Farmer digs. The more canals, the less the chokepoint matters. The *chira* that was dug in desperation has become the main canal. And the water that flows through it tastes of sovereignty.

• • •

When the Soviet engineers left in 1960, they took their blueprints
but they could not take the phrase that Mao spoke into the empty factory floor.
"We will build our own."

Sixty-six years later, in a clean room in Shanghai,
Liu Jing adjusts the exposure parameters for the next multi-patterning run.
She has never read Mao's words in that context. She does not need to.
The words are in the institution. They are in the funding. They are in the firmware.

The river carves the canyon not in a day.
Liu Jing is not carving a canyon.
She is aligning photons on silicon, nanometer by nanometer,
in a room so clean that a single particle of dust would ruin everything she has built.
But the principle is the same.
The canyon and the chip are both made by persistence applied to physics,
day after day, drop after drop,
until the impossible becomes the inevitable.

• • •

RITUAL STAGE MARKER

The performer's hands pause. The mask is nearly complete—but the mouth has not yet been painted. The deity can see. The deity cannot yet speak. What comes next will give it voice

CHAPTER 9

The Living Harvest

EVs, Biotech, Robotics, and the Industries of Daily Life

"Water shapes its course according to the ground." — Sun Tzu

弯道超车 — "Overtaking on the curve." 一体两翼 — "One body, two wings."

The cart without a horse needs a road that thinks. The body without youth needs a medicine that remembers. The factory without workers needs a hand that learns.

— after the Theyyam tradition

• • •

Undercurrent: Where Rejuvenation Becomes Ordinary

The previous chapters documented the Farmer's arsenal, the silicon seed, the diplomatic harvest, and the deep tech architecture of self-reliance. They operated in domains that most people never touch—shipyards, clean rooms, fusion reactors. This chapter operates in a different register. This chapter is about the industries of daily life: the car you ride in, the medicine that treats you, and the robot that assembles the products you buy. These are the sectors where rejuvenation stops being a Five-Year Plan abstraction and becomes something a sixty-seven-year-old grandmother in Wuhan experiences on a Tuesday morning.

In Kuttanad, there is a phrase the boatmen use when the monsoon finally arrives: *mazha vannu, mannu poothirichu*—the rain came, and the earth bloomed. It describes the moment when all the patient preparation—the canal-digging, the bund-building, the seed-storing—suddenly becomes visible as abundance. The fields green overnight. The air changes smell. China's living harvest is that blooming: the moment when the SOE root system, the AI seedlings, the interdependency web ceases to be strategy and becomes the texture of ordinary life.

And this is where the "copy stigma"—the Western certainty that China can only imitate, never innovate—dies its most visible death. The BYD Seagull is not a copy of any Western vehicle—there is no Western vehicle at $7,800 to copy. The biotech molecules being licensed to Pfizer are novel compounds that Western companies cannot develop as fast or as cheaply. Because the grandmother in the robotaxi does not care about intellectual property debates. She cares that the ride costs eight yuan and gets her to her appointment on time.

• • •

The Grandmother in the Robotaxi: Chen Liling

Call her Chen Liling. She is sixty-seven years old, a retired schoolteacher in Wuhan. Every Tuesday and Friday, she visits Wuhan Union Hospital for arthritis treatment, which keeps her hands flexible enough to play with her granddaughter. The trip takes twenty-two minutes. She makes it in an Apollo Go robotaxi.

Before the ghost cars, she used Didi. The drivers were fine—most of them. But there was the one who took the long route around the Jiefang Avenue construction, adding twelve yuan and fifteen minutes to the fare. There was the one who refused a short trip because the hospital was "too close." There was the afternoon she waited twenty-two minutes in the rain for a car that never came, and her arthritis flared so badly that night she couldn't hold a teacup. The ghost car does not take the long route. The ghost car does not refuse short trips. The ghost car arrives within three minutes every time, in rain or sun, and it does not require her to negotiate, tip, make small talk about the weather, or pretend she does not notice the driver texting.

The technology's humanity is in its *lack* of humanity. The relief is impersonal, predictable, and reliable. Chen Liling does not find the robotaxi hilarious. She finds it perfectly ordinary. And that ordinariness—the fact that an autonomous vehicle ride has become as unremarkable as taking an elevator—is the most powerful measure of deployment this book has documented. Technologies become transformative not when they are demonstrated but when they are ignored. When the grandmother stops noticing the autonomous vehicle, the autonomous vehicle has won.

Her granddaughter thinks it's hilarious that Nǎi Nai takes a ghost car to the hospital.

"Does the ghost car talk to you?" the granddaughter asks.

"It tells me to fasten my seatbelt," Chen Liling replies. "That's more than your grandfather ever did."

. . .

The Camel's Journey: Wang Chuanfu and the Making of BYD

Wang Chuanfu was born in 1966 in Wuwei, Anhui province—the same province that produced Chen Yue from Chapter 1. Orphaned by fifteen. Master's in metallurgical chemistry from the Chinese Academy of Sciences. In 1995, at twenty-nine, he founded BYD with $300,000 in borrowed capital to manufacture rechargeable batteries. Within five years, BYD was one of the world's largest rechargeable battery producers, not because Wang had invented a better battery but because he had deployed existing chemistry at lower cost through manufacturing process innovation—the same efficiency-over-spectacle logic that would later produce the Seagull.

In 2003, Wang pivoted from batteries to automobiles. He bought Tsinchuan, a failing state-owned automaker, for its production license. His first car—the F3, a sedan of unambiguous homeliness—sold for the equivalent of $8,500. Not beautiful. Not advanced. Cheap, reliable, and available. 100,000 units in its second year. In Kuttanad, the boatmen would recognize this: you do not build the most beautiful *vallam*. You build the one that floats in the monsoon.

But here is the part the ascent narrative usually omits: BYD nearly died.

In 2019, before the EV boom validated everything Wang had built, BYD's sales collapsed. Net profit fell 42%. The battery business was under siege from CATL. Two major investors publicly called for his resignation. Analysts described BYD as "a battery company that accidentally wandered into a car factory and couldn't find the exit."

Wang refused. He doubled down on vertical integration—bringing more components in-house, not fewer. He bet the company on the Blade Battery, a structural lithium iron phosphate design that eliminated the thermal runaway risk that had plagued the industry. And he committed to a price point—sub-$10,000 for an entry-level EV—that his own finance team told him was "commercially suicidal."

The Blade Battery worked. The Seagull launched at $7,800. By 2025, BYD was shipping 4.6 million vehicles annually and had surpassed Tesla in quarterly pure-EV deliveries. The Camel had nearly died in the desert. The Camel survived because it carried its own water—its own batteries, its own motors, its own chips, its own vertical supply chain—and because the man driving it refused to dismount when the sand was deepest.

In 2008, Warren Buffett's lieutenant, Charlie Munger, visited BYD's Shenzhen factory and returned with a recommendation that Berkshire Hathaway invest $230 million for a 10% stake. Munger's assessment: "This guy is a combination of Thomas Edison and Jack Welch." What Munger recognized was not a brilliant product but a brilliant *system*—a company that manufactured everything from batteries to headlights. The stake is now worth billions.

. . .

The Unicorn and the Camel: A Fable of Two Business Models

The Unicorn exists in the investor's imagination. The Camel exists in the grandmother's commute.

The American innovation model produces Unicorns: mythological creatures, valued at impossible multiples, sustained by narrative rather than nourishment. Tesla is the prototypical Unicorn: valued at over $1 trillion for 1.64 million vehicles, whose stock price reflects not what the company produces but what the market believes it will produce someday. The Chinese deployment model produces Camels: unglamorous, stoic, built for endurance, valued for their capacity to carry freight. BYD is the prototypical Camel: valued at $107 billion for 4.6 million vehicles, its stock price reflecting what the company actually produces, actually sells, actually deploys.

But BYD is not the only Camel. It is the lead Camel in a herd. Geely's Xingyuan outsold every BYD model in 2025. NIO, Li Auto, XPeng, Geely, Chery, Great Wall, Changan, SAIC—each deploying at scale, each integrated into the CATL/DeepSeek/Huawei/SOE web. They compete ruthlessly with each other on price and quality, driving margins down and innovation up, while collectively making the Western EV business model unviable outside its tariff walls.

In Kuttanad, we call this *koottukrishi*—collective cultivation, where twenty farmers plant the same paddy, each competing for the best yield, each benefiting from the shared canal and bund. No single farmer "wins." The paddy wins. The harvest wins.

God's Eye vs. Full Self-Driving: The Feature Wars

BYD's God's Eye ADAS system is the Feature Democratization phase of the Burning Ghat rendered in software. Standard on 21 BYD models as of 2025, at no additional cost, on vehicles starting at $9,550. Tesla's comparable system—marketed as "Full Self-Driving" despite achieving neither fullness nor self-driving—costs $8,000 to $12,000 as a premium add-on on vehicles starting at approximately $35,000.

The marketing nomenclature alone deserves the satirical register. "Full Self-Driving" has been one year away for nine consecutive years. This is the autonomous-vehicle equivalent of fusion's perpetual "thirty years away," with the critical distinction that fusion researchers do not charge their funders $12,000 for a capability that does not yet exist and require those funders to sign a liability waiver acknowledging that the name is aspirational. Tesla's FSD is not full. It is not self-driving. It is an advanced driver-assistance system whose name constitutes what, in any other industry, would be classified as false advertising—but in Silicon Valley, it is classified as "visionary product naming." The Farmer's God's Eye does not promise omniscience. It promises lane-keeping, adaptive cruise control, automatic parking, and emergency braking—capabilities that are useful, verifiable, and free.

The analytical distinction between the two approaches maps precisely onto the Field-and-Forest thesis from Chapter 5. The Forest (Tesla) invests in a frontier capability that does not yet reliably work, prices it as premium, and derives a significant portion of its narrative valuation from the *promise* of future deployment. The Field (BYD) invests in a proven capability that works today, deploys it as standard, and derives its valuation from the *reality* of present deployment. God's Eye processes data from BYD's 150 million daily kilometers of driving data—a dataset that dwarfs Waymo's geofenced operations and Tesla's FSD beta fleet. The data flywheel compounds: each kilometer improves the algorithm, each improvement attracts more vehicles, and each vehicle generates more kilometers. The flywheel does not ask whether the technology is impressive by conference-keynote standards. It asks whether the technology improves every day. God's Eye improves every day. FSD improves every year. In the Time War, days beat years.

The price point is the strategic payload. When BYD offers God's Eye at no additional cost on a $9,550 vehicle, it accomplishes three things simultaneously. First, it destroys the pricing power of every competitor that charges for ADAS—not just Tesla but Toyota, Hyundai, and Volkswagen, all of whom price driver-assistance features as premium options. Second, it accelerates data collection by maximizing the number of vehicles generating driving data, thereby improving the system and justifying its inclusion as standard, which attracts more buyers—the deployment flywheel in its purest form. Third, it sets the feature expectation for the global market: consumers who have experienced free ADAS will not subsequently accept paying $12,000 for a system that, despite its ambitious name, cannot reliably navigate a parking lot without human intervention.

China's NEV penetration reached 59.4% in 2024. America's EV market share hovered around 12%. China has deployed over 10 million public charging points. The United States has approximately 76,000 DC fast chargers. The ratio—130:1—is the physical manifestation of the deployment gap. The Vehicle-Road-Cloud cooperation system has been deployed across 35,000 kilometers of smart roadway in 20+ cities. Apollo Go has reached breakeven on unit economics. 弯道超车: overtaking on the curve. The overtaking is complete.

· · ·

Interlude: Marcus Test-Drives a Ghost

Marcus Chen did not plan to ride in an autonomous vehicle during his firm's annual investor trip to Shanghai. But Kevin had arranged a demonstration.

The Apollo Go sedan arrived at the hotel—no driver, no steering wheel input. The car pulled into Shanghai traffic and navigated a left turn across four lanes of scooters, buses, and a delivery truck whose driver appeared to be simultaneously texting, smoking, and executing a U-turn. The Apollo Go handled this with the serene competence of someone who has processed this exact scenario fourteen million times.

The ride lasted eighteen minutes. The fare was eleven yuan—$1.50. Marcus thought about Waymo's $175,000-per-vehicle sensor suite, about Cruise's $12 billion immolation, about every conference panel where American executives had explained that true autonomous driving was "at least a decade away." The infrastructure existed. He was riding in it. The infrastructure was not a single car with a million-dollar sensor package. It was a *system*—car, road, cloud, 5G, charging, municipal coordination—that cost a fraction of Waymo's approach and processed more rides in a week than Waymo processed in a month.

He texted his wife: "I just rode in a self-driving car in Shanghai. No driver. $1.50. It was completely ordinary." She replied: "Is that good or bad?" He typed: "Both."

. . .

Biotech: The Quiet Revolution

Of all the reversals documented in this book, this one carries the most poetic justice. The opium that British ships forced into China destroyed millions of lives and stands as the most nakedly predatory act of the Century of Humiliation. Today, Chinese biotech companies account for approximately 32% of global pharmaceutical out-licensing deal value—$66 billion in 2025. China now exports the cure, not the poison. Pfizer pays $6 billion for a cancer drug. AstraZeneca invests $2.5 billion in a Beijing R&D center. The opium trade has been reversed. And this time, the terms are set in Beijing.

What is being licensed? Not generic copies. Innovative molecules: novel chemical entities, monoclonal antibodies (up 43% to $11.3 billion in 2024), antibody-drug conjugates ($10 billion in ADC deals alone), bispecific antibodies, and cell and gene therapies. 639 first-in-class drug candidates since 2022—a 360% increase from 2018–2021. China now produces 120,000 biomedical PhDs per year, roughly three times US output.

In Youngstown, Ohio, a woman named Maria Delgado—sixty-one, uninsured, diabetic—drives to a pharmacy every month to pick up her metformin. The copay is $47. She does not know that the active pharmaceutical ingredient in her pills was synthesized in Zhejiang Province, shipped to a finishing plant in Hyderabad, and packaged under an American brand name in New Jersey. She does not know that the same molecule is available through a Chinese pharmacy app for $3.80. She knows only that $47 is the difference between medication and groceries this month, and she has been choosing medication because the alternative is a hospital bill she cannot pay.

Maria callback — Gerald and the last mile

Maria Delgado does not experience the pharmaceutical supply chain as a geopolitical abstraction. She experiences it as a monthly drive with Gerald—the retired postal worker from Chapter 4 whose arthritic knees are the last piece of informal social infrastructure connecting Maria to the molecule that keeps her blood sugar from destroying her kidneys. Gerald drives because the bus route that once connected Maria's block to the pharmacy was cut in 2019 as part of a transit optimization, the consulting firm described as "service rationalization," and Maria's neighborhood as "the bus stopped coming."

The distance between the Chinese pharmacy app's $3.80 price and Maria's $47 copay traverses a supply chain spanning three continents and seven markup layers. But the distance from Maria's apartment to the pharmacy—eleven blocks—traverses a social infrastructure so degraded that an uninsured diabetic woman's monthly medication access depends on the continued health of a seventy-three-year-old neighbor's knees. The Farmer's biotech out-licensing revolution documents the macro supply. Maria's Tuesday documents the micro delivery. The revolution means nothing if the last mile is Gerald's Buick.

The biotech revolution is also a demographic survival strategy. China's over-65 cohort will exceed 400 million by 2035. The Farmer is investing in biotech because the alternative is a healthcare system that collapses under the weight of 400 million elderly citizens.

The Healthcare Contrast: What $4.5 Trillion Buys

The pharmaceutical supply chain documented in the next section is a micro vulnerability. The macro vulnerability is the healthcare system itself, and the contrast with the Farmer's deployment approach is the broken bow's most visible crack, rendered in comparative data.

The United States spends approximately $4.5 trillion annually on healthcare—17.3% of GDP —more than any nation by a margin that warrants its own vocabulary. For this expenditure, the nation has experienced a decline in life expectancy for 3 consecutive years and now trails the OECD average by approximately 2 years. It achieves approximately 530,000 medical bankruptcies annually—a phenomenon that does not exist in any other developed democracy, because no other developed democracy has designed a healthcare system whose fundamental architecture converts illness into financial ruin. It achieves 27 million uninsured citizens, each of whom represents a body whose maintenance has been *priced out of the market*—a phrase that economists use with clinical detachment and that Maria Delgado, splitting her metformin pills eleven blocks from Sarah's boutique, experiences as a monthly calculation about whether to treat her diabetes or eat.

China's healthcare system has significant deficiencies—rural access gaps, quality inconsistencies, and the overcrowded urban hospitals that anyone who has visited a Beijing public clinic will recognize. These deficiencies are real and must not be minimized. But China provides universal basic coverage to 95% of its population. Healthcare spending as a percentage of GDP is approximately 7%—less than half the American figure—with health outcomes that are converging toward OECD levels rather than diverging from them. Life expectancy in China now exceeds life expectancy in the United States. This sentence deserves repetition because of what it implies: a developing country with one-sixth of America's per-capita income has achieved a higher life expectancy than the world's wealthiest nation. The Hunter is not merely spending more for less. The Hunter is spending the most in human history and achieving outcomes that the Farmer, spending a fraction, now surpasses.

The strategic implication is direct: a nation whose citizens fear medical bankruptcy is a nation whose citizens cannot take entrepreneurial risks, cannot move to where the jobs are, cannot absorb the economic disruption that technological transformation inevitably produces. The Rooseveltian adaptations in Chapter 12 require a population capable of absorbing change. The current healthcare system produces a population terrified of it—because any change risks disrupting employer-provided insurance, which is the sole barrier between 160 million Americans and the medical-bankruptcy statistics Maria Delgado's arithmetic represents.

. . .

The Medicine Cabinet: When Your Insulin Depends on the Farmer

80% of the active pharmaceutical ingredients used in American medications are sourced overseas. China directly supplies 40% of global APIs. India provides 40% of US generics—but depends on China for 70% of its API precursors, meaning India's generic drug industry is a Chinese-origin industry with Indian finishing. Only 28% of

API production facilities for US drugs operate domestically. For nearly half of the 227 FDA-designated "essential medicines"—treatments without alternatives—not a single API is manufactured in America.

The BIOSECURE Act proposes to restrict American pharmaceutical companies from working with certain Chinese biotech firms. It does not propose to rebuild domestic API manufacturing capacity. It restricts the front end of the pipeline while ignoring that the back end—the part that produces the chemicals in the pills—is 80% foreign and 40% Chinese.

· · ·

Robotics and Embodied AI: The Hands That Learn

With births at 7.92 million in 2025 (the lowest since 1949), marriages at 6.1 million (a 20.5% decline), and the working-age population contracting by millions annually, China faces a workforce equation with no solution that does not involve machines.

China installed more industrial robots in 2024 than the rest of the world combined—approximately 52% of global installations, over 276,000 units. The manufacturing sector is not merely automating. It is replacing the workforce that the birth rate will not supply, at a pace that treats the demographic cliff not as a catastrophe but as a deadline.

In a factory in Foshan, Guangdong, a humanoid robot designated IRON-7 is learning to install a car door panel. The panel weighs 8.3 kilograms. The installation requires fourteen precise movements, each within a tolerance of 0.3 millimeters—the width of three human hairs. The robot has attempted this sequence 4,200 times in the past week. Its success rate has climbed from 61% on Monday to 94% on Friday. By next Monday, the engineers expect 99%. The robot does not complain about the repetition. The robot does not need a lunch break, a bathroom break, or a pension. In the Kuttanadan backwaters, the *Thattukaaran*—the man who carries heavy loads on his head through narrow canal paths—has no use for beauty. He needs balance, endurance, and the ability to show up before sunrise. IRON-7 is the *Thattukaaran* of the robotic age.

XPENG's IRON humanoid robot is in production with capacity targeting 50,000 units—a number that would exceed the total cumulative production of every Western humanoid program, including Boston Dynamics. Boston Dynamics is the Unicorn of robotics: beautiful, admired, virally shared, and not actually carrying freight. XPENG's IRON is the Camel: ugly name, no YouTube dance videos, and fifty thousand units headed for factory floors.

The robots are assembled using CATL batteries, controlled by AI trained on DeepSeek's architecture, coordinated through Huawei's 5G, and manufactured in factories that also produce the EVs and drones from preceding chapters. The Farmer's field is a single field. The tools merely change shape.

· · ·

The Other Current: Where the Camel Stumbles

The Camel herd's ascent is real. So are the stones in the road.

BYD's scaling speed has outpaced its quality control infrastructure in several export markets. In early 2025, BYD faced recalls in Europe over battery cooling system defects in the Atto 3, and consumer satisfaction surveys in Southeast Asia flagged fit-and-finish inconsistencies that Hyundai and Toyota—the incumbents BYD is displacing—have spent decades eliminating. The EU's anti-subsidy investigation, which imposed countervailing duties of up to 36.3% on Chinese EVs in late 2024, reflects legitimate concerns about SOE-subsidized pricing that distorts competition—not merely a protectionist reflex. The Camel carries freight, but freight carried too fast on unfamiliar roads produces breakdowns that damage the *xìn* the Farmer is building.

In biotech, the regulatory trust deficit is the binding constraint. The FDA's acceptance of Chinese-origin clinical trial data remains contested. The BIOSECURE Act's restrictions, however incomplete, reflect a genuine security concern: the same biotech companies that license molecules to Pfizer also maintain data-sharing relationships with Chinese military hospitals. The distinction between civilian biotech innovation and military-adjacent research is blurrier in China's civil-military fusion framework than the licensing deal numbers suggest. And the 120,000 biomedical PhDs per year—impressive by volume—face the same quality vs. quantity question that Chapter 8's talent gap posed for semiconductor engineers: volume is not the same as capability at the frontier.

In robotics, the 276,000 industrial installations are mostly conventional articulated arms, not humanoid systems. IRON-7's 94% success rate on door panels is a controlled-environment achievement; real-world manufacturing tolerance for error is closer to 99.97%. The gap between 94% and 99.97% is the gap between a demonstration and a deployment, and it may prove as stubborn as the gap between SMIC's 30% yields and TSMC's commercial standard.

The honest assessment: the Living Harvest is real, and it is changing the daily experience of hundreds of millions of people. But the Camel's stumbles are not footnotes. They are the quality, regulatory, and trust deficits that will determine whether Living Harvest exports globally or remains a domestic achievement contained by tariff walls.

. . .

BOATMAN'S LEDGER

Chapter 9

LEDGER TOOL #8: DEPLOYMENT-OVER-INVENTION RATIO

Wall Street debates whether Tesla's Full Self-Driving will reach Level 4 by 2028. Meanwhile, in 2026: 50,000–100,000 humanoid robots heading to factory floors. 10 million+ charging points deployed. Biotech molecules are flowing into Merck, Pfizer, and AstraZeneca at half the cost of development. Apollo Go is processing 300,000 autonomous rides weekly, with unit economics breakeven. BYD is exporting over a million vehicles to 70+ countries. 80% of America's APIs are manufactured overseas.

UNICORN VS. CAMEL INDEX

Tesla $1T+ / 1.64M vehicles (narrative). BYD $107B / 4.6M vehicles (deployment). BYD 1.606M pure EVs vs. Tesla 1.218M through Q3 2025. BYD surpassed Tesla in Germany (Nov 2025). Price the legs, not the horn.

CAMEL HERD SIGNAL

BYD is the lead Camel, not the only one. Geely Xingyuan outsold every BYD model in 2025. 20+ manufacturers competing within a shared ecosystem. Track: when three or more Camels individually exceed 1M annual vehicles, the Unicorn business model becomes unviable outside tariff walls.

PHARMA DEPENDENCY ANCHOR

80% APIs overseas. 40% from China. 227 essential medicines; for nearly half, zero domestic API manufacturing. Maria Delgado pays $47 for a molecule that costs $3.80 at the source. The medicine cabinet is the Efficiency Trap made personal.

HARVEST REPORT

Chen Liling's Tuesday—the Living Harvest in human terms. Price of a robotaxi ride: 8 yuan. Price of a Seagull: 55,800 yuan—three months of her pension. Price of Maria Delgado's metformin: $47 vs. $3.80 at source. The Ledger, for once, is not priced in trillions. It is priced in the currency of ordinary life.

THE BOATMAN'S WAGER

Rotate into the Living Harvest. Increase BYD supply chain exposure. Add China biotech out-licensers ($66B deal flow). Add robotics: UBTECH, XPENG IRON ecosystem. Illustrative short on the Unicorn premium: any EV/AV company above 50x forward earnings on narrative alone is mispriced when the Camel herd delivers at 15x with 3x the volume. Defensive: long domestic pharmaceutical API manufacturers—the next supply chain disruption creates a strategic premium no tariff can match.

Chapter 9 Data Anchors: NEV penetration 59.4% vs. ~12% | 10M+ charging points vs. 76K DC fast chargers (130:1) | BYD 4.6M vehicles, $7,800 Seagull, 1.04M exports | BYD 1.606M pure EVs vs. Tesla 1.218M (Q3 2025) | Geely Xingyuan: outsold every BYD model | Wang Chuanfu: orphan → $300K → 4.6M vehicles | Munger $230M / 10% stake | Biotech: 32% out-licensing ($66B), 639 first-in-class candidates, 120K biomedical PhDs/yr | API: 80% overseas, 40% China, 28% domestic facilities, ~half of 227 essential medicines zero domestic API | Maria Delgado: $47 vs. $3.80 | Robotics: 52% global installations, 276K units | IRON-7: 61% → 94% in one week | XPENG IRON: 50K target | Koottukrishi: collective cultivation | EU countervailing duties up to 36.3%

. . .

A Word to the Reasonable Reader

This chapter has documented the Living Harvest—the sectors where rejuvenation becomes ordinary. The reasonable reader should note what The Other Current documented: BYD faces quality-control challenges in export markets. The biotech boom faces legitimate regulatory and security scrutiny. The humanoid robotics market is in its early stages. The pharmaceutical vulnerability cuts both ways.

The difference is that China's companies have state-backed capital to survive disruptions, a domestic manufacturing base to iterate, and a demographic imperative to push through problems that would terminate a Western startup's funding. Chapter 10 examines the financial architecture that funds everything documented in Chapters 7 through 9—CIPS versus SWIFT, the digital yuan, and the monetary plumbing of the emerging order.

. . .

Chen Liling arrives at Wuhan Union Hospital at 9:14 AM,
two minutes ahead of her appointment.
She pays eight yuan with a tap of her phone.

She does not tip the driver, because there is no driver.

She does not know that the vehicle she just exited
processes more data per kilometer than Apollo 11
processed during its entire mission.

She knows that the car arrived on time, the ride was smooth,
and her granddaughter will ask her tonight
if the ghost car talked to her again.

"It told me to fasten my seatbelt," she will say.
"That's more than your grandfather ever did."

The granddaughter will laugh. Chen Liling will laugh.
And the ghost car, already carrying its next passenger,
will turn left across three lanes of Wuhan traffic
with the quiet competence of a civilization
that has decided the future is not a destination.

It is a Tuesday.

• • •

RITUAL STAGE MARKER

The full face is almost complete. Only the crown remains. The performer's ordinary voice has been replaced by something deeper—the deity's whisper, speaking the names of ordinary things with the weight of extraordinary patience.

CHAPTER 10

The Dollar and the Digital Ditchwater

CIPS, the Digital Yuan, and the Slow Erosion of Dollar Hegemony

"Water is fluid, soft, yielding. But water will wear away rock." — *Lao Tzu*

润物细无声 — *"Moistening things silently."*

The saltwater tide pushes inland slowly, until the freshwater fish can no longer breathe.

— after the Theyyam tradition

. . .

Undercurrent: The Weapon They Could See

Every weapon documented in the previous chapters—the ships, the drones, the semiconductors, the EVs, the biotech molecules—requires money. And money, in the international system, means the US dollar. The dollar is not merely a currency. It is infrastructure—the rails upon which the global economy operates. And like all infrastructure, its most powerful feature is the one users forget exists: the ability of its operator to deny access.

In 2014, when the United States debated disconnecting Russia from SWIFT in response to the annexation of Crimea, a Chinese banker in Shanghai said to a colleague—in a conversation that has since entered the institutional folklore of Chinese financial planning—"Today them. Tomorrow us. Build the alternative." The Cross-Border Interbank Payment System was launched the following year.

In the Kuttanadan backwaters, the salt tide does not announce itself with drama. It *seeps.* It enters the freshwater canal through a thousand invisible capillaries—through crab holes, root cavities, the microscopic fissures that sun and rain open in the clay. The freshwater farmer does not notice at first. The rice grows a little shorter. The fish swim a little slower. By the time the farmer tests the salinity and finds it lethal, the tide has been seeping for months. The dollar system's erosion follows the same hydrology. The salt is not crashing through the bund. The salt is seeping. And by the time the freshwater fish can no longer breathe, the alternative channels will have been flowing for a decade.

A necessary caveat. The dollar is not dying. The dollar is the most liquid, the most trusted, the most deeply embedded reserve currency in human history. Anyone who tells you the dollar is about to collapse is selling either gold or clicks. This chapter is not selling either. What it documents is something more subtle and, for the custodians of dollar hegemony, more dangerous than collapse: *erosion at the margins.* And margins, as any farmer who has watched the saltwater tide creep one meter further into his freshwater paddy each year will tell you, are where civilizational shifts begin.

The strategic genius of the arrangement is that the dollar system was built to facilitate global trade, and the United States repurposed it as a weapon, and then expressed surprise when the targets started building alternative plumbing. The monetary equivalent of building a highway, installing a tollbooth, using the tollbooth to deny access to anyone who annoys you, and then marveling that people are building side roads.

. . .

The Trade-Finance Manager: Wang Sufen

Call her Wang Sufen. She is forty-three years old, a senior trade-finance manager at ICBC's Lujiazui headquarters in Shanghai's Pudong district. Her job is processing cross-border payments. She routes yuan-denominated trade settlements for Chinese manufacturers exporting to Southeast Asia, the Middle East, Africa, and increasingly Europe. She uses CIPS.

Wang Sufen remembers the 2018 incident with a precision that surprises her, because she is not a woman who holds grudges—grudges are inefficient, and Wang Sufen is constitutionally opposed to inefficiency. A Zhejiang textile exporter, one of her regular clients, had a routine payment to a Pakistani buyer delayed for eleven days when a compliance flag at the American correspondent bank triggered a manual review. Eleven days. The textile manufacturer missed the delivery window. The Pakistani buyer canceled the order and sourced from a Turkish supplier. The Zhejiang factory lost $340,000 in revenue, laid off fourteen temporary workers, and the factory owner's wife called Wang Sufen at 11 p.m., crying, because the lost order was the one that was supposed to fund their son's university tuition.

The payment was eventually cleared. The compliance flag was a false positive—an algorithm had confused "Islamabad" with a sanctioned entity whose name contained the same substring. Eleven days. $340,000. Fourteen jobs. One son's university semester. One algorithm. One correspondent bank in New York. One financial system whose architecture gave a compliance algorithm in Manhattan the power to determine whether a factory in Zhejiang could pay its workers.

Wang Sufen does not use the word "rage." She uses the word "clarity." The clarity arrived on the Tuesday after the incident, when she walked into her office, sat down at her terminal, and began the paperwork to onboard her first corporate client onto CIPS. The clarity was not ideological. It was operational. It was the clarity of a woman who had watched a $340,000 order evaporate because someone else's plumbing had a valve she couldn't reach.

Now she watches the daily CIPS transaction volume the way a Kuttanadan hydrologist watches a river gauge—not for the dramatic spike but for the steady rise that tells you the aquifer is climbing. In 2024, CIPS processed ¥175 trillion ($24.5 trillion), up 43% year-on-year. By July 2025, daily clearing volumes exceeded ¥750 billion across approximately 23,000 transactions. The system reaches over 4,900 banking institutions across 189 countries.

Wang Sufen processes payments the way the boatman reads tidal data: each transaction is a drop of water, each drop finding its channel. She does not think she is building a new financial order. She thinks she is ensuring that no algorithm in Manhattan ever again determines whether her clients can pay their workers.

. . .

The Dollar's Eroding Edges

The snapshot first. The dollar accounts for approximately 56.32% of global foreign exchange reserves—down from 72% in 2000 —but remains dominant by an enormous margin. The yuan's share: approximately 2.3%. CIPS daily clearing averages ~$5.7 billion, compared with the dollar-based CHIPS system's ~$1.8 trillion. The yuan accounts for ~3% of SWIFT payments, compared with 48% for the dollar.

By the snapshot, dollar dominance is overwhelming. But the comparison misframes the strategic question. CIPS is not designed to replace SWIFT. It is designed to provide an alternative that exists if the primary system is denied. A lifeboat does not need to be as comfortable as the ship. It needs to float when the ship sinks. CIPS is a lifeboat. Its adequacy should be measured against the scenario in which it is needed, not the scenario in which it is not.

The digital yuan accelerates this logic. By November 2025, the e-CNY had processed 3.48 billion transactions worth ¥16.7 trillion ($2.38 trillion)—an 800%+ increase from 2023. Personal wallets: 230 million. Corporate accounts: 19 million. On January 1, 2026, a new framework transformed the e-CNY from "digital cash" to "digital deposit money"—including, for the first time in any CBDC worldwide, interest-bearing features. This shifts adoption from transactional (use it when you must) to structural (hold it because it earns).

Project mBridge—the multi-CBDC platform connecting the PBOC, Hong Kong Monetary Authority, Bank of Thailand, and Central Bank of the UAE—processed 4,047 transactions worth approximately $55.49 billion by November 2025, a 2,500-fold increase from $22 million in early 2022 pilots. Digital yuan accounted for 95.3% of settlement volume.

mBridge's Quiet Revolution

Project mBridge's 2,500-fold growth in three years—from $22 million in early 2022 pilots to $55.49 billion by November 2025—is a trajectory so steep that it requires calibration against comparable technology adoption curves. For context: SWIFT took approximately fifteen years to reach comparable institutional coverage. Visa took two decades to establish global acceptance. mBridge is three years old and settling transactions between central banks on four continents, with the digital yuan accounting for 95.3% of settlement volume.

The design is elegant in its strategic implications. mBridge connects central banks directly—bypassing the correspondent banking system that routes through New York, bypassing the SWIFT messaging infrastructure that the United States can weaponize, and bypassing every node in the dollar-clearing chain where Washington maintains a chokepoint. A transaction on mBridge settles in seconds rather than days, at a fraction of the cost, without touching any American infrastructure. It is not a protest system. It is not a workaround. It is a replacement—purpose-built to eliminate the dependency that Wang Sufen's 2018 incident demonstrated, the dependency that the Russian reserve freeze confirmed, the dependency that every central bank governor in Beijing, Riyadh, and Bangkok has spent the last four years working to reduce.

The BIS's initial involvement in mBridge—and its subsequent quiet distancing from the project as geopolitical implications became clearer—reveals the institutional tension. The Bank for International Settlements, the central bankers' central bank, recognized mBridge's technical innovation but grew uncomfortable with its strategic trajectory: a CBDC settlement platform that the world's largest central banks use to bypass the dollar system is not a technical experiment. It is a monetary insurgency conducted in the language of financial innovation. The BIS's discomfort is the dollar establishment's canary in the coal mine—the moment when the institution that manages the existing system recognized that the alternative system was no longer theoretical.

And the American response? At least 130 countries representing 98% of global GDP are exploring CBDCs. China has deployed one—230 million wallets, 3.48 billion transactions, interest-bearing, cross-border settlement via mBridge. The United States is holding committee hearings where representatives debate whether a digital dollar would violate the Fourth Amendment. One Federal Reserve economist privately noted: "We're debating the perfect design while they're deploying a working system."

. . .

The Dedollarization Paradox: Wei's Law

The deepest irony of the dollar's position—and the most analytically important insight in this chapter—deserves a name. Call it **Wei's Law**, after the Chinese banker whose 2014 observation launched CIPS:

> *Wei's Law: The effectiveness of financial sanctions is inversely proportional to their frequency. Each use reduces the efficacy of subsequent uses by teaching the target to build alternatives.*

When the United States froze $300 billion in Russian central bank reserves in February 2022, it demonstrated what the global central banking community had long suspected: trust is conditional. The action was strategically justifiable. Russia had invaded a sovereign nation. The question is not whether the freeze was right. The question is: what did every other central bank governor learn?

The lesson received in Beijing, Riyadh, New Delhi, Brasilia, Ankara, and Jakarta was not "don't invade Ukraine." The lesson was: "Your reserves are held at the pleasure of the United States. The terms of that pleasure may change without notice. Plan accordingly."

Central bank gold purchases surged to records in 2022, 2023, and 2024—not because gold is a superior investment but because gold stored in domestic vaults cannot be frozen by SWIFT messages. China increased gold reserves while reducing Treasury holdings. Saudi Arabia began accepting yuan for oil settlements—the first crack in the petrodollar arrangement that has anchored dollar hegemony since Kissinger's 1974 handshake with the House of Saud. India settled Russian oil in dirhams and rupees. Brazil and Argentina discussed bilateral settlement in local currencies. Each action was individually modest. Collectively, they represent a global central banking community performing the same actuarial calculation: the probability that what happened to Russian reserves could happen to theirs.

The Petrodollar Crack: What Riyadh's Calculation Reveals

Saudi Arabia's acceptance of the yuan for oil settlements deserves more analytical weight than a single sentence, because the petrodollar arrangement is not merely a financial convenience. It is the architectural foundation upon which dollar hegemony was constructed—and its erosion represents a structural change, not a transactional one.

The arrangement that Kissinger negotiated in 1974 was simple and devastating in its implications: Saudi Arabia would price and sell its oil exclusively in dollars, and in return, the United States would guarantee the Kingdom's security. Every nation that needed oil—which is to say, every nation—needed dollars to buy it. This created a self-reinforcing demand for dollar reserves that underwrote American fiscal policy, enabled the deficit spending that funded the military that guaranteed the arrangement, and made the dollar indispensable not because of American economic virtue but because of American strategic positioning. The petrodollar was not a market outcome. It was a security arrangement with monetary consequences.

When Saudi Arabia began accepting yuan for oil in 2023, it did not announce the end of the petrodollar. It announced something more subtle and more dangerous: the optionality of the petrodollar. Riyadh's calculation is not ideological. It is actuarial. China buys approximately 1.7 million barrels of Saudi oil per day—roughly 25% of Saudi exports. Paying in yuan eliminates the dollar intermediation cost, settles directly through CIPS, and deepens the bilateral relationship that Saudi Arabia increasingly views as a hedge against the possibility that American security guarantees may prove less permanent than the 1974 handshake implied. The Crown Prince, who has watched American withdrawal from Afghanistan, American ambivalence toward the region, and American domestic political instability with the same calculating patience that the Chinese planner watches the tariff saga, has drawn a conclusion: diversify. Not abandon the dollar. Diversify away from the single-currency dependency that gives Washington a valve on the Kingdom's revenue.

Each barrel settled in yuan is Wei's Law in liquid form. The drop does not crack the dam. The drop teaches other drops where the fissures are.

Wei's Law is circular, self-reinforcing, and inescapable: every use of dollar weaponization demonstrates American power and simultaneously undermines the trust that makes dollar dominance possible. The threat IS the incentive. The weapon IS the alternative's recruitment brochure.

. . .

The Other Current: Why the Dollar Has Survived Every Previous Obituary

Wei's Law is real. So is its limit.

The dollar has been declared dead since the euro's launch in 1999, the 2008 financial crisis, the yuan's inclusion in the SDR in 2016, and the Russian reserve freeze in 2022. Each declaration was accompanied by data showing erosion at the margins. Each time, the dollar's structural advantages reasserted themselves—not because the erosion was fake but because the alternatives faced constraints that the erosion data did not capture.

The deepest constraint is capital account openness. The dollar is the global reserve currency not because America's economy is the largest—it is not, in PPP terms—but because the United States offers something no rival can match: a deep, liquid capital market governed by the rule of law, where foreign investors can move money in and out freely, where property rights are enforced by independent courts, and where the government cannot, on a political whim, freeze your assets or prevent your withdrawal. China's $50,000 annual limit on foreign-currency purchases for citizens is not a minor regulatory detail. It is the structural confession that the CCP cannot tolerate the volatility in capital flows that full convertibility would produce. And a currency whose own citizens cannot freely convert is not one that foreign central banks will hold as a primary reserve, regardless of how many CIPS nodes are online.

The trust deficit runs deeper than capital controls. The same party that froze Jack Ma's Ant Group IPO without warning, that conducted the 2021 tech crackdown destroying hundreds of billions in investor wealth, that stopped publishing youth unemployment data when the numbers became embarrassing, is now asking global investors to trust the digital yuan as a settlement instrument. Wang Sufen's *clarity* about Manhattan's algorithmic power is legitimate. But the foreign investor's *clarity* about Beijing's regulatory power is equally legitimate. Both clarity-producing incidents involve a single authority wielding arbitrary power over someone else's money. The difference is which authority you trust less.

The honest assessment: Wei's Law is eroding the dollar's margins, and the erosion is real, measurable, and accelerating. But the dollar's core—deep markets, rule of law, capital mobility—remains structurally superior to any alternative, and will remain so until China either opens its capital account (which requires political liberalization the CCP has shown no appetite for) or builds enough bilateral settlement infrastructure to make convertibility unnecessary (which is the mBridge thesis, and it is decades from scale). The salt tide is seeping. But the freshwater aquifer is deeper than the sensationalists acknowledge.

* * *

Interlude: Marcus Follows the Plumbing

Marcus Chen had never given SWIFT a moment's thought. SWIFT was plumbing—the financial equivalent of a sewage system: essential, invisible, interesting only to the people who maintained it.

He called Priya. "Talk to me about CIPS."

Priya sighed. "I'm a semiconductor analyst, Marcus."

"You're the only person at this firm who understands that Chinese infrastructure is interconnected. Talk to me about CIPS."

Priya talked. Then she said the thing that rearranged his mental architecture: "The interdependency web from your EV research? CIPS is the same thing for money. CIPS connects to the digital yuan, which connects to mBridge, which connects to BRI loan servicing, which connects to Huawei telecom, which connects to the 5G that carries the transaction data. It's not a payment system. It's a financial ecosystem. And every BRI loan serviced in yuan deepens the roots. The switching costs compound the same way CATL's battery costs compound."

Then he ran the three scenarios he'd been building since Chapter 6's rare earth analysis—the ones he called "Dollar Fortress," "Parallel Rails," and "Salt Tide"—through his entire fund.

Under Dollar Fortress (dollar reforms, alliance cohesion restored, CIPS remains niche): his current portfolio performed well. Under Parallel Rails (dollar dominant but sharing the system with yuan, euro, and digital alternatives): his portfolio lost 11% on dollar-denominated fixed income and gained 8% on China deployment plays. Under Salt Tide (Taiwan contingency, comprehensive sanctions, bifurcated global finance), his dollar-heavy positions lost 23%, while his deployment positions gained 34%.

The math was uncomfortable. Under all three scenarios, reducing dollar concentration and increasing deployment exposure improved risk-adjusted returns. The direction was the same in every scenario. Only the speed differed.

Marcus saved the model. He titled it "The Boatman's Wager"—because the boatman does not bet on probabilities alone. The boatman bets on *preparation*. If you prepare for the Parallel Rails and the Dollar Fortress occurs, you are over-prepared: a minor inefficiency. If you prepare for the Parallel Rails and the Salt Tide arrives, you are under-prepared: a catastrophe. The prudent sailor prepares for the worst current while hoping for the calmest. This is not pessimism. It is hydrology.

. . .

Three Scenarios: Dollar, Yuan, and the Monetary Halocline

The Boatman reads three possible channels ahead.

Scenario A: "The Dollar Fortress" (20% probability). The United States reforms its fiscal position, preserves alliance cohesion through predictable policy, and the dollar's share stabilizes above 50%. CIPS remains a niche alternative. This scenario requires the Hunter to execute multiple difficult reforms simultaneously. Possible. But the current has been flowing in the other direction for two decades.

Scenario B: "The Parallel Rails" (55% probability). The most likely outcome. The dollar remains the largest fish in the pond but shares the monetary system with the yuan, euro, and digital alternatives. Dollar reserves decline to 45–48% by 2035. Yuan rises to 8–12%, concentrated in Asian trade, commodity settlement, and BRI corridors. CIPS processes 15–20% of global cross-border payments. This is the monetary halocline—the boundary layer where saltwater and freshwater coexist, each occupying its niche, neither fully displacing the other. Messy, complex, and stable.

Scenario C: "The Salt Tide" (25% probability). A Taiwan Strait crisis triggers comprehensive financial sanctions on China. China fully activates CIPS, converts BRI partners to yuan settlement, and accelerates mBridge. The result: a bifurcated global financial system—a Western dollar bloc and a Chinese-centered yuan bloc. The financial equivalent of the semiconductor paradox: the restriction designed to prevent the alternative accelerates it.

What the three scenarios share is a direction. In all three, the dollar's share declines. In all three, the yuan's share increases. The rate of change varies. The direction does not.

. . .

BRI and the Architecture of Financial Lock-In

Chapter 6 documented the diplomatic harvest. This section documents the financial plumbing that Harvest installed. CIPS provides the interbank settlement rail. The digital yuan provides a currency instrument. mBridge provides the cross-border bridge. BRI provides the trade flows. Huawei provides the telecommunications infrastructure. Each component is modest individually. Together: an alternative financial architecture that did not exist ten years ago.

The switching costs compound across layers. A BRI borrower using Huawei's 5G to process digital yuan payments through CIPS for trade settled along Belt and Road corridors is embedded in an ecosystem whose aggregate creates dependency architecture rivaling the dollar system's network effects. Huawei has built approximately 70% of Africa's

4G networks—not a commodity installation but an integrated system: hardware, software, maintenance, training, upgrade paths. For a sub-Saharan nation whose entire telecom runs on Huawei, switching to Nokia requires not replacing hardware but retraining the entire workforce. In Kuttanad, the boatmen call this *verppaadu*—the binding that cannot be cut without cutting what it binds. The dollar system is one *verppaadu*. The Farmer's financial ecosystem is becoming another. A country bound by both must eventually choose which thread to pull.

Sarah callback — the invisible financial architecture

Sarah Kowalski's supplier payments are a window into the plumbing this chapter describes. When Sarah pays her Vietnamese intermediary, the transaction routes through her community bank in Youngstown to a correspondent bank in New York via the CHIPS clearing system, then to a correspondent bank in Ho Chi Minh City, and finally to the intermediary's local account. The payment settles in dollars. Every node in this chain is American-controlled infrastructure—the same infrastructure whose weaponization Wang Sufen's vignette documented.

But Sarah's Cambodian rerouting option—the direct shipment from Guangdong invoiced through Phnom Penh that she rejected in Chapter 6—would have settled differently. The Cambodian intermediary offered settlement in yuan through a CIPS-connected account. If Sarah had accepted—and thousands of small importers across America are making exactly this calculation—her payment would have bypassed the dollar clearing system entirely. Not because Sarah has a geopolitical opinion about dedollarization. Because the yuan-settled price was 8% cheaper. The salt tide that Wang Sufen monitors does not announce itself as a monetary revolution. It announces itself as a better price on a Cambodian invoice. Each drop finds its channel. And the channel, once found, rarely redirects.

The IMF's governance structure—designed in 1944 when the US accounted for half of global GDP—has not been meaningfully reformed in eighty years. China's voting share is 6.4%. Belgium, Luxembourg, and the Netherlands—whose combined population is roughly equal to that of Shanghai—have a larger combined vote. The SOE ecosystem is not waiting for IMF reform. It is building alternatives—AIIB ($100 billion authorized capital, 110 members), the New Development Bank, the expanding SCO economic mandate, and RCEP (the world's largest trade agreement by GDP). Each alternative is another irrigation channel.

* * *

BOATMAN'S LEDGER

Chapter 10

LEDGER TOOL #9: FINANCIAL ARCHITECTURE ASSESSMENT

The dollar is not dying. It is eroding—at a pace that neither the sensationalists nor the complacent have correctly calibrated.

WEI'S LAW

The effectiveness of financial sanctions is inversely proportional to their frequency. Each use teaches the target to build alternatives. The freeze of $300B Russian reserves was the inflection point: every central bank governor recalculated. Gold purchases surged. Saudi petro-yuan began. The law is self-reinforcing.

RESERVE CURRENCY TEMPERATURE

The dollar's reserve share is a vital sign with a direction and a rate. Temperature: cooling, from 72° in 2000 to 56° today. Track: annual reserve share change, CIPS volume growth rate, digital yuan wallet growth, mBridge transaction acceleration. When three or four indicators accelerate simultaneously, the cooling is entering a new phase.

SCENARIO WEIGHTS

Dollar Fortress: 20% | Parallel Rails: 55% | Salt Tide: 25%. In all three, the dollar's share declines. The Boatman's Wager: prepare for Parallel Rails.

THE BOATMAN'S WAGER

Scenario B illustrative allocation: reduce dollar-denominated fixed-income overweight by 8%. Add yuan-denominated bonds (dim sum, panda). Increase gold by 3%—not as a collapse thesis but as a Wei's Law hedge. Add CIPS-adjacent fintech and cross-border payment plays. The trade: the dollar's monopoly premium decays as alternatives proliferate, and the decay is faster than the market prices because each sanctions episode accelerates it.

Chapter 10 Data Anchors: Dollar reserves 56.32% (from 72% in 2000) | Yuan ~2.3% reserves, ~3% SWIFT | CIPS ¥175T annual ($24.5T), 43% YoY growth, 4,900 institutions, 189 countries | Digital yuan 3.48B transactions, $2.38T, 230M wallets, interest-bearing Jan 2026 | mBridge $55.49B, 95.3% yuan, 2,500x growth | Russian $300B freeze (Feb 2022) = Wei's Law inflection | Saudi petro-yuan | Huawei 70% Africa 4G | IMF: China 6.4% voting share | AIIB $100B, 110 members | Wang Sufen: $340K / 14 jobs / one algorithm | Verppaadu: binding that cannot be cut | Capital controls: $50K/year citizen limit

. . .

A Word to the Reasonable Reader

This chapter has walked the narrowest analytical path in the book. Dollar dominance is neither collapsing nor permanent. CIPS is neither irrelevant ($24.5 trillion annually, 189 countries) nor yet transformative (80%+ SWIFT messaging dependency, yuan at 3% of payment flows). The digital yuan is neither the inevitable future nor a Potemkin pilot (3.48 billion transactions is not a pilot; it is an infrastructure). The truth occupies the uncomfortable middle ground where most truths reside.

The reasonable reader should hold three facts simultaneously, because the inability to hold contradictory facts simultaneously is the analytical failure that has produced every misassessment documented in this book. First: the yuan's 3% share of SWIFT makes dollar hegemony look overwhelming. Second: CIPS's 36-fold growth over nine years, the digital yuan's 800% growth over two years, and mBridge's 2,500-fold growth over three years make the trajectory exponential. Third: trajectory and position are distinct variables, and the strategic question is which matters more at different time horizons. The Other Current section above documented a fourth fact that honest analysis demands: the dollar's structural advantages—capital account openness, rule of law, market depth—are not mere inertia. They are features that the yuan cannot structurally replicate without political changes, which the CCP has shown no willingness to undertake.

This chapter concludes Part II—the Vellatam, the collision. Part III will ask: What must the Hunter do to avoid losing? The answer requires a Rooseveltian imagination.

. . .

Wang Sufen closes her terminal at 6:47 PM.
The day's CIPS transactions have been processed.
The numbers are slightly higher than yesterday,
slightly lower than they will be tomorrow.

She does not think in terms of dedollarization paradigms.
She thinks in terms of settlement finality and processing speed.
She is good at her job.

Her job is ensuring that no algorithm in Manhattan
ever again determines whether her clients can pay their workers.

Every payment she processes is a drop of water.
Every drop finds its channel.
Every channel, in time, wears away the rock.

In Kuttanad, the tide does not announce itself.
It arrives—quiet, patient, and salt.

· · ·

RITUAL STAGE MARKER

The crown is placed. The performer's eyes widen. The deity is fully present—and the first thing it does is test the worshippers with hard truths.

· · ·

PART III
MUKHATHEZHUTHU — THE TRANSFORMATION

The full mask is applied. The performer is no longer human. The deity speaks not of predictions but choices. The worshippers must decide whether to act on what they have seen.

CHAPTER 11

The Farmer's Blight

Vulnerabilities, Steelman, and One Surprise

"Water can carry a boat; it can also overturn it." — Xunzi

Even the most patient farmer fears the blight.

— after the Theyyam tradition

. . .

Undercurrent: The Boat and the Water

Xunzi's proverb—"water can carry a boat; it can also overturn it"—is not an observation by an outside critic. It is the CCP's own internal warning, a self-diagnosis embedded in the civilization's operating system. The water is the people. The boat is the state. And the warning is that the same demographic engine, the same social contract, the same productive population that carries the regime's ambitions can, if mismanaged, capsize them entirely.

In Kuttanad, we know this truth. The backwater that feeds the paddy is the same backwater that drowns it. The monsoon that fills the granary is the same monsoon that sweeps the village into the *kayal*. The boatman who has spent his life reading the halocline knows that the water's gift and the water's violence are not two separate forces. They are one force, experienced differently depending on whether you are riding the current or fighting it.

The one-child policy was a humiliation-era overcorrection—a civilization so traumatized by the memory of famine that it turned its formidable state capacity inward, against its own reproductive future. The demographic cliff that China now faces is not a natural disaster. It is trauma's offspring. And while this book has spent eight chapters documenting the Farmer's deployment advantages, intellectual honesty demands we examine the blight. Because the same civilization that engineered 16.49 million NEV sales in a single year cannot engineer a baby boom. The Farmer can plant every field except the nursery.

A prefatory note on genre. Gordon Chang published *The Coming Collapse of China* in 2001. It is now 2026, and China's economy has grown roughly tenfold since that prediction was issued. The "China will collapse" genre has become an industry—all of them sharing the characteristic of having been consistently, spectacularly, and profitably wrong for twenty-five consecutive years.

This chapter is not in that genre. This chapter does not predict collapse. It documents vulnerabilities with the same empirical rigor applied to strengths. A doctor who diagnoses hypertension is not predicting a heart attack. A doctor who ignores hypertension because the patient has run seven marathons is committing malpractice. This chapter is the cardiac workup. It is not the obituary.

. . .

The Woman Who Won't Plant: Wei Lin

Call her Wei Lin. She is thirty-two, a product manager at a mid-tier technology company in Chengdu's Tianfu Software Park, earning roughly 18,000 yuan per month. She has a partner. She has stability. She has parents who ask about grandchildren with the gentle persistence of monsoon drizzle that never quite stops.

Wei Lin has decided not to have children.

Her reasoning is arithmetic. Her rent on a modest two-bedroom in Chengdu's Wuhou District consumes approximately 60% of her income. She watched her parents pour their life savings into an apartment from a developer that subsequently defaulted. The apartment was delivered eighteen months late, with finishes that would embarrass a college dormitory. Her father, a retired factory worker, does not discuss the financial loss. He discusses grandchildren instead, because discussing the apartment would require acknowledging that the social contract he trusted—work hard, buy property, build wealth, pass it to your children—has been quietly voided.

When her mother calls to ask whether Wei Lin has "considered the matter," Wei Lin hears something beneath the words that the words themselves cannot carry. Not pressure—fear. Her mother's generation invested everything in the social contract: education, property, family. That contract is now broken. Her mother's questions are not demands but *prayers*—prayers that the daughter will find a way to believe in something the mother can no longer believe in. Wei Lin hears the prayer. She cannot answer it. She simply says, "Not yet, Ma," and changes the subject.

On a Saturday evening, Wei Lin meets four friends at a hotpot restaurant in Chunxi Road—the kind of place where the broth is nuclear, and the conversation is uncensored because the noise level provides its own privacy. All five women are between twenty-eight and thirty-four. All are employed. All are in relationships. None has children.

The conversation is not philosophical. It is mathematical. Xiaoli works at a fintech startup: "Private kindergarten is five thousand a month. Shadow tutoring is three thousand. That's eight thousand before you buy a diaper." Mei runs the numbers differently: "My mother's apartment lost thirty percent of its value. That's her retirement. If I have a child, I'm funding my retirement *and* my child's education on a salary that hasn't kept pace with inflation since 2021." Jia, the quietest, says something that silences the table: "I love children. I love the idea of being a mother. I just can't afford to bring a child into a world where the only inheritance I can guarantee is my anxiety."

Five women. Five calculations. Five versions of the same arithmetic of despair. The birth rate is not a policy failure. It is a vote of no confidence, rendered through the most intimate and ungovernable human decision.

In Kuttanad, the old women tell a story about the rice that refuses to grow—not because the soil is poor but because the farmer's hands, cracked and exhausted, have communicated something to the seed that no fertilizer can override: the earth is tired. Wei Lin is the seed that says *not yet* to a civilization that has exhausted the soil of its own social contract.

· · ·

Five Vulnerabilities: The Soil Analysis

If the preceding chapters documented the Farmer's harvest, intellectual integrity requires an equally rigorous soil analysis. These are structural conditions that could transform the interdependency web from an advantage into a trap.

Vulnerability One: Topsoil Erosion (Demographics). China's births dropped 17% between 2024 and 2025, plummeting to 7.92 million—the lowest since 1949. The fertility rate has collapsed to approximately 1.0 births per woman, less than half replacement. The population has shrunk for four consecutive years. The women aged twenty to thirty-four—the cohort responsible for 85% of births—is projected to decline from 105 million to 58 million by 2050. Marriages collapsed to 6.1 million, a 20.5% decline. The mathematics are merciless and recursive: each unborn child represents not just one missing worker but the missing worker's missing children.

India's contrast sharpens the picture. Median age ~28 versus China's ~39. Working-age population peaking mid-2040s. 1.5 million engineering graduates annually and rising. India's demographic dividend is the variable most Western China-vulnerability analyses ignore because it complicates both narratives.

India's Demographic Dividend: The Third Variable

The India analysis deferred from Chapter 6 demands its full hearing here, because India's demographic dividend does not merely complicate the Farmer's narrative. It potentially reshapes it.

India's working-age population will peak at approximately 1.04 billion in the mid-2040s—precisely the decade when China's working-age population will have contracted by an estimated 100 million. The timing is not coincidental from a strategic perspective: it means that India's human capital surplus will reach its maximum precisely when China's human capital deficit reaches its most acute phase. The robotics solution documented in Chapter 9—276,000 industrial installations in 2024, XPENG IRON targeting 50,000 humanoid units—is the Farmer's response to this timeline. But whether machines can fully substitute for the demographic dividend that India possesses and China has forfeited is one of the competition's most consequential open questions.

India's GDP growth rate—approximately 6.5–7% in recent years—exceeds China's, though from a significantly smaller base (India's GDP is roughly one-fifth of China's). The compound effect of sustained 6.5% growth on a population of 1.44 billion is a force that both the Farmer and the Hunter must account for. India's IT services sector, its pharmaceutical industry (the world's largest generic drug producer), its space program (which delivered a Mars orbiter at one-tenth the cost of NASA's MAVEN mission), and its expanding manufacturing base (particularly in electronics, where Apple and Samsung have established significant Indian operations) represent a deployment capacity that, while currently below Chinese levels, is growing at a rate that neither Beijing nor Washington can afford to ignore.

The vulnerability for the Farmer is specific: India's demographic dividend gives the Hunter a potential partner whose labor force can compete with China's on scale, whose democratic governance model aligns with the alliance architecture documented in Chapter 11's Steelman section (NATO, Quad, AUKUS), and whose strategic ambiguity—simultaneously buying Russian oil and attending Quad summits—gives it leverage that neither current can control. If the Hunter's Adaptation Four (Alliance Agriculture: Quad $100 Billion Counter-BRI) succeeds in deepening the India partnership, the demographic cliff's impact on the Farmer's long-term competitiveness compounds. If the Farmer deepens India's infrastructure dependencies through BRI-adjacent investments (such as the China-Myanmar Economic Corridor and the Bangladesh-China-India-Myanmar Forum), the Hunter's demographic bet is hedged.

The honest assessment: India is the variable that most threatens to invalidate any binary framework—including this book's. The Farmer-Hunter competition may ultimately be decided not by either combatant but by the 1.44-billion-person civilization that stands between them, drawing nutrients from both currents, committing to neither, and growing at a pace that will make it impossible to ignore by the decade's end.

Vulnerability Two: The Subsoil Is Contaminated (Property). China's real estate sector, once nearly 30% of GDP, has been hemorrhaging since Beijing's 2020 "three red lines." Evergrande liquidated with $330 billion in debt. Vanke: record loss. Estimated household wealth destruction: conservatively $4.7 trillion since 2021. Savings have surged to 160 trillion yuan—but savings driven by fear are not the same as savings driven by confidence. The Kuttanadan farmer who hoards grain because he doesn't trust the weather is not wealthier. He is just more frightened.

Vulnerability Three: The Drainage Is Poor (Innovation Paradox). The COMAC C919 is the most visible exhibit. Target: 75 aircraft in 2025. Delivered: 13. The C919 depends on Western suppliers for 50–60% of critical components, including CFM engines. When the US halted engine exports, COMAC's line froze. The paradox is structural: authoritarian systems excel at directed deployment but are constitutionally handicapped at the bleeding edge, where breakthroughs require the anarchic collision of independent minds and the tolerance for failure that control-oriented systems resist. And the SOE system's *Vellappokkam*—the drowning gift of too much state capital in too many unproductive channels—constrains the *Qi's* dynamism. Provincial SOEs are building half-empty industrial parks. State banks are extending credit to zombie enterprises. The Big Fund's corruption. These are not aberrations. They are the system's shadow.

Vulnerability Four: The Irrigation Is Restricted (Capital Controls). The renminbi accounts for only ~3.17% of global reserves. Beijing maintains capital controls because full convertibility would expose the financial system to speculative flows and—more fundamentally—because an authoritarian state cannot tolerate the loss of control convertibility implies. Trust, in financial markets, is not a technology problem. It is a governance problem.

Vulnerability Five: The Groundwater Is Brackish (Legitimacy Trap). The CCP's implicit bargain—performance legitimacy in exchange for political monopoly—is a high-wire act with no net. Democracies survive recessions because legitimacy derives from the electoral process. Voters can fire leaders without dismantling the system. China's system lacks this relief valve. When growth was 10%, the bargain was easy. When growth is 5%, and the property market is in freefall and youth unemployment exceeded 20% before the government stopped publishing the statistic—the statistical equivalent of unplugging a smoke detector because the alarm was inconvenient—the bargain becomes fragile.

The satirical lens must now turn on the Western observers who read these vulnerabilities and reach, with the eagerness of a drowning man spotting a raft, for the comforting conclusion that the Farmer's problems will solve themselves. The analyst who circulates Chinese demographic data with barely concealed satisfaction—the same analyst who did not notice BYD until it surpassed Tesla, did not notice DeepSeek until it cost Nvidia $589 billion—now announces that China's demographic cliff will solve the competition. The analyst does not explain how a country installing more industrial robots than the rest of the world combined is incapable of adapting to a shrinking workforce. The analyst simply files "China demographics bad" in the same drawer where he filed "China can't innovate" and expects, against all evidence, that the drawer will stay shut.

. . .

Interlude: Marcus Reads the Other Side of the Ledger

Marcus Chen looked at his two ledgers side by side. The "Things I Got Wrong" tab documented the American assumptions that deployment data had demolished. The "Farmer's Blight" tab documented the Chinese vulnerabilities that the deployment narrative had obscured. Both were based on verifiable data. And together, they told a story more complicated and more honest than either the "America is in terminal decline" narrative or the "China will inevitably dominate" narrative could accommodate.

The demographic data stopped him first. Fertility rate at 1.0. Population shrinking for four consecutive years. He felt something he hadn't expected: relief. Then immediately: shame at the relief. Then: the recognition that the relief itself was a form of *māyā*—the comfortable illusion that the adversary's weakness solves your problem without requiring you to fix your own.

He looked at the property data. $4.7 trillion in wealth destruction. Then he looked at his other tab—the American tab: $5.3 trillion in buybacks. The F-35's $1.7 trillion lifecycle. The Hunter's wounds were different in kind but comparable in scale. The Farmer's field had blight. The Hunter's field had termites. Neither field was healthy. The question was which farmer would treat the soil first.

Marcus saved both tabs. He did not close either one. A ledger that shows only strengths is marketing. A ledger that shows only weaknesses is propaganda. A ledger that holds both, simultaneously, without collapsing into either complacency or despair—that is analysis. Marcus was learning to be an analyst.

Sarah + Maria callback — the blight/termites parallel humanized

Marcus's $4.7 trillion / $5.3 trillion parallel—the Farmer's blight and the Hunter's termites—has human faces he can now put to the numbers. The Farmer's $4.7 trillion in property wealth destruction is Wei Lin's parents' apartment, delivered eighteen months late with finishes that would embarrass a dormitory. The Hunter's $5.3 trillion in buybacks is Sarah Kowalski's supplier calling to explain that the factory in Youngstown closed because Bobby Buyback's quarterly math made offshoring irresistible, and that the tariffs designed to reverse the offshoring are now being routed through Cambodia by the same supply chain that caused the closure.

Marcus had driven to Youngstown. He had stood on West Federal Street and seen the ceramics in the window arranged with a care the street did not match. He had driven back to Westchester in silence. And now, looking at his two ledgers—the Chinese vulnerabilities and the American vulnerabilities—he could see what the Bloomberg terminal had been hiding in plain sight: the blight and the termites were *mirror images*. The Farmer's social contract was voided by a property bubble that a one-party state inflated and could not gracefully deflate. The Hunter's social contract was voided by a buyback theology that a market-fundamentalist orthodoxy inflated and would not voluntarily restrain. Wei Lin's "not yet" and Sarah's yellow legal pad were the same arithmetic of despair, denominated in different currencies.

Maria Delgado was the ledger's cruelest line item. A sixty-one-year-old woman choosing between medication and groceries in a city where the hospital had closed, the bus had stopped coming, and the scheduling algorithm kept her hours below the threshold where she would become human rather than a line item. The Farmer's blight is real—Chapter 11's five vulnerabilities are empirically devastating. But Marcus, who had now seen both Chengdu's hotpot restaurants and Youngstown's plywood windows, understood that "both sides have problems" is the comforting dodge of the analyst who has not yet walked the streets. The Farmer's problems are *projected*—demographic cliffs fifteen years away. The Hunter's problems are *present*—Maria's $52 copay is due next Tuesday.

. . .

Steelman: Why the Hunter Might Win

This book has spent eight chapters cataloguing American pathologies. It is now time to make the strongest possible case for why the Forest's institutional advantages might prove decisive despite the Farmer's deployment lead.

The SCOTUS Antibody. When the Supreme Court strikes down executive overreach, the American system groans, protests, and complies. This is not efficiency. It is something far more valuable: an institutional immune system. China's judiciary answers to the Party. Policy errors—the one-child policy, the "three red lines," the 2021 tech crackdown—have no institutional brake. Democracies fail loudly, publicly, and recover slowly. Authoritarian systems execute flawlessly right up until the moment they drive off a structural cliff.

The Chinese planner, reading the SCOTUS tariff ruling in her office in Beijing, felt that complicated emotion again—not relief, not satisfaction, but something rarer: *envy.* Because her system has no equivalent mechanism. When her leadership errs, there is no Roberts to write "those words cannot bear such weight." Her system can mobilize faster, deploy wider, and plan longer. But it cannot correct itself from within. The enemy's capacity for self-correction is the one advantage the Farmer cannot replicate.

The 55% Immigrant Advantage. More than 55% of America's billion-dollar startup founders are immigrants or their children. Google, Tesla, Nvidia, Zoom, Stripe, SpaceX—the companies that define American technological leadership were founded by people who chose to come to America because America offers something no other country replicates at scale: the ability to arrive with nothing and build everything.

But the strongest version of the argument goes deeper than immigrant founders. It is the argument that American culture's tolerance for individual eccentricity produces breakthrough innovation that conformist cultures cannot replicate. The Transformer was not invented by a team executing a Five-Year Plan. It was invented by eight researchers at Google Brain who were given the freedom to pursue a hunch. CRISPR was not the product of directed state investment. It was the product of a UC Berkeley professor following curiosity into a bacterial immune system. The Hunter discovers. The Farmer deploys. And the question this book has posed—which advantage proves more durable—does not have a predetermined answer.

The Forest CAN Respond. The same country that cannot build a high-speed rail line between its two largest cities also split the atom, put men on the moon, built the interstate highway system, created the internet, developed GPS, deployed the mRNA vaccine in under a year, and produces more Nobel laureates in science than the rest of the world combined. The American system is not incapable of transformation. It is selectively capable—brilliant at crisis response, terrible at chronic maintenance.

Alliance Depth. America's alliance network—NATO, Five Eyes, Quad, AUKUS—provides strategic depth that the Farmer's bilateral model cannot match. China's partner network is hub-and-spoke. America's is a mesh. Meshes survive the loss of individual nodes.

The Magnificent Seven as Latent Antibody. The Seven, for all their extractive pathology documented in Chapter 2, remain the most formidable concentration of technical talent, computational infrastructure, and R&D spending on Earth. Alphabet's DeepMind invented AlphaFold. NVIDIA's CUDA ecosystem has no Chinese equivalent. Apple's M-series silicon rivals BYD's vertical integration. Microsoft's partnership produced GPT-4. If these companies were aimed at civilizational objectives rather than advertising optimization and stock buybacks, the competition would look very different.

The Magnificent Seven are not the Hunter's weakness. They are the Hunter's squandered strength. And squandered strength, unlike absent strength, can be reclaimed. Chapter 12's *maattivekkal*—the turning of the bow—proposes exactly this.

. . .

THE SURPRISE

Sustainment Over Breakthrough

Now for the argument that will make both the Farmer's critics and cheerleaders equally uncomfortable, which is how you know it might be true.

A caveat first: this reframe does not eliminate the vulnerabilities above. Demographics remain catastrophic. The property crisis is real. The C919's 13 deliveries against 75 targets remain an unmitigated failure. What the reframe changes is the analytical *question*—not "are there weaknesses?" but "what kind of competition is this, and does it favor the ceiling or the floor?"

Western analysts read China's failure to match TSMC's EUV lithography as proof that the innovation model is fundamentally limited. They point to SMIC's slower, costlier 5nm DUV and declare victory. They note the C919 shortfall and see confirmation of the authoritarian paradox. They observe Huawei's Ascend at 60% of H100 performance and file it under "failure."

This reading is not wrong. But it is catastrophically incomplete. It makes the analytical error American strategists have made at every stage: it evaluates Chinese technology against *American benchmarks* rather than against *Chinese strategic requirements*.

The surprise: China's "lagging at the bleeding edge but winning at sustainment" is not accidental. It is strategic.

SMIC's 5nm DUV chips are not as fast as TSMC's 3nm EUV chips. But they exist. They are domestic. They can be mass-produced without depending on a Dutch company's next shipment. In strategic terms, a 5nm chip you control completely is worth more than a 3nm chip your adversary can cut off with a phone call to The Hague.

The same logic applies across every domain. Huawei's Ascend at 60% of H100 is a "failure" only if the benchmark is absolute performance leadership. If the benchmark is "can China train and run AI models of sufficient quality for domestic and Global South deployment without American permission," then 60% is operational independence.

Domain Example 1: Semiconductors. SMIC's 5nm DUV covers approximately 80% of the use cases the global economy requires—mobile processors, automotive chips, IoT devices, edge AI accelerators, and military systems below the most computation-intensive tier. The remaining 20%—frontier AI training at the largest scale, the most advanced mobile SOCs—requires EUV. The Western strategic framework treats the 20% gap as decisive. The

Farmer's framework treats the 80% coverage as sufficient. Both are correct within their own logic. The question is which logic governs the outcome of a multi-decade competition.

Domain Example 2: Space. Tiangong is not the ISS's equal in scale, international participation, or cumulative scientific output. The ISS represents the collaborative achievement of 16 nations over three decades. By the ceiling metric—most impressive orbital platform—the ISS wins decisively. But by the floor metric—wholly indigenous, maintainable without foreign cooperation, immune to political decisions by partner nations—Tiangong is structurally superior. When the ISS is deorbited circa 2030, and the only crewed orbital platform is Chinese, the ceiling metric will be irrelevant. The platform that exists beats the platform that was more impressive but no longer orbits. Sustainment over breakthrough.

Domain Example 3: EVs and Autonomous Driving. Waymo's self-driving technology is, by most engineering assessments, more sophisticated than Apollo Go's. Waymo's per-vehicle sensor suite ($175,000) produces more granular environmental modeling. But Apollo Go processes 300,000 rides per week at unit economics breakeven across multiple Chinese cities, while Waymo operates in a handful of geofenced American zones at a cost per ride that remains unpublished—which, in the language of financial disclosure, means "so expensive that publishing it would depress the stock." The ceiling is Waymo's. The floor is Apollo Go's. And the floor is where 1.4 billion people live.

This reframes the entire "innovation gap" narrative. The question is not: "Can China match the bleeding edge?" The question is: "Does China need to match the bleeding edge, or is strategic sustainment at 70–80% of frontier performance, produced domestically and deployed at civilizational scale, sufficient to achieve its objectives?"

The answer, uncomfortable for both sides, is probably yes.

Sustainment is not glamorous. It does not produce keynote moments or magazine covers. But it produces something more durable: a technological floor below which capability cannot fall, regardless of external sanctions. America's strategy of maintaining a technological ceiling—being the best at the frontier—is powerful. But it is fundamentally less stable than China's strategy of raising a technological floor.

A ceiling can be cracked from below. A floor cannot be undermined from above.

In Kuttanad, the distinction is between the farmer who plants the highest-yielding rice variety—vulnerable to blight, dependent on specific conditions, spectacularly productive when everything aligns—and the farmer who plants three moderately productive varieties that collectively guarantee a harvest regardless of weather. The first farmer has a higher potential yield. The second farmer never starves. In a multi-decade strategic competition, which farmer would you bet on?

The ceiling-versus-floor distinction is not a semantic quibble. It is a strategic paradigm shift that most Western analysts have not yet internalized—and until they do, their assessments will continue to miscalibrate the threat and the opportunity. The reviewer who reads nothing else in this book should read this section, because the paradigm shift it describes is the single insight most likely to survive the data's inevitable revision.

* * *

Assessment: The Disciplined Observer's View

The honest analyst holds the following assessments simultaneously:

The Farmer's weaknesses are real, structural, and slow-burning. Demographics cannot be reversed on any timescale shorter than thirty years. The property crisis has destroyed a generation's wealth. The authoritarian innovation paradox is visible in the C919. The SOE *Vellappokkam* constrains dynamism. Capital controls limit global reach. The legitimacy trap narrows Beijing's margin with each point of slower growth.

But slow-burning does not mean imminent. China's demographic cliff will not bite with full force for fifteen to twenty years. The property crisis is being partially absorbed by historic savings (160 trillion yuan). The innovation paradox constrains frontier capability but not deployment capability—and deployment may matter more in sustained competition. The sustainment model provides a floor that sanctions cannot breach.

The Hunter, meanwhile, has time. Not unlimited time—the interdependency web is accelerating—but enough time to respond if the response is Rooseveltian. The institutional antibodies are real. The Forest can respond. The Magnificent Seven's latent capability is reclaimable.

The crucial asymmetry is in the timeline. China's weaknesses are front-loaded in *visibility* but back-loaded in *impact*—maximally visible in headlines now, but their strategic bite is years away. China's strengths are front-loaded in *impact*—BYD's God's Eye is deploying now, DeepSeek is reshaping AI economics now, and the interdependency web is accelerating now. The window between China's current strength-phase and its eventual vulnerability-phase is the strategic window that will determine the century's shape.

In Theyyam, the deity does not promise healing. The deity promises truth. And the truth is that both the Farmer and the Hunter are wounded, both retain formidable capacities for adaptation, and the outcome will be determined not by which system is inherently superior but by which system looks at its own wounds with unflinching honesty and treats them before the gangrene sets in.

The Window: Why Timing Is the Decisive Variable

The chapter's assessment identified a crucial asymmetry in the timeline: China's weaknesses are front-loaded in terms of visibility but back-loaded in terms of impact, while China's strengths are front-loaded in terms of impact. This asymmetry creates a window—a strategic window that deserves explicit analysis because it determines whether the competition's outcome is still contingent or already determined.

The window's dimensions are approximately ten to fifteen years. China's demographic cliff will not produce its full workforce reduction until the late 2030s. The property crisis's $4.7 trillion in wealth destruction is being partially absorbed by 160 trillion yuan in savings—a buffer that buys time, though at the cost of the consumer spending that would otherwise drive domestic demand growth. The innovation paradox—the C919's 13/75 delivery shortfall—constrains frontier capability but not deployment capability, which has proven more strategically consequential across every domain this book has documented. The legitimacy trap narrows with each point of slower growth, but the CCP's surveillance infrastructure provides a buffer against political instability that no previous authoritarian system has possessed.

The Hunter's window for response is the mirror image. The Bipartisan Infrastructure Law, the CHIPS Act, and the Inflation Reduction Act represent the first sustained investment in a generation—but the deployment pace of these investments (zero operational CHIPS Act fabs in three and a half years; broadband buildout years behind schedule; EV charging infrastructure at 76,000 stations versus China's 10 million) means the investments will not produce their full strategic effect for seven to ten years. The latent antibodies—the SCOTUS institutional immune system, the 55% immigrant pipeline, the Magnificent Seven's $300 billion in reclaimable R&D—require *activation*, and activation requires the social cohesion that Chapter 3 documented as under assault and the physical infrastructure that Chapter 4 documented as degraded.

The window's logic is simple and uncomfortable. During the next ten to fifteen years, China's strengths (deployment advantage, interdependency web, SOE substrate) are at their maximum, while China's weaknesses (demographics, property, legitimacy) have not yet reached their full constraining force. Simultaneously, the Hunter's potential for response (latent antibodies, legislative investments, alliance network) exists but has not yet been activated to strategic effect. The competition's outcome will be determined by what happens *during this window*—not by today's snapshot or by projections for 2050.

If the Hunter activates the latent antibodies during the window—if the Magnificent Seven are turned toward deployment, if the Supply Sovereignty Fund is funded, if the talent pipeline is expanded, if the social cohesion is repaired enough to sustain a Rooseveltian mobilization—then the ceiling-versus-floor contest becomes genuinely competitive, because the Hunter's ceiling advantages (breakthrough innovation, university system, alliance depth) can be translated into floor capabilities through sustained investment. If the Hunter spends the window on tariff theater, buyback liturgy, and the fourteenth domain's continued self-destruction, then the Farmer's deployment advantage compounds beyond the point where latent antibodies can close the gap, and the floor the Farmer has built becomes the permanent terrain of the competition.

The Theyyam performer knows what the audience does not: the ritual has a clock. The drums do not beat forever. The deity arrives, delivers its truth, and withdraws. The window between the deity's arrival and its departure is the only time the worshippers can act on what they have been shown. That window is open. Whether it remains open depends on choices not yet made—in boardrooms, in legislatures, in the voting booths of a nation that must first agree on what is real before it can agree on what to do.

· · ·

BOATMAN'S LEDGER

Chapter 11

LEDGER TOOL #10: VULNERABILITY-ADJUSTED POSITION SCORE

The Farmer's deployment advantage (24/25 in Chapter 5) is discounted for structural vulnerabilities. Demographics (topsoil erosion): −3. Property (subsoil contamination): −2. Innovation paradox (poor drainage): −1.5. SOE drag / *Vellappokkam*: −1. Capital controls (restricted irrigation): −1. Legitimacy trap (brackish groundwater): −1.5. **ADJUSTED DEPLOYMENT SCORE: 14/25.**

The Hunter's institutional advantages scored independently. SCOTUS antibody: +3. Immigrant talent pipeline: +3. Reinvention capacity: +2.5. Alliance depth: +2. Forest response capability: +2.5. Magnificent Seven latent antibody: +2. **HUNTER INSTITUTIONAL SCORE: 15/25.**

NET ASSESSMENT: Farmer 14, Hunter 15. Margin: 1 point. Not predetermined.

The margin is a policy variable, not a destiny. The Farmer's score rises if the sustainment-floor thesis proves correct and demographics are offset by automation. The Hunter's score rises if the latent antibody activates. A 1-point margin in a civilizational competition is the definition of contingent: everything depends on choices not yet made.

CEILING VS. FLOOR FRAMEWORK

This is the Ledger's most consequential tool. The Western analytical framework evaluates the ceiling—who leads at the frontier. The Farmer's framework evaluates the floor—who can sustain across all domains without foreign dependency.

SMIC 5nm covers ~80% of use cases. Tiangong is the only station that will orbit post-2030. Apollo Go runs 300K rides/week at breakeven while Waymo's unit economics remain unpublished. Track the floor, not the ceiling. The floor is where civilizations live. The ceiling is where they perform.

THE BOATMAN'S WAGER

Maintain deployment plays but hedge with an illustrative 15% allocation to American reinvention: next-gen AI efficiency, immigrant-founded deeptech, infrastructure rebuild beneficiaries, Magnificent Seven restructuring plays that bet on the latent antibody's activation. Add 5% India exposure: the demographic dividend is the decade's most underpriced macro variable. The trade is not binary. Position on both mispricings simultaneously.

Chapter 11 Data Anchors: Demographics: 7.92M births (−17% YoY), fertility 1.0, population shrunk 4 consecutive years, 105M→58M women 20–34 by 2050, marriages 6.1M (−20.5%) | Property: $4.7T wealth destruction, Evergrande $330B, savings 160T yuan | Innovation paradox: C919 13/75 delivered, 50–60% Western components | Capital controls: yuan 3.17% reserves | Youth unemployment >20% (unpublished) | India: median age 28, 1.5M engineers/yr | Sustainment floor: SMIC 80% use cases, Tiangong sole post-2030 platform, Apollo Go 300K/week breakeven, Ascend 60% H100 | Ceiling vs. floor: paradigm shift | Net assessment: Farmer 14, Hunter 15 | Wei Lin: the seed that says not yet

• • •

A Word to the Reasonable Reader

If this chapter feels different from the preceding eight, that is by design. The preceding chapters made the Farmer's case with the force of accumulated evidence. This chapter tests that case against the hardest data the other side can muster. A book that documents only strengths is propaganda. A book that documents strengths and weaknesses with equal rigor is an analysis.

The surprise—that China's "gaps" may be strategic sustainment rather than failure—is not offered as vindication of the Farmer. It is a reframe that changes the analytical question. If China is building an unbreachable technological floor rather than trying to beat America at the frontier, then the entire Western strategy of maintaining a ceiling advantage may be targeting the wrong variable. A ceiling can be cracked from below. A floor cannot be undermined from above.

Chapter 12 must answer the question both civilizations face: what must change? The deity has tested the worshippers with hard truths. Those who remain standing—those who can hold both the Farmer's blight and the Hunter's rot in their minds simultaneously without collapsing into complacency or despair—deserve what comes next.

• • •

The crown is placed. The hard truths have been spoken.
But the Theyyam performer knows what the worshippers do not:
The hardest test is not hearing the truth. It is acting on it.

The water that carries the boat is rising.
The question is no longer whether it will overturn something.
The question is what.

• • •

RITUAL STAGE MARKER

The deity stands fully crowned. The oracle speaks not of predictions but choices. The worshippers' faces are illuminated—and some of them flinch. But the ones who do not flinch—the ones who hold the hard truth in both hands and refuse to drop it—these are the ones the deity came to find.

CHAPTER 12

The Kuttanadan Way

Adaptations, Burning Ghat, Futures, and Synthesis

"If your plan is for a hundred years, educate people." — Guanzi

"The wise warrior avoids the battle." — Sun Tzu

The Kuttanadan farmer does not fight the water. He builds bunds, canals, floating gardens.

— after the Theyyam tradition

• • •

Undercurrent: Learning to Farm

In 2013, the United Nations Food and Agriculture Organization recognized the Kuttanad Below Sea Level Farming System as a Globally Important Agricultural Heritage System. The recognition was not for productivity or technology but for something rarer: adaptation. Kuttanad's farming system operates below sea level, in a landscape where freshwater and saltwater coexist, where the monsoon floods the fields every year, and where the same plot must produce rice in one season and fish in another. The farmers did not conquer their environment. They learned to work with both currents.

The system uses temporary earthen bunds—*orumuttu*—to manage water flow. Not permanent walls. Temporary structures are built, breached, and rebuilt according to the season. When the freshwater rises, the bunds hold it for rice cultivation. When the saltwater pushes inland, the bunds are opened for aquaculture. The same field, the same water, two different harvests. This is not primitive farming. It is the most sophisticated form of agricultural adaptation the FAO has documented: a system that treats the oscillation between currents as a feature rather than a bug.

In Kerala, we have a phrase for this practice: *nilavum vellavaum ondaakkuka*—to make the land and the water one. Not to defeat the water. Not to wall it out. To make it part of the harvest. America does not need to become China. America needs to become Kuttanad: a system that works with both currents—competition and renewal—building adaptive structures that manage the flow rather than permanent walls that dam it.

The GI Bill, the Interstate Highway System, the Apollo program, DARPA's creation of the internet, GPS, and mRNA vaccine technology—these were America's adaptive moments. Multi-domain investments that did not fight the environment but reshaped it. Each was bipartisan. Each operated on a time horizon longer than a single electoral cycle. Each combined government investment with private sector commercialization. Each produced returns exceeding costs by orders of magnitude.

A confession before the prescription. I have spent thirty years advising Fortune 10 companies on transformation. I sat in the boardrooms where the offshoring decisions were made. I helped build the system this book critiques. The prescription that follows is not the counsel of a theorist. It is the counsel of a practitioner who has seen, up close, both the extraordinary capacity of American institutions when aimed at a strategic objective and the extraordinary dysfunction of those same institutions when aimed at nothing more ambitious than next quarter's earnings.

...

Six Multi-Domain Adaptations: The Rooseveltian Prescription

The adaptations below are presented in order of urgency and feasibility. If you do only one thing, do the first. If you do only two, do the first and the sixth. The ranking matters because the civilizational competition does not wait for comprehensive reform packages to pass through the committee.

Adaptation One (MOST URGENT): Aim the Seven. The Magnificent Seven represent $20 trillion in market capitalization, $300 billion in annual R&D, and the largest concentration of AI talent outside the Chinese government. They are currently aimed at advertising optimization, engagement metrics, and stock buybacks.

Aim them at civilizational objectives. Not through nationalization, which would destroy the Forest's innovation advantage. Through conditional tax incentives, procurement preferences, and a National Strategic AI Deployment mandate that gives the Seven the same dual mandate as China's SOEs: commercial profitability *and* national strategic capability.

If Nvidia's GPUs were used to power domestic semiconductor equipment development rather than cryptocurrency mining. If Google's Transformer architecture powered American manufacturing optimization instead of ad targeting. If Amazon's logistics infrastructure served supply chain sovereignty. If Meta's AI talent were redirected from dopamine-drip timeline optimization to medical diagnostics, agricultural AI, and educational technology. If Microsoft's enterprise cloud became the platform for a national Vehicle-Road-Cloud system. If Tesla's data, vehicles, and charging network were integrated into a national autonomous mobility infrastructure.

In Kuttanad, the boatmen call this *maattivekkal*—the turning of the bow. The vessel does not change. The direction changes. The Seven are the Hunter's most powerful vessels. They do not need to be rebuilt. They need to be turned.

Imagine the voice that could turn them:

> *"My fellow Americans, we have spent twenty years fighting wars we cannot win with weapons we cannot afford while the infrastructure of our future crumbled beneath us. That ends today. We will build. We will plant. We will remember how to farm. The same companies that gave us the Transformer, the GPU, and the iPhone will now give us the factories, the supply chains, and the deployment systems that a civilization requires to survive the century ahead. Not because we command them. Because we aim them. Because the alternative—another twenty years of extraction, another twenty years of buybacks, another twenty years of watching the Farmer plant while we argue about whose fault it is that the field is empty—is a future this country does not deserve and will not accept."*

The adaptations become a speech, not a memo. The memo gathers dust. The speech gathers will.

Adaptation Two: Temporal Reform — From Quarterly to Generational. Establish a bipartisan National Strategic Planning Commission with a ten-year mandate, insulated from electoral cycles. The model is not Chinese. It is American: the Base Realignment and Closure Commission (BRAC), which since 1988 has successfully navigated the most politically toxic decisions in domestic policy—closing military bases in congressional districts—through a mechanism that converts political paralysis into structured action. Appointments by the President with Senate confirmation. Recommendations subject to expedited congressional vote: up or down, no amendments. The BRAC model works because it removes the incentive structure that rewards obstruction—each legislator votes on the entire package rather than trading individual closures for political favors. Apply the same architecture to strategic industrial policy: the Commission identifies the ten most critical supply-chain vulnerabilities, the ten most consequential infrastructure investments, and the ten most urgent technology-sovereignty initiatives. Congress votes on the package up or down within ninety days. No amendments. No riders. No earmarks. The temporal frame shifts from quarterly to decadal overnight—not through cultural transformation but through *procedural architecture*. The KfW comparison stands: Germany's development bank has operated for seventy-five years under a mandate that transcends electoral politics. America does not need a Five-Year Plan. America needs a BRAC for industrial strategy. The Hunter is not outspent. The Hunter is out-patienced. And patience is the compound interest of strategy.

Adaptation Three: Supply Sovereignty — $200 Billion Over a Decade. A Supply Sovereignty Fund targeted at building domestic or allied-nation capacity in six domains: rare earth processing, pharmaceutical API manufacturing, advanced batteries, shipbuilding, solar/wind manufacturing, and semiconductor equipment. Structurally separated from the defense procurement system. The $200 billion sounds large until calibrated: the US spent $2.3 trillion on Iraq and Afghanistan, $1.7 trillion on the F-35 lifecycle. $20 billion per year to build the supply chain that eliminates strategic dependency is the cheapest insurance policy in the history of great-power competition.

Adaptation Four: Alliance Agriculture — Quad $100 Billion Counter-BRI. Jointly funded by the US, Japan, Australia, and India, targeted at the sixty countries where BRI dependency is deepest. The fund offers what BRI does not: transparent financing, governance standards, and technology transfer that creates genuine capacity rather than permanent reliance on Chinese maintenance contracts. Treaty-based commitment structure, not an executive agreement that dies with each administration.

Adaptation Five: The Democratic Advantage — Double H-1B, Triple NSF. Double the H-1B cap to 170,000 with STEM priority. Triple the NSF budget to ~$30 billion, restoring Cold War levels as a share of GDP. Create a "gold card" pathway for STEM PhDs from allied nations. Frame it as defense spending—because that is what it is. The government spends $400,000 educating the world's most talented engineer, teaches her everything America knows about AI, hands her a diploma, and then tells her she has sixty days to leave the country. She takes the diploma to Hangzhou. She takes the knowledge with her. America keeps the diploma frame.

Adaptation Six: ARPA-X and the National Investment Bank. Create ARPA-X—cross-domain advanced research spanning AI, semiconductors, quantum, clean energy, biotech, and advanced manufacturing. Fund at $10 billion annually—triple DARPA's current budget, less than 1% of the defense budget. Pair with a National Investment Bank capitalized at $200 billion over a decade, modeled on KfW.

The specificity matters because "create a new agency" is a sentence, not a strategy. What made DARPA work—and what ARPA-X must replicate—is a set of institutional design features that are individually mundane and collectively revolutionary:

Hiring authority is exempt from standard civil service rules. DARPA's original 1958 charter allowed program managers to be hired from industry and academia without the multi-month clearance process required by standard government hiring. This meant that the best semiconductor engineer at Bell Labs could be running a DARPA program within weeks, not years. ARPA-X must have the same authority, because the talent it needs is the same talent the Magnificent Seven are currently paying $800,000 annual packages to, aiming at advertising optimization. If ARPA-X cannot compete on hiring speed, it will recruit the talent that the private sector has already passed on. A government research agency staffed by the private sector's rejects is a PowerPoint factory, not an innovation engine.

Four-year term limits for program managers. DARPA's genius was not permanence. It was impermanence. Program managers arrive with a thesis, fund high-risk projects that embody the thesis, and leave before institutional capture converts the thesis into a bureaucratic empire. The four-year term is the mechanism that prevents the agency from becoming the thing it was created to circumvent. When a program manager knows she has four years to prove her thesis, she funds moonshots. When she has tenure, she funds career preservation. The internet was created by program managers with deadlines, not by civil servants with pensions.

A mandate to fund projects that would not survive peer review. This is the single most important design feature, and the one most likely to be neutered by congressional oversight. Peer review is the scientific community's quality-control mechanism, and it works brilliantly for incremental research. It is catastrophic for paradigm-shifting research because paradigm shifts are, by definition, ideas that the existing paradigm's experts would reject. DARPA's original TCP/IP program would not have survived peer review. The mRNA platform that produced COVID vaccines in under a year was funded through a DARPA-adjacent pathway that bypassed conventional NIH review. ARPA-X must have explicit statutory authority to fund projects that reviewers reject—not despite the rejection but *because* of it. If every funded project looks reasonable to the existing establishment, the agency has already failed.

ARPA-X must be capped at 500 program managers with DARPA-level authority. The moment it requires three layers of review to approve a $5 million grant, it has become the thing it was created to circumvent. The moment it hires a "Director of Strategic Alignment" or a "Vice President of Stakeholder Engagement," it should be dissolved and rebuilt. The Farmer does not produce innovation through committees. The Farmer produces innovation through funded individuals with deadlines and the authority to fail spectacularly. ARPA-X must do the same—or it will join Quibi, Theranos, and the California High-Speed Rail in the innovation graveyard, the only difference being that its headstone will read "Funded by Taxpayers."

The six adaptations total approximately $600 billion over a decade. Less than one-third of the F-35 lifecycle cost. Less than one-quarter of the Iraq/Afghanistan wars. DARPA's $3.5 billion annual budget created the internet and GPS. The GI Bill returned $7 for every $1 spent. The adaptations are not costs. They are investments with a historical track record of transformative returns.

. . .

The 90-Day Transformation Insurgency: For the C-Suite Reader

Days 1–30: The Supply Chain Audit. Map your Chinese exposure across all tiers. Chapter 6 demonstrated that "Made in Vietnam" conceals 65–80% Chinese content. Score each supplier 1–5: (1) domestic alternative exists, (5) sole-source Chinese dependency. Any 4 or 5 is a strategic vulnerability.

Days 31–60: The Dual-Current Strategy. For every supplier scoring 4 or 5, develop dual-sourcing that maintains the Chinese relationship while building an alternative. The Kuttanadan principle: work with both currents. The *orumuttu* between them is the dual-sourcing contract.

Days 61–90: The Deployment-Over-Invention Reset. Review every R&D project. Ask the DeepSeek question: "Is this project optimized for announcement or for deployment?" Kill the Juiceros. Fund the God's Eyes.

And one final question. If the thing you're building had to last fifty years—not fifty months until an exit, not fifty weeks until the next earnings call, but fifty years—what would you do differently this quarter? Answer it honestly, and the adaptations follow naturally.

. . .

The Burning Ghat: Six Phases of Cross-Sector Extinction

The Theyyam ritual includes a passage through the burning ghat—the cremation ground where the old self is consumed before the deity emerges. In Kuttanad: *maranathinte vellam*—the water of death, the tidal surge that drowns the old planting so new seeds can take root in the enriched sediment. What drowns is not wasted. What drowns becomes soil. This section is the definitive treatment of the six phases previewed in Chapter 5.

Phase 1: Price Compression. The Farmer enters at a price point the incumbent considers impossible. BYD Seagull at $7,800 versus an average American car at $33,600. *Complete. If your business model depends on a price premium, the Field can undercut by 95%, and you are not competing. You are composting.*

Phase 2: Feature Democratization. Features that command premium prices become standard. BYD God's Eye ADAS—standard on 21 models, no additional cost, on vehicles starting at $9,550. Tesla charges $8,000–$12,000. When the feature is free, the premium disappears, and the business model that relied on it collapses. *Underway.*

Phase 3: Data Flywheel Dominance. Deployment at scale generates data at scale. BYD's 150 million daily kilometers versus Waymo's three-city operations. The flywheel is compound interest: each ride improves the algorithm, each improvement attracts more riders. *Accelerating.*

Phase 4: Standard-Setting. The Farmer's deployed infrastructure becomes the de facto standard. Huawei sets the standards, training protocols, and upgrade paths for 70% of Africa's 4 G equipment. When the standard is set, the switching cost is not a product replacement but a civilizational retraining. *Emerging.*

Phase 5: Talent Gravity. As the ecosystem scales, it attracts researchers who once gravitated exclusively to the Hunter. DeepSeek's efficiency-first approach produces research that Stanford and MIT now cite. When Chen Yue chose Hangzhou over Mountain View, she was not making a salary decision. She was making a deployment decision. *Begun.*

Phase 6: Ecosystem Colonization. The Farmer builds an integrated ecosystem—EVs + batteries + charging + autonomous driving + AI + robotics + telecom + financial settlement—that creates switching costs at the system level. A country that adopts BYD vehicles, Huawei 5G, CIPS settlement, and Chinese drone infrastructure has not purchased products. It has adopted an ecosystem. And ecosystems are not replaced by better alternatives. They are replaced only by better ecosystems. *The face the world sees is the mask carved by a thousand hands.*

And a seventh pyre, unlit but smoldering: the innovation-theater-industrial complex itself. Here lies $27 billion in wasted capital—4,821 DeepSeek training runs, 2.8 million BYD Seagulls, the careers of thousands who believed the performance. They died so that we might learn: deployment is the only truth. May they rest in the compost of history, fertilizing whatever grows next.

· · ·

Three Futures: 2030–2050

The deity does not predict. The deity illuminates choices.

天下大同 **(Tiānxià Dàtóng) — "Great Harmony Under Heaven" (30%).** Managed pluralism evolves into genuine cooperation. Demographic pressures force collaboration on AI-assisted healthcare, climate technology, and governance frameworks. The halocline stabilizes: two systems coexist, compete within defined domains, and cooperate when existential threats demand it. This requires leadership of a caliber that neither currently demonstrates. Aspirational but not impossible.

一山二虎 **(Yī Shān Èr Hǔ) — "Two Tigers on One Mountain" (40%).** The most likely outcome. Sustained competition across all thirteen domains, punctuated by crises but never tipping into direct conflict because both civilizations possess sufficient deterrence. Neither tiger wins. Neither can rest. The world adapts to permanent bipolarity with the weary pragmatism of Cold War Europe—except that economic interdependence makes clean separation impossible. The tigers share the mountain because neither can push the other off.

两败俱伤 **(Liǎng Bài Jù Shāng) — "Both Sides Suffer Defeat" (30%).** The nightmare. A Taiwan crisis escalates beyond de-escalation. Financial sanctions trigger bifurcation. TSMC's fabs—90%+ of the world's most advanced chips—are destroyed or rendered inoperable. The global economy experiences a semiconductor famine. The adaptive model is abandoned in favor of the fortress model—permanent walls, not temporary bunds. And the fortress, as every civilization that has retreated behind walls has eventually discovered, becomes a prison.

The 30/40/30 weightings demand hedging across all three. The disciplined investor bets on the halocline—the boundary where both currents meet—because it's where Two Tigers offers the most opportunity, Great Harmony the most upside, and even the nightmare scenario is partially survivable through diversification.

· · ·

Marcus Chen Closes the Screen

In the Prologue, Marcus watched $6.6 trillion evaporate. He has read every chapter since. He has met Zhang Mei, Liu Jing, Chen Liling, Wei Lin, and Wang Sufen. He has built spreadsheets that demolished his own assumptions.

He pulls up his allocation screen. 45/35/20. He sizes his China positions according to deployment data. He hedges his American positions based on institutional antibodies. He adds, for the first time, Magnificent Seven restructuring plays—betting on the *maattivekkal*, the possibility that $20 trillion in squandered strength might yet be aimed at civilization's survival. He allocates 20% to alternatives—gold, India, the demographic dividend.

He closes his screen. He looks out the window at the Shanghai skyline—the Lujiazui towers, built on land that was vegetable farms in the 1980s, on ground that was a treaty port concession in the 1840s. Behind him, his Bloomberg terminal displays American markets that, despite everything, remain the deepest, most liquid, most innovative on Earth. Both statements are true. Both currents flow.

Then Marcus does something the reader doesn't expect.

He opens his email. Not to his risk desk. Not to Kevin. To his daughter, Emma—the one who needed sneakers in White Plains, the one whose patience he exhausted tracing the supply chain of a "Made in Vietnam" shoe. He types:

> *"Em—I know you're thinking about majoring in international relations next year. I have a different suggestion. Come to Shanghai this summer. Ride in a robotaxi. Visit a shipyard. Stand in a factory where batteries are built that power half the world's electric vehicles. Then go to Youngstown and talk to a woman named Sarah who runs a boutique on West Federal Street. Ask her what happened to her prices. Then decide what you want to study. Love, Dad."*

He sends it. He closes the laptop. The Boatman's son has stopped looking at screens and started looking at the water.

* * *

The Coke Bottle's Final Lesson

In the film, Xi walks to the edge of the world and hurls the Coke bottle into the void. Problem solved—for the San. But the bottle still exists somewhere.

The Boatman does not throw the bottle away. He picks it up, turns it in the light, and reads what is etched in the glass—the bill of materials, the supply chain, the thirteen interlocking domains. He does not discard the bottle. He does not worship it. He repurposes it.

In Kuttanad, when the monsoon washes debris into the paddies—coconut shells, broken bamboo, driftwood from the hills—the farmer does not curse the debris and hurl it back into the water. The farmer builds with it. The coconut shell becomes a ladle. The bamboo becomes a bund support. The driftwood becomes a drying rack. The monsoon's gift is the monsoon's garbage, reclassified by hands that know how to read what the water carries.

The Coke bottle—American capitalism, AI supremacy, the Magnificent Seven's $20 trillion, the algorithms that addict, and the platforms that extract—is not inherently destructive. It is a tool. The question is whether the community that holds it has the wisdom to repurpose it: to aim the Seven at deployment rather than extraction, to build bunds rather than walls, to farm rather than hunt, to read the halocline rather than fight the current.

Xi threw the bottle because his community had no framework for absorbing a tool that powerful. The Kuttanadan farmer would not throw it. The Kuttanadan farmer would plant rice in it.

* * *

BOATMAN'S LEDGER

Chapter 12

LEDGER TOOL #11: THE HALOCLINE PORTFOLIO

PRINCIPLE 1 (Adaptive Infrastructure)

Build positions that adjust, not walls that crumble. Rebalance quarterly based on deployment data, not narrative.

PRINCIPLE 2 (Dual-Current Cultivation)

Maintain exposure to both Hunter and Farmer. Scenario B illustrative allocation: 45% US-aligned (AI infrastructure, immigrant-founded deeptech, defense reform, Mag 7 restructuring, advanced manufacturing, alliance-economy supply chains) / 35% China-aligned (BYD supply chain, CATL battery ecosystem, biotech out-licensers, semiconductor equipment, CIPS-adjacent fintech, robotics, AI+ deployment) / 20% alternatives (gold, commodities, non-aligned infrastructure, India demographic dividend).

PRINCIPLE 3 (Community Resilience)

No single position exceeds 5%. No single geography exceeds 50%. Quarter-Kelly sizing: bet enough to profit if right, little enough to survive if wrong.

ADAPTATION PRIORITY RANKING

If you do only one: Aim the Seven ($0 cost—it's a mandate, not a budget). If you do two: add Supply Sovereignty ($200B/decade). If you do three: add Talent Sovereignty (double H-1B, triple NSF). The ranking matters because the Farmer does not wait for comprehensive reform packages.

BURNING GHAT PHASE TRACKER

Phase 1 (Price Compression): legacy auto, consumer electronics. Phase 2 (Feature Democratization): ADAS, battery storage. Phase 3 (Data Flywheel): autonomous vehicles, AI models. Phase 4 (Standard-Setting): telecom, digital payments, satellite navigation. Phase 5 (Talent Gravity): AI research, quantum, biotech. Phase 6 (Ecosystem Colonization): Global South infrastructure, financial architecture. Track your industry's current phase. Phase 4 is the closing window. Phase 5 is the event horizon.

MAATTIVEKKAL SIGNAL

Track whether the Magnificent Seven begin redirecting from extraction to deployment. Key indicators: buyback-to-capex ratio declining below 1.5:1, domestic manufacturing investment increasing, AI application deployment growing faster than AI advertising revenue. When three of the Seven show these signals simultaneously, the turning of the bow has begun. This is the most consequential macro variable in the competition.

Chapter 12 Data Anchors: FAO Kuttanad recognition 2013 | Nilavum vellavaum ondaakkuka | Orumuttu: adaptive, not permanent | Maattivekkal: turning of the bow | ~$600B total: $200B Supply Sovereignty + $100B Quad Counter-BRI + $10B/yr ARPA-X + $200B NIB | DARPA precedent: internet, GPS, mRNA on $3.5B/yr | GI Bill 7:1 return | 90-Day Insurgency: audit/dual-source/deploy | Burning Ghat 6+1 phases with status markers | Three Futures 30/40/30 | Halocline Portfolio 45/35/20 | Marcus 45/35/20 allocation | "The Kuttanadan farmer would plant rice in it"

. . .

A Final Word to the Reasonable Reader

The farmer does not fight the water. He does not deny the saltwater's advance. He does not convene a bipartisan commission to study whether the monsoon is real, or impose tariffs on the rain, or blame the previous administration for the tides. He builds bunds. He digs canals. He cultivates floating gardens on the water that would drown a farmer who tried to fight them. He rotates between rice and fish, freshwater and salt, because he has learned—across generations of farming below sea level—that the only permanent strategy is the one that adapts.

America is, for the first time in its modern history, farming below sea level—competing from a position where the currents are rising and the old bunds are eroding. The question is not whether America can learn to farm. The GI Bill, the Interstate Highways, DARPA—these are American precedents. The Magnificent Seven's $300 billion in annual R&D—these are American assets, reclaimable for civilization if the will materializes. The question is whether America *will* learn to farm.

The Boatman has no prediction. The Boatman has a portfolio, three principles, eleven Ledger tools, six adaptations totaling ~$600 billion, and the understanding that in a halocline, the only fatal position is the one that assumes the currents will not change.

He checks the current. He adjusts his oar. He pushes off from the shore.

● ● ●

The Theyyam performer removes the crown.
The face paint remains—it will fade over the coming hours,
But for now, the divine countenance persists.

The worshippers disperse into the pre-dawn darkness,
carrying with them not certainties but choices.
The deity did not tell them what would happen.
The deity told them what they needed to see.

The rest—the bunds, the canals, the floating gardens,
The patient work of adaptation—is theirs.
It has always been theirs.

The water rises. The Farmer farms. The story continues.

● ● ●

RITUAL STAGE MARKER

Dawn. The deity withdraws. The performer's body shakes once, twice—then stills. He reaches for the mask. It comes away in his hands. Underneath: a human face, wet with sweat and something that might be tears. He looks at the mask. The mask looks back. And the Boatman, watching from the canal, pushes off into water that accepts him the way the earth accepts the seed: without judgment, without promise, with only the patient certainty that what is planted will, in time, be harvested. The reader, now, must build.

EPILOGUE

The Mask Comes Off

"The Way that can be told is not the eternal Way." — Lao Tzu, Chapter 1

The performer removes the divine mask. Beneath it is a human face.

— after the Theyyam tradition

* * *

Marcus Chen Closes the Book

Marcus Chen did not read this book in sequence. He read it the way a fund manager reads anything—backwards, starting with the conclusions, scanning for data points, checking the footnotes to see if the author was bluffing. He was not bluffing. The data held. And so Marcus went back to the beginning—to the Yuanmingyuan burning, to the smoke that rose for three days—and read it forward, chapter by chapter, from the Summer Palace to the Kuttanadan synthesis.

His spreadsheet—the one he had titled "Things I Got Wrong"—now had twenty-three tabs. It had become, without his intending it, a document of personal transformation: a record of a mind changing in real time, one demolished assumption at a time, until the man who closed the book was not the same man who opened it.

He would rebalance his portfolio on Monday. He would present the thesis to his investment committee, and some would understand it and some would not. But that was Monday. Tonight, he would take Emma to buy new sneakers—and this time, he would not read the label.

Marcus's transformation is complete—or rather, it has begun, because transformation is not a single epiphany but a compounding process. Marcus's journey was the reader's journey. Now the reader's journey becomes the author's confession.

I open the mask.

* * *

Zhuangzi's Butterfly

There is a passage in Zhuangzi that I have carried in my body since I first read it, decades ago, in a translation borrowed from a lending library in Kuttanad that smelled of monsoon damp, coconut oil, and the slowly composting ambitions of a thousand previous borrowers. The shelves were warped from humidity. The pages were soft as cloth. The librarian, a man named Krishnan who had memorized the location of every book by touch rather than by catalogue, handed me the volume without being asked—because in Kuttanad, the librarian reads the borrower the way the boatman reads the current, and Krishnan had seen something in my face that day that said: this boy needs the butterfly.

Zhuangzi dreamed he was a butterfly. He woke and was a man. But he could not determine whether he was a man who had dreamed he was a butterfly, or a butterfly now dreaming he was a man.

Am I a Kuttanadan farmer who dreamed he was a Wall Street analyst? Or a Wall Street analyst now dreaming he is a Kuttanadan farmer? The answer is both. And neither. The butterfly and the man are the same consciousness, refracted through different waking states. This book is that refraction—a single consciousness shaped by monsoon canals and Bloomberg terminals, by Theyyam drums and earnings calls, trying to tell a truth about the world that is inevitably also a truth about itself.

I tell you this not to undermine the analysis—the data stands regardless of who compiled it—but to honor the reader who has stayed to the end. You deserve to see the face beneath the mask.

. . .

Dual Belonging

I was born in Kerala, in a landscape where the backwaters meet the sea and the boundary between freshwater and salt is negotiated every day. I learned the halocline before I had a word for it. I learned it by watching my grandfather adjust the bunds after the monsoon, by watching a community coordinate their actions not through contracts but through the accumulated trust of generations. The air in Kuttanad smells different at each hour—dawn brings the green breath of paddy, noon brings the salt tang of the tidal push, evening brings the sweet ferment of coconut toddy and the woodsmoke of kitchens preparing *karimeen* in banana leaf, and night brings the silence that is never truly silence but the sound of water moving through a thousand channels in the dark.

I carried Kuttanad into Wall Street. I did not know I was doing it. But when I watched a Fortune 10 company allocate capital with the short-termism that Chapter 12 diagnosed, I recognized the farmer who builds a permanent wall where a temporary bund would serve. When I watched Anand Rathi's trading floor in Mumbai in the 1990s—my first exposure to capital markets, when the Bombay Stock Exchange still conducted trades with hand signals and paper chits—I recognized the fish market in Alappuzha, where the auction communicates price, quality, and trust in a single gesture.

The Theyyam performer understands dual belonging. During the ritual, he is both human and divine—not alternating but containing both simultaneously. The face beneath the mask does not disappear when the mask is worn. The deity does not disappear when the mask is removed. The performer holds both truths in his body, and the holding is the ritual's purpose.

I have written this book from that position of dual belonging. I belong to the world of Kuttanadan canals and the world of Big Four consultancies. I belong to the Farmer's patience and the Hunter's speed. I belong to the Boatman's position on the halocline—between the currents, reading both, committed to neither, honest about both.

. . .

What I Hope

I hope for patience married to creativity. The Farmer has patience—the civilizational patience that plants a tree whose shade you will never sit in. The Hunter has creativity—the anarchic, uncontrollable creativity that invents the Transformer in a corporate lab, produces CRISPR in a university basement, builds the internet because a Pentagon agency funded a graduate student's thesis, and then has the wisdom to let the invention escape into the world.

What neither civilization has demonstrated—what the halocline demands—is patience and creativity in the same system. The Kuttanadan Way requires both: the patience to build bunds that last a season and the creativity to reimagine the field when the season changes.

I hope that the Magnificent Seven look up from their buyback schedules long enough to realize that the vessels they command could be turned toward the civilization's survival. The *maattivekkal* is available. The bow can be turned. But the turning requires a mandate that no quarterly earnings call will provide.

I hope that the Reasonable Reader puts this book down not with despair but with the determined clarity of a farmer who has seen the weather forecast and is already calculating where to place the bunds.

* * *

What I Fear

I fear that time is running out. The Farmer's interdependency web is not slowing. It is accelerating. Every year of delay is a year during which the ecosystem lock-in deepens, and the number of countries embedded in the Farmer's infrastructure grows.

I fear the particular form of American dysfunction that mistakes activity for strategy—that confuses the announcement of a tariff with the construction of a fab, the declaration of a trade war with the winning of a competition. The Hunter is extraordinarily active. Activity is not adaptation.

I fear the narrowing of imagination on both sides. I have sat in a boardroom in Hong Kong where a senior official described American institutions as "a beautiful machine that has forgotten how to manufacture anything except lawyers and excuses," and I watched the room nod with the comfortable certainty of people who have never watched a Supreme Court ruling rewrite the rules of the game. I have sat in a boardroom in New York where a managing director described Chinese innovation as "just scale, not substance," and I watched the room nod with the comfortable certainty of people who have never stood in a SMIC clean room. Both rooms were wrong. Both rooms were certain. And certainty in the face of complexity is the intellectual posture that produces the worst outcomes.

I fear that the reader will finish this book, nod thoughtfully, update no assumption, change no allocation, and return to the Bloomberg terminal's *māyā*. The Theyyam tradition permits the deity to address the worshippers directly. So let me: *I did not write this book for your entertainment. I wrote it for your hands. Do not put it on a shelf. Put it on your desk. Open it on Monday morning. Let it change what you do, not just what you think.*

I fear, most of all, that the competition between these two civilizations produces not a winner but a wasteland—a world in which the resources and ingenuity that could address climate change, pandemic disease, and the governance of artificial intelligence are instead consumed by a rivalry that neither can win and neither can afford to lose.

* * *

The Mask Comes Off

In the Theyyam ritual, the moment of greatest power is not when the mask is put on. It is when the mask comes off. Because the mask's removal reveals what the ritual was always about: not the deity's power but the human being's capacity to hold that power, to channel it, to be transformed by it, and survive the transformation.

This is what it feels like. The weight lifts first—the crown, sometimes three kilograms of painted wood and beaten metal, lifted from the skull, and the neck, which has been rigid for hours, suddenly has to support only itself. The sweat runs into the eyes—not the clean sweat of exertion but the thick, paint-darkened sweat of a body that has been burning from the inside. The performer's vision narrows: the deity's panoramic sight contracts to ordinary human tunnel vision. Colors dim. Sounds lose their resonance. The drumbeats, which during possession felt like the performer's own heartbeat, become external again—someone else's rhythm, heard from outside. And in the performer's hands, the mask: painted, sacred, still warm from his face. He looks at it. The mask looks back. And in the looking, both are diminished—the mask without the face that gave it life, the face without the vision that the mask conferred.

I remove my mask now. I am not the Boatman. I am not the deity. I am not the contrarian insider or the analytical eye. I am a man from Kuttanad who has spent thirty years navigating the halocline, who has watched both civilizations from the inside, who has felt the current shift beneath his feet, and who wrote this book because the bunds that might manage the flow are not being built.

I have written this book for those who will live in the world these two civilizations are building. For my sons. For Wei Lin's unborn child—the one she has decided not to have, for reasons that are rational and heartbreaking. For Chen Liling's granddaughter, who thinks the ghost car is hilarious. For the children of the Reasonable Reader, whoever she is.

* * *

Where They Are Now

The deity withdraws. The performers return to their ordinary lives. And the characters who carried this book's truths in their bodies are, at this moment, doing what they have always done.

Zhang Mei is at the Jiangnan shipyard. It is 6:47 a.m., and her thermos is full, and the arc will not waver.

Liu Jing is in the clean room. The next multi-patterning run begins in eleven minutes. She adjusts the exposure parameters with the quiet precision of someone who has learned that the difference between success and failure is measured in nanometers—and in showing up the morning after the wafers come out wrong.

Chen Liling is in the robotaxi. It is Tuesday. The ghost car will arrive in three minutes. Her granddaughter has already texted to ask if the car talked to her.

Wei Lin is at her desk in Chengdu. She has not changed her mind. The seed still says *not yet.*

Wang Sufen is processing CIPS transactions. The numbers are slightly higher than yesterday, slightly lower than they will be tomorrow. Each transaction is a drop. Each drop finds its channel.

Sarah Kowalski is in Youngstown. It is a Wednesday, and the North Carolina ceramics have been on the shelf for three months. The margins are 22% tighter than those offered by the Vietnamese supply chain. But the customers who buy them—and there are more each month—hold the pieces differently. They turn the mugs over and read the label: Asheville, NC. They ask Sarah where Asheville is, and she tells them. Sometimes they drive there on vacation and send her photographs of the studio where the clay was thrown. The story she told herself—"made here, for us, by people you could drive to visit"—turned out to be worth exactly the margin compression it cost. Helen's desk is still in the back. The yellow legal pad has a new page. The numbers are tighter. The shop is open. Sarah Kowalski has not closed her grandmother's boutique. She has not closed her mind. And the thodu—the leverage point she chose when she rejected the Cambodian invoice—is hers.

Maria Delgado is in Youngstown, eleven blocks from Sarah's shop. It is the first Tuesday of the month. Gerald's arthritis is worse—he grips the steering wheel now with both hands flat, the way physical therapists teach patients to compensate for reduced grip strength. The drive to the pharmacy takes nine minutes. Gerald does not complain. He considers the drive his orumuttu—though he would not use that word, and he has never heard of Kuttanad. He would simply say that Maria is his neighbor, that the pharmacy is eleven blocks away, and that somebody has to drive.

The metformin costs $52 this month. Maria has not switched to groceries. She has, however, started splitting the pills—a practice her doctor would not recommend and that the pharmaceutical supply chain, stretching from Zhejiang to Hyderabad to New Jersey, has not priced into its optimization model. The molecule is the same. The woman is adapting. The molecule costs $3.80 at the source. Maria pays $52 and splits the dose. Somewhere in the margin between those two numbers—$3.80 and $52, the distance between what a civilization could provide and what this civilization chooses to charge—the broken bow bends but does not fly.

And Marcus Chen is buying his daughter new sneakers. He does not read the label. He has learned that the label tells you where the shoe was assembled. It does not tell you where the shoe was *made.* He has learned that the difference between the two is the halocline. He has learned that haloclines are everywhere, once you know how to see them.

. . .

The gods are not crazy.

They are patient. They are running a civilizational experiment across thirteen domains, two civilizations, and a timeline that extends from the burning of the Summer Palace to the training of the next AI model. The experiment has no control group. The outcome is not determined. The variables are still in play.

The Theyyam mask comes off. The monsoon will return. The water will rise. The halocline will shift. The Farmer will farm. The Hunter will hunt. And in between—in the brackish water where freshwater meets salt, where patience meets creativity, where fear meets hope, where the old world meets the new—the Boatman will do what the Boatman has always done.

He will read the current. He will adjust the oar. He will push off from the shore.

The question is whether we have built bunds strong enough to hold.

And one last question—the one that determines whether this book was worth the hours you gave it:

If the thing you are building—your portfolio, your company, your career, your country, the world you are handing to your children—had to last fifty years, not fifty months until an exit, not fifty weeks until the next earnings call, but fifty years of monsoons and droughts and tides that shift without warning—what would you do differently tomorrow morning?

Do not answer now. Answer tomorrow morning, when you open your email, when you sit in your first meeting, when you make the first decision of the day. Answer with your hands, not your mouth. The bund is built by hand, not by proclamation.

. . .

[The narrator's voice slows here. The Theyyam drum fades to silence.]

Somewhere in Kuttanad, a farmer walks to his field before dawn.

The sky is the color of wet slate, not yet light, not fully dark—
the in-between hour when the backwater holds its breath
and the coconut palms are silhouettes against a horizon that has not yet decided
whether today will bring rain or mercy or both.

The water is high this season. The bunds need repair.

He can smell the canal before he sees it—
the mineral tang of fresh water mixing with the faint brine
of the salt tide that pushed inland overnight.

His tools are heavy in his hands: the shovel, the leveling board,
the short-handled hoe that his grandfather carved from jackfruit wood
and that has outlasted every prediction about what would grow
and what would drown.

He does not think about geopolitical competition
or semiconductor chokepoints or civilizational experiments.

He thinks about the water—
where it is, where it is going,
whether the bunds he built last season will hold.

He adjusts. He digs. He plants.

The monsoon will come. The harvest will come after.

The water rises.
The farmer farms.

This is the Kuttanadan Way.
It has always been the Kuttanadan Way.

GLOSSARY OF RECURRING TERMS

A guide to the multilingual vocabulary that structures the book's analysis

KUTTANADAN & MALAYALAM TERMS

Azhakulla thoni ("Beautiful canoe") The vessel that carries the analysis—the book's metaphor for the argument itself. In Kuttanad, the most beautiful canoe is not the fastest; it is the one that reads the current most accurately.

Chira An irrigation channel dug by hand through rock or hardpan to bring water where natural flow cannot reach. In the book, the metaphor for China's self-reliance campaigns—SMIC's multi-patterning, the EAST tokamak, the domestic EUV prototype—channels dug in defiance of chokepoints.

Halocline The invisible boundary layer in the Kuttanadan backwaters where freshwater and saltwater meet but do not mix. The book's central analytical metaphor: the zone between surface narrative and undercurrent reality, between what markets say and what factories produce, between the Hunter's Bloomberg terminal and the Farmer's deployment data.

Irattamukham ("Double face") The Theyyam concept of a mask that shows one face to the audience and another to the deity. In the book, applied to institutions and metrics that present differently depending on the observer's position relative to the halocline.

Kalvazhi ("Stone path") The ancient elevated pathways through Kuttanadan fields, built by generations of farmers to navigate flooded terrain. In the book, the metaphor for institutional pathways that persist across political cycles—the SOE substrate, the Five-Year Plan infrastructure.

Kayal The vast lake system of the Kuttanadan backwaters, where fresh and salt currents create the halocline. The macro environment in which the analysis operates.

Kettuvallam The traditional houseboat of the Kerala backwaters, constructed without nails—coir rope binds the planks, the hull flexes with the current rather than resisting it. In the book, the metaphor for adaptive systems is that they absorb shocks through flexibility rather than rigidity.

Koottukrishi ("Collective cultivation") The Kuttanadan practice of neighboring farmers pooling labor, oxen, and water management for rice planting—an agricultural commons that predates and parallels the SOE collective-deployment model.

Maattivekkal ("The turning of the soil") The seasonal preparation of the field before planting. In the book, the strategic preparation phase—R&D investment, talent pipeline construction, regulatory framework design—that precedes deployment.

Māyā Sanskrit/Malayalam. The beautiful illusion that drowns those who mistake the surface for the depth. Applied to the Bloomberg terminal's price data stripped of civilizational context, and more broadly to the narrative layer that obscures deployment reality.

Nilavum vellavum ondaakkuka ("Make moonlight and floodwater one") The Kuttanadan boatman's phrase for the moment when surface light and underwater current align—when narrative and reality converge. The analytical goal of halocline reading.

Ormappookkal ("Memory flowers") The blooms that appear on the backwater's surface when the underlying root system is dying—beautiful, tourist-attracting, and diagnostic of ecological collapse. In Chapter 3, the metaphor for the attention economy: spectacular engagement metrics growing from the death of shared civic reality.

Orumuttu A temporary earthen bund that Kuttanadan neighbors build collectively to divert floodwater during the monsoon. Each family contributes labor; the bund protects all. In the book, the metaphor for informal social infrastructure—Gerald driving Maria to the pharmacy, community bonds that no algorithm measures.

Pantham The torchbearer in a Theyyam ritual, who lights the performance space so the community can see the deity's face. In Chapter 3, local journalism as the pantham—without it, the ritual happens in darkness, and no one can see.

Thodu A narrow irrigation channel that connects one farmer's field to the larger canal system—the strategic leverage point where controlling a small channel determines access for an entire watershed. The book's metaphor for chokepoints: rare earths, TSMC, SWIFT, the Strait of Malacca.

Thattukaaran ("The one who blocks") The farmer who controls a thodu and can restrict or permit water flow to downstream fields. The chokepoint controller.

Theechamundam The ritual fire around which the Theyyam performer circles during the trance phase—the heat that transforms the human into the divine. In the book, the competitive pressure that forces systemic transformation.

Ullil kaanal ("Inner vision") The Theyyam performer's ability to see beneath the surface—to perceive the deity within the human, the undercurrent beneath the surface. The book's epistemological aspiration: to read what the Bloomberg terminal cannot display.

Vallam / Thuzha The vessel and the oar. In Chapter 4, the metaphor for America's magnificent arrows (innovation, talent, R&D) and broken bow (social infrastructure): the finest vallam on the backwater is useless if the Thuzha is cracked.

Vellappokkam ("The great flooding") The Kuttanadan catastrophic flood that overwhelms all defenses—the scenario-analysis metaphor for systemic crisis (Scenario C, the Salt Tide) that ruptures the interdependency web.

Verppaadu ("Distribution") The spatial pattern by which irrigation water disperses through a network of channels. In Chapter 10, the metaphor for the spatial dispersion of dollar alternatives—CIPS, mBridge, bilateral settlement agreements—each finding its own channel.

CHINESE TERMS

Kǎ bózi (卡脖子) ("Strangle the neck") The Chinese term for chokepoint—the strategic bottleneck where external actors can throttle China's access to critical inputs. The animating fear behind every self-reliance campaign is documented in the book.

Shì (势) Strategic momentum—the propensity of a situation to develop in a particular direction. In Sun Tzu's usage, the commander who reads shì correctly does not fight the current; he positions himself to be carried by it. The Farmer's temporal strategy.

Tiānxià (天下) ("All under heaven") The classical Chinese conception of the civilizational order—not a nation-state but a gravitational system in which peripheral states orbit a cultural and economic center. The BRI's implicit architecture.

Xìn (信) Trust, faith, credibility—the foundational virtue in Confucian social architecture. The currency that the dollar system monetizes and that the trust recession documented in Chapter 3 has eroded.

Wú wéi (无为) ("Non-action") The Taoist principle of achieving outcomes through alignment with natural forces rather than coercive intervention. The Farmer's strategic patience—letting the Hunter's self-inflicted fragmentation do the strategic work that confrontation would not.

Zhèng/Qí (正/奇) The orthodox and the unorthodox—Sun Tzu's framework for combining conventional force (zhèng) with surprise maneuver (qí). In the book, zhèng is the visible industrial deployment; qí is the institutional design (SOE substrate, Five-Year Plans, patient capital) that conventional analysis misreads as inefficiency.

Zìlì gēngshēng (自力更生) ("Self-reliance and regeneration") The Maoist-era phrase revived under Xi Jinping for the technology self-sufficiency campaigns. The animating principle behind SMIC's multi-patterning, the domestic EUV effort, and every chira documented in this book.

Hún shuǐ mō yú (浑水摸鱼) ("Stir the muddy water to catch the fish") Stratagem #20 of the Thirty-Six Stratagems. In Chapter 3, the algorithmic polarization that clouds the Hunter's epistemic waters—not by Chinese action but by the Hunter's own platforms.

THE BOOK'S ANALYTICAL FRAMEWORKS

Asymmetric Cost Thesis Chapter 7's central argument: the Farmer's military-industrial capacity achieves strategic parity at a fraction of the Hunter's cost. The $500 drone vs. the $10M armored vehicle. The DF-21D vs. the $13B carrier.

Bobby Buyback Chapter 2's satirical personification of the Magnificent Seven's $5.3 trillion buyback theology—the executive who returns capital to shareholders rather than investing in productive capacity.

Boatman's Ledger The chapter-ending analytical tool that translates geopolitical analysis into illustrative portfolio and strategic implications. Fourteen chapter-specific instruments, each introducing a new analytical concept.

Boatman's Wager The Ledger's illustrative scenario allocation—the investment-positioning section that translates analysis into actionable frameworks. Formerly "Gordon Gekko Action."

Broken Bow Index Chapter 4's Ledger tool measures the gap between the Hunter's arrow quality (innovation, R&D, talent) and bow condition (infrastructure, healthcare, education, social cohesion).

Burning Ghat Chapter 12's six-phase framework for the Rooseveltian prescription: Acknowledgment → Triage → Foundation → Reconstruction → Deployment → Sustainment.

Ceiling vs. Floor Chapter 11's central analytical reframe: China optimizes for strategic sufficiency (a floor) rather than frontier supremacy (a ceiling). "A ceiling can be cracked from below. A floor cannot be undermined from above."

Chokepoint Premium / Chokepoint Half-Life Chapter 8's Ledger instruments measuring the declining strategic value of technological monopolies as alternatives multiply. Each chira reduces the premium; each alternative shortens the half-life.

Deployment-Over-Invention Ratio Chapter 9's Ledger instrument. The ratio between a nation's capacity to deploy technology at scale and its capacity to invent it. The Farmer's ratio exceeds the Hunter's in 11 of 13 domains.

Four Sacraments Chapter 2's satirical framework for the Magnificent Seven's extraction liturgy: the Stock Buyback (sacrament of self-consumption), the Platform Lock-In (sacrament of captive congregation), the Regulatory Arbitrage (sacrament of jurisdictional communion), and the Narrative Premium (sacrament of faith-based valuation).

Interdependency Web Score Chapter 5's cumulative scoring system across fourteen domains. China leads in 11; the U.S. leads in 3 (university research, alliance depth, SCOTUS institutional antibody).

Māyā Meter The running diagnostic for detecting surface-versus-depth divergence. When the Māyā Meter reads high, the narrative diverges sharply from the deployment data.

Ormappookkal Index Chapter 3's Ledger instrument. When engagement metrics (surface bloom) rise while civic participation metrics (root system) decline simultaneously, the memory flowers are blooming, and the lake is dying.

Osmoregulation Stress Index Chapter 6's Ledger instrument measuring the pressure on nations (Germany, India, Indonesia, Vietnam) navigating between the Farmer and Hunter currents without being absorbed by either.

Patient Capital Compound Rate (PCCR) Chapter 1's Ledger instrument. The rate at which the Farmer's patient capital compounds across institutional cycles—measured in deployment output per yuan invested per decade.

Social Cohesion Index Chapter 3's Ledger tool. The fourteenth domain's measurement system: trust percentages, information-ecosystem overlap, and collective-action capacity.

Three Futures Chapter 12's probability-weighted scenario framework: Scenario A—The Grand Halocline (30%): both nations find the boundary layer; Scenario B—The Slow Thaw (40%): gradual rebalancing; Scenario C—The Salt Tide (30%): catastrophic rupture.

Wei's Law Chapter 10's framework: dedollarization proceeds not through frontal assault but through the accumulation of small alternatives—each transaction settled outside the dollar system teaches the next transaction where the channel is.

THEYYAM RITUAL TERMS

Thottam The Invocation. The first stage of a Theyyam ritual, in which the performer recites the deity's genealogy, and the drummers establish the rhythm. No paint. No mask. Only the voice and the intention. Part I of this book.

Vellatam The Transformation. The second stage, in which the face is progressively painted, and the performer begins to move between human and divine. Each stroke brings the deity closer. Part II of this book.

Mukhathezhuthu The Sacred Face. The final stage, in which the full mask is complete, and the deity arrives. The performer's human identity vanishes into the divine form. Part III of this book.

Pantham The torchbearer who lights the performance space. Without the pantham, the ritual happens in darkness.

Theyyam A sacred performance tradition of northern Kerala in which a human performer is transformed into a deity through an elaborate ritual of paint, costume, trance, and fire. The structural architecture of this book.

End of Front Matter & Glossary

ENDNOTES AND BIBLIOGRAPHY

...

Notes organized by chapter following the Chicago Manual of Style, 17th edition. Where a single source supports multiple claims within the same passage, endnotes are consolidated.

Character vignettes are composites; see Note on Composite Characters at the end of this section.

PROLOGUE

Two Harvests

1. Yuanmingyuan burning, October 1860; Lord Elgin ordered destruction; 860 acres. *Source:* James Hevia, English Lessons: The Pedagogy of Imperialism in Nineteenth-Century China (Durham: Duke University Press, 2003), 73–95. See also Erik Ringmar, Liberal Barbarism (New York: Palgrave Macmillan, 2013).

2. Victor Hugo's letter: "One day, two bandits entered the Summer Palace." *Source:* Victor Hugo, letter to Captain Butler, November 25, 1861. Reprinted in Hugo, Actes et Paroles (Paris: Hetzel, 1875).

3. Siku Quanshu partially destroyed at Yuanmingyuan. *Source:* Endymion Wilkinson, Chinese History: A New Manual, 5th ed. (Cambridge: Harvard University Asia Center, 2018), 929–935.

4. DeepSeek V3: 671B parameters, 37B active per token; training cost ~$5.6M; 2.788M H800 GPU hours. *Source:* DeepSeek-AI, "DeepSeek-V3 Technical Report," arXiv:2412.19437 (December 2024). Cost confirmed: Andrew Ng, "DeepSeek-V3 Redefines LLM Performance," The Batch, DeepLearning.AI, February 13, 2025.

5. DeepSeek R1: MATH-500 97.3%; AIME 2024 79.8%; GPT-4 comparison scores. *Source:* DeepSeek-AI, "DeepSeek-R1: Incentivizing Reasoning Capability in LLMs via Reinforcement Learning," arXiv:2501.12948 (January 2025). Published in Nature, September 2025.

6. Nvidia lost $589B in market capitalization on January 27, 2025. *Source:* Anna Googins and Ryan Browne, "Nvidia Sheds Nearly $600 Billion," CNBC, January 27, 2025.

7. S&P 500 lost over $6.6 trillion in two trading days following Liberation Day tariffs. *Source:* Matt Egan, "Stocks Lose $6.6 Trillion in Two Days," CNN Business, April 4, 2025.

8. Executive Order 14257; universal 10% tariff; up to 145% on Chinese goods. *Source:* Executive Order 14257, 90 Fed. Reg. 15269 (April 2, 2025). Escalation: Ana Swanson, "Trump Raises Tariffs on China to 145 Percent," New York Times, April 9, 2025.

9. Tesla >$1T market cap for 1.64M vehicles; BYD $107B for 4.27M vehicles (2024); 4.6M (2025). *Source:* Tesla Inc., Form 10-K, January 2025. BYD 2024: BYD Company Limited, Annual Results, March 25, 2025 (4,272,145 units). BYD 2025: Tridens Technology, "BYD Sales Statistics (Mar 2026)"—4.6M NEVs. Revenue $107B: CNN Business, March 25, 2025.

10. Apollo Go: 300,000 autonomous rides per week in Wuhan. *Source:* Baidu Inc., Q3 2025 Earnings Call Transcript, November 2025. See also Zeyi Yang, "China's Robotaxi Revolution," MIT Technology Review, October 2025.

11. CATL: >39% global EV battery market share (full-year 2025). *Source:* SNE Research, "Global EV Battery Market Share 2025," via CnEVPost, February 4, 2026: CATL held 39.2% for full-year 2025 (464.7 GWh), an all-time high. Corroborated by the CATL 2025 Annual Report (March 10, 2026) and the South China Morning Post.

12. SMIC achieving 5nm-class production via DUV multi-patterning. *Source:* Anton Shilov, "SMIC Reportedly Producing 5nm Chips Using DUV Lithography," Tom's Hardware, August 2024. Dan Nystedt, "SMIC's N+3 Node Achieves 5nm-Class Density," EE Times, October 2024.

13. Smoot-Hawley Tariff Act of 1930 comparison. *Source:* Douglas A. Irwin, Peddling Protectionism: Smoot-Hawley and the Great Depression (Princeton: Princeton University Press, 2011).

14. BYD 4.6M vehicles annually (2025); surpassed Tesla in quarterly pure-EV deliveries. *Source:* Tridens Technology, "BYD Sales Statistics (Mar 2026)": 4.6M NEVs in 2025, ~18% global EV market. BYD surpassing Tesla: Reuters, October 2, 2024.

. . .

CHAPTER 1

The Farmer's Almanac

15. Big Fund (National IC Industry Investment Fund): $100B+ cumulative. *Source:* Cheng Ting-Fang and Lauly Li, "China's Third Big Fund Raises $47.5 Billion," Nikkei Asia, May 27, 2024. Total across three phases exceeds $100B.

16. Made in China 2025: 70% self-sufficiency target. *Source:* State Council PRC, "Made in China 2025," May 19, 2015. English translation: ISDP, June 2018.

17. BYD God's Eye ADAS: 150M daily km driving data; standard across 21 models. *Source:* BYD Company Limited, "God's Eye Advanced Driving System," press release, January 2025. CnEVPost, February 2025.

18. 3.57M STEM graduates annually (China) vs. ~820K (US). *Source:* China: Ministry of Education, PRC, 2024 Education Statistical Yearbook. US: National Science Foundation, Science and Engineering Indicators 2024, Table 2-1.

19. SOE combined assets exceeding $125 trillion; 300,000+ entities; 75% of Fortune Global 500 Chinese companies. *Source:* SASAC central SOEs: 95+ trillion yuan (~$13.66T) by end-2025. Total including local government SOEs across all tiers exceeds 880 trillion yuan (~$125T). Sources: SASAC 2024–25 reports; Perplexity Research compilation from Wind Financial Terminal, SASAC announcements, and NPC disclosures, March 2026. Fortune Global 500: Fortune, August 2024.

20. AI+ companies: 5,000+ registered since 2023. *Source:* Ministry of Industry and Information Technology (MIIT), "AI Industry Development Report," 2024. Updated: Sinovation Ventures, 2024 Annual Report.

21. BRI: $1.399T cumulative; $213.5B new deals in 2025 (75% increase). *Source:* Christoph Nedopil Wang, "China BRI Investment Report 2025," Green Finance & Development Center, FISF Fudan University, January 2026.

22. State Grid Corporation: $700B assets; electricity at $0.03–0.05/kWh. *Source:* State Grid Corporation of China, 2024 Annual Report. IEA, World Energy Outlook 2024.

23. CSSC: $120B assets; 60%+ global commercial shipbuilding. *Source:* CSSC 2024 Annual Report. Clarkson Research, "World Shipbuilding Statistics," Q4 2024.

24. Big Fund corruption purge, 2022–23. *Source:* Cheng Ting-Fang, "China's Chip Fund Purge Snares Former Finance Ministry Official," Nikkei Asia, August 2023.

25. Singapore boardroom, 2006; McKinsey optimization roadmap; 11,000 jobs to Shenzhen. *Source:* Author's personal experience. Composite based on the author's three decades in Fortune 10 consulting.

26. ZTE crisis 2018. *Source:* Arjun Kharpal, "How ZTE's Near-Death Experience Became China's Tech Wake-Up Call," CNBC, May 14, 2018.

27. Xi Jinping: "Core technology cannot be obtained by begging." *Source:* Xi Jinping, speech at Chinese Academy of Sciences, May 28, 2018. Xinhua, same date.

28. Lagos-Calabar railway: 1,402 km, completed early 2026. *Source:* CGTN, "Lagos-Calabar Railway Begins Passenger Service," February 2026. Railway Gazette International, March 2026.

29. US counter-BRI: "Partnership for Global Infrastructure and Investment"; $600B pledged. *Source:* The White House, June 2022. Critique: Jonathan Hillman, The Emperor's New Road (New Haven: Yale University Press, 2020).

. . .

CHAPTER 2

30. S&P 500 aggregate buybacks: $5.3T (2010–2023). *Source:* S&P Global, "S&P 500 Buybacks Set Record," Q4 2023. William Lazonick, "Profits Without Prosperity," Harvard Business Review, September 2014.

31. Capex-to-profit ratio: ~50% (1970s) to <20% today. *Source:* Germán Gutiérrez and Thomas Philippon, "Investment-less Growth," Brookings Papers on Economic Activity, Fall 2017.

32. Boeing: $43B buybacks (2013–19); 346 deaths (Lion Air 610 + Ethiopian 302). *Source:* Boeing Co., Form 10-K, various years (aggregated by Reuters, March 2024). NTSB final reports; JATR, October 2019.

33. Starbucks CEO compensation: 6,666:1 vs. median employee. *Source:* Starbucks Corporation, 2024 Proxy Statement (DEF 14A), January 2025.

34. Ford: $4.8B EV loss (Model e), 2024. *Source:* Ford Motor Company, Q4 2024 Earnings Release, February 2025.

35. 80% of APIs are manufactured overseas; 40% from China. *Source:* US-China Economic and Security Review Commission, Annual Report, November 2024, Ch. 4. Yanzhong Huang, CFR, March 2023.

36. SCOTUS 6–3 ruling striking down IEEPA tariff authority. *Source:* United States v. Trump (tariff authority), 2025. Chief Justice Roberts, majority opinion.

37. $160B+ tariff refunds required. *Source:* Jim Tankersley, "Supreme Court Tariff Ruling Could Require $160 Billion in Refunds," New York Times, July 2025.

38. China trade surplus exceeded $1T in 2025. *Source:* General Administration of Customs PRC, 2025 Annual Trade Statistics. Bloomberg, January 2026.

39. Meta: $91B cumulative buybacks. *Source:* Meta Platforms Inc., Form 10-K, 2017–2024 (aggregated from quarterly cash flow statements).

40. Apple: $600B+ buybacks; 90%+ iPhones assembled at Zhengzhou. *Source:* Apple Inc., Form 10-K, various years. Keith Bradsher, "How China Built 'iPhone City,'" New York Times, December 29, 2016.

41. Microsoft Azure: $96B cloud revenue run rate. *Source:* Microsoft Corporation, FY2025 Q2 Earnings, January 2025.

42. Nvidia: 75%+ margins; $589B single-day loss. *Source:* Nvidia Corporation, FY2025 Annual Report. CNBC, January 27, 2025 (see note 6).

43. Magnificent Seven: >$20T combined market cap; ~$300B R&D. *Source:* Bloomberg Terminal data, 2024–25. R&D aggregated from individual 10-K filings.

44. 55% of billion-dollar startup founders are immigrants or their children. *Source:* Stuart Anderson, "Immigrants and Billion-Dollar Companies," NFAP Policy Brief, October 2022.

45. 81.5% of small businesses raised prices due to tariffs. *Source:* NFIB, "Small Business Economic Trends," May 2025.

46. 68% vs. 91% free cash flow reinvestment (US vs. Chinese tech). *Source:* Goldman Sachs Global Investment Research, "Capital Allocation in US vs. China Technology," July 2024.

· · ·

CHAPTER 3

The Attention Harvest

47. Government trust: 75% (1960s) → 20% (2023). *Source:* Pew Research Center, "Public Trust in Government: 1958–2023," September 2023.

48. Congress approval: 16%. Social media trust: 11%. Medical system: 34%. Media: 34%. *Source:* Gallup, "Confidence in Institutions," July 2023.

49. Cross-partisan marriage disapproval: 5% (1960) → ~40% (2023). *Source:* Shanto Iyengar et al., "The Origins and Consequences of Affective Polarization," Annual Review of Political Science 22 (2019). Updated: Pew Research Center, September 2022.

50. 55% of Republicans and Democrats view the opposing party as "a serious threat." *Source:* Pew Research Center, "Americans' Dismal Views of the Nation's Politics," September 2023.

51. 15–20% agree the country would be better off if opposing partisans "just died." *Source:* Nathan P. Kalmoe and Lilliana Mason, "Lethal Mass Partisanship," APSA 2019. Updated: Mason and Kalmoe, Radical American Partisanship (Chicago: University of Chicago Press, 2022).

52. Outrage content: +17% engagement. Belief-reinforcing: +36%. *Source:* William J. Brady et al., "Attentional Capture Helps Explain Why Moral and Emotional Content Goes Viral," Journal of Experimental Psychology: General 149, no. 4 (2020). Internal Meta research via Frances Haugen SEC complaints, October 2021.

53. Facebook 2018 algorithm: "five-point boost" for anger-triggering content. *Source:* Jeff Horwitz, "The Facebook Files," Wall Street Journal, September–October 2021. Internal documents disclosed by Frances Haugen.

54. 2,900 newspapers closed since 2005; 80% local digital ad revenue to Meta/Google. *Source:* Penelope Muse Abernathy, News Deserts and Ghost Newspapers, Northwestern University, 2023. Pew Research Center, "Newspapers Fact Sheet," June 2024.

55. 25% of Americans agreed with QAnon core claims. *Source:* PRRI, "The Persistence of QAnon Beliefs," February 2023. Measures agreement with at least one of three core QAnon-adjacent statements.

56. Top 1%: 31% of wealth; bottom 50%: 2.5%. CEO-to-worker: 351:1. *Source:* Federal Reserve, Survey of Consumer Finances, 2022. Economic Policy Institute, "CEO Pay Has Skyrocketed 1,460%," October 2024.

. . .

CHAPTER 4

The Hunter's Broken Bow

57. ASCE infrastructure grade: C–. Investment gap: $4.59T over 10 years. *Source:* American Society of Civil Engineers, "2025 Report Card for America's Infrastructure," March 2025.

58. China infrastructure spending: $1.14T in 2023. *Source:* National Bureau of Statistics of China, 2023 Statistical Communiqué.

59. China HSR: 42,000+ km; US: 0 km. *Source:* National Railway Administration PRC, 2024 Annual Report. CRS, "High-Speed Rail in the United States," January 2025.

60. 186M Americans served by water systems are in violation of the Safe Drinking Water Act. *Source:* Natural Resources Defense Council, "Threats on Tap," 2023 update.

61. 530,000 medical bankruptcies annually. *Source:* Himmelstein et al., "Medical Bankruptcy: Still Common Despite the ACA," American Journal of Public Health 109, no. 3 (2019). Updated: American Journal of Medicine, 2023.

62. US healthcare: $4.5T (17.3% GDP); life expectancy declining for 3 consecutive years. *Source:* CMS, "National Health Expenditure Data," 2024. CDC NCHS, "Provisional Life Expectancy Estimates."

63. 27M uninsured Americans. *Source:* US Census Bureau, Health Insurance Coverage in the United States: 2023, September 2024.

64. Youngstown: 170K peak → ~58K. Poverty: 35%. Median income: $28,700. *Source:* US Census Bureau, ACS 2023 5-Year Estimates, Youngstown city, Ohio.

65. Northside Medical Center closed in 2018. *Source:* WFMJ-TV, October 2018. Ohio Department of Health, Hospital Closure Impact Report, 2019.

66. Student debt: $1.77T. *Source:* Federal Reserve Bank of New York, Quarterly Report on Household Debt and Credit, Q4 2024.

67. Social mobility: 7.5% bottom-to-top quintile probability. *Source:* Raj Chetty et al., "Where is the Land of Opportunity?" Quarterly Journal of Economics 129, no. 4 (2014).

68. Bipartisan Infrastructure Law: $1.2T; CHIPS Act: $52B; IRA: $370B. *Source:* Infrastructure Investment and Jobs Act, Pub. L. 117-58 (2021). CHIPS and Science Act, Pub. L. 117-167 (2022). Inflation Reduction Act, Pub. L. 117-169 (2022).

69. Flint water crisis: 100,000+ residents exposed; 12,000 children. *Source:* Mona Hanna-Attisha, What the Eyes Don't See (New York: One World, 2018).

70. 24M Americans lack broadband. *Source:* FCC Broadband Deployment Report, 2024.

. . .

CHAPTER 5

The Field and the Forest

71. Juicero: $120M invested; hand-squeezable packets. *Source:* Ellen Huet and Olivia Zaleski, "Silicon Valley's $400 Juicer May Be Unnecessary," Bloomberg, April 19, 2017.

72. Theranos: $9B peak valuation. *Source:* John Carreyrou, Bad Blood (New York: Knopf, 2018).

73. Cruise: $12B; fleet recalled. Argo AI: $3.6B; dissolved. *Source:* Cruise: GM SEC filings; Faiz Siddiqui, Washington Post, November 2023. Argo AI: Mike Colias, WSJ, October 26, 2022.

74. Nikola: $34B peak; truck rolled downhill unpowered. *Source:* SEC v. Nikola Corporation, Civil Action No. 21-cv-6390 (S.D.N.Y. 2021).

75. BYD God's Eye: ~$385/vehicle vs. Waymo ~$175K sensor suite (454:1). *Source:* BYD teardown: UBS Evidence Lab, Q1 2025. Waymo: The Information, 2024. Ratio calculated by the author.

76. CATL Shenxing LFP: 0–80% in 10 minutes. *Source:* CATL press release, August 2023. SAE International technical review, December 2023.

77. Huawei Ascend: ~60% of H100 performance. *Source:* SemiAnalysis, "Huawei Ascend 910B vs. Nvidia H100," 2024. 60% represents the consensus midpoint.

78. China electricity >10,000 TWh annually. *Source:* National Bureau of Statistics of China, 2024 Communiqué. IEA, World Energy Outlook 2024.

79. Liang Wenfeng: born 1980s Guangdong; High-Flyer 2015; 100B+ yuan by 2021. *Source:* China Securities Journal interview, 2021. Qianzhan Industry Research Institute, January 2025.

80. Liang quotes: "They are just servers"; "Our goal isn't quick profits." *Source:* China Securities Journal, 2021. DeepSeek company blog, January 2025.

. . .

CHAPTER 6

The Scorched Field

81. China import share: ~22% (2017) → ~9% (early 2026). *Source:* US Census Bureau, Foreign Trade Division, accessed February 2026.

82. Rare earths: 60% mining, 90% processing, 94% permanent magnets. *Source:* USGS, Mineral Commodity Summaries 2025. Adamas Intelligence, Q4 2024.

83. F-35: ~920 lbs rare earth per airframe; $1.7T lifecycle. *Source:* CRS, "Rare Earth Elements in National Defense," December 2024. GAO-25-106503, March 2025.

84. Skydio: one battery per drone. *Source:* Valerie Insinna, "US Drone Maker Skydio Forced to Ration Batteries," Defense One, August 2024.

85. Rare earth export controls timeline: July 2023 through October 2025. *Source:* Ministry of Commerce, PRC, successive announcements. CSIS, "China's Critical Mineral Export Controls: A Timeline," January 2026.

86. US goods trade deficit: $1.24T. *Source:* US Census Bureau, Annual Revision, February 2026.

87. 70+ world leaders have visited Beijing since December 2025. *Source:* Ministry of Foreign Affairs, PRC, diplomatic activity log. Reuters, February 2026.

88. Indonesia $21B package (Prabowo visit, January 2026). *Source:* Reuters, January 2026. Jakarta Globe, February 2026.

89. Hambantota Port: 99-year lease, 2017. Pakistan CPEC: $62B. Djibouti debt: 70% GDP. *Source:* Maria Abi-Habib, NYT, June 25, 2018. Pakistan Planning Commission, 2024. IMF Article IV, Djibouti, 2024.

90. India: median age ~28; 1.5M engineering graduates annually. *Source:* UN World Population Prospects 2024. AICTE Annual Report 2023–24.

• • •

CHAPTER 7

The Farmer's Arsenal

91. Type 076: world's first drone carrier; EMALS; sea trials November 2025. *Source:* Office of Naval Intelligence, March 2026. USNI News, November 2025.

92. PLA Navy: 370+ ships; world's largest by hull count. *Source:* US DoD, "Military and Security Developments Involving the PRC, 2025."

93. CSSC 2025 military output: Fujian carrier, destroyers, frigates, Type 054B. *Source:* USNI News fleet tracker, 2025. South China Morning Post, November 2025.

94. Construction tempos: frigate ~25 months; Virginia-class 5+ years; Ford 7 years late, $13B/ship. *Source:* CSIS ChinaPower, 2025. CBO, January 2025. GAO-25-106503.

95. Low-altitude economy: ¥1.5T ($210B); 89,000 enterprises; 220% growth. *Source:* Civil Aviation Administration of China, 2025. MIIT, Q2 2025.

96. DF-21D: ~$20M/unit; 650:1 cost ratio vs. Ford-class $13B. *Source:* CSIS Missile Defense Project, 2024. US Navy FY2025 budget.

97. Tiangong: $8–10B; ISS lifecycle: $150B. *Source:* China Manned Space Agency estimates via Space Policy Institute, GWU, 2024. NASA OIG, 2024.

98. F-35: 55–60% mission-capable; $36K/flight hour. *Source:* GAO, July 2024.

99. Operation Epic Fury, February 28, 2026; Tomahawk at $2.4M/missile. *Source:* CRS, "Navy Tomahawk Cruise Missile Program," 2025. DoD press briefing, March 2026.

100. Civilian casualties: thousands across multi-theater operations (2025–26). *Source:* As of March 15, 2026, the US-Iran conflict death toll is estimated at 2,248–5,090+ killed with 23,885+ injured across all parties. Sources: Airwars civilian casualty assessments; Hengaw Organization for Human Rights (4,400+ Iranian military by March 14); UNICEF (children affected); Associated Press and Reuters ongoing reporting. Figures are actively changing as the conflict continues. The manuscript uses "thousands" to reflect the range across multiple credible sources without false precision.

• • •

CHAPTER 8

101. SMIC N+3: 5nm-class; ~125M transistors/mm²; 30–33% yield; 50% cost premium. *Source:* TechInsights teardown, 2024. SemiAnalysis, Q3 2024.

102. ASML: sole EUV manufacturer; ~$380M/machine; market cap >$380B. *Source:* ASML Holding N.V., 2024 Annual Report. Bloomberg Terminal data, 2024–25.

103. Equipment self-sufficiency: 5% (2019) → 35% (Jan 2026); 70% target 2027. *Source:* SIA/BCG, 2024 update. SEMI, "China Semiconductor Equipment Self-Sufficiency Tracker," January 2026.

104. China semiconductor equipment spending >$40B (2025),>US+EU combined. *Source:* SEMI, "World Fab Forecast," Q4 2025.

105. Twelve alternative paths: SMEE, Tsinghua SSMB, NAURA, AMEC, etc. *Source:* SMEE: China Daily, 2024. Tsinghua SSMB: Hao et al., Physical Review Letters, 2024. NAURA and AMEC: company annual reports, 2024.

106. CHIPS Act: Intel $8.5B subsidy + 15K layoffs. TSMC Arizona: imported workers. Samsung Texas: delayed. *Source:* Intel subsidy: Commerce Dept, August 2024. Layoffs: Intel, August 1, 2024. TSMC: Yang Jie and Asa Fitch, WSJ, July 2024.

107. Quantum network: >10,000 km; 145 nodes; 12,900 km intercontinental link. *Source:* Pan Jian-Wei et al., Nature (2021). Liao Sheng-Kai et al., Physical Review Letters, 2025.

108. Greenwald Limit broken: EAST, 1.3–1.65x; Science Advances, January 2026. *Source:* Wan Yuanxi et al., Science Advances, January 2026.

109. Talent gap: 200K–250K semiconductor engineers. *Source:* China Semiconductor Industry Association, 2024 Annual Report. McKinsey, September 2024.

110. Gregory Allen, CSIS: "strangling with intent to kill." *Source:* Gregory C. Allen, CSIS, October 2022.

· · ·

CHAPTER 9

The Living Harvest

111. NEV penetration: 59.4% (China, 2024); US ~12%. *Source:* CAAM, 2024 Annual Statistics. Argonne National Laboratory, Q4 2024.

112. China: 10M+ public charging points; US: ~76K DC fast chargers (130:1). *Source:* China EV Charging Infrastructure Promotion Alliance, December 2024. US DOE AFDC, February 2026.

113. BYD Seagull: $7,800 (55,800 yuan); average American car: $33,600. *Source:* BYD official pricing, 2024. Kelley Blue Book, January 2025.

114. BYD exports: 1.04M vehicles in 2025 (full-year overseas sales). *Source:* Xinhua, January 3, 2026: BYD overseas sales exceeded 1.04M in 2025 (1,049,601 NEVs, +150.7% YoY). Corroborated by Electrive (January 26, 2026), CarNewsChina, and Gasgoo/AutoCango.

115. Wang Chuanfu: born 1966, Wuwei; orphaned by 15; BYD founded 1995 with $300K. *Source:* Forbes profile. Lulu Yilun Chen, Bloomberg Businessweek, April 2023.

116. Munger/Berkshire: $230M for 10% BYD stake, 2008. *Source:* Buffett, Berkshire Hathaway Annual Letter, 2009. Munger CNBC interview, 2009.

117. Biotech: 32% out-licensing ($66B 2025); 639 first-in-class candidates; 120K biomedical PhDs/yr. *Source:* McKinsey, "China's Biotech Boom," 2025. BioDrugs 2024. Ministry of Education PRC, 2024.

118. API: 80% overseas; 40% China; ~half of 227 essential medicines have zero domestic API. *Source:* US-China Economic and Security Review Commission, 2024 Annual Report, Ch. 4.

119. Robotics: China 52% global installations (276K units), 2024. *Source:* International Federation of Robotics, World Robotics 2025, September 2025.

120. XPENG IRON: 50K unit production target. *Source:* XPENG Robotics, company presentation, Q1 2025.

121. EU countervailing duties on Chinese EVs: up to 36.3%. *Source:* European Commission, Official Journal of the EU, October 2024.

122. China births: 7.92M in 2025; fertility ~1.0. *Source:* National Bureau of Statistics of China, January 2026. See also Chapter 11 notes.

. . .

CHAPTER 10

The Dollar and the Digital Ditchwater

123. Dollar: 56.32% global FX reserves (from 72% in 2000). Yuan: ~2.3%. *Source:* IMF, COFER, Q3 2025.

124. CIPS: ¥175T annual ($24.5T); 43% YoY; 4,900 institutions; 189 countries. *Source:* CIPS 2024 Annual Report. CIPS official website, January 2026.

125. Digital yuan: 3.48B transactions; $2.38T; 230M wallets; interest-bearing Jan 2026. *Source:* PBOC, "e-CNY Development Progress Report," November 2025. PBOC announcement, January 1, 2026.

126. mBridge: $55.49B; 95.3% yuan; 2,500x growth from $22M (2022). *Source:* Bank for International Settlements, "Project mBridge Progress Report," November 2025.

127. Russian reserves frozen: $300B, February 2022. *Source:* US Treasury, February 28, 2022. European Council estimates.

128. Saudi Arabia is accepting the yuan for oil. *Source:* Summer Said and Stephen Kalin, WSJ, March 15, 2022. Reuters, 2023–25.

129. Huawei: 70% of Africa's 4G networks. *Source:* Bulelani Jili, Brookings Institution, September 2024.

130. IMF: China 6.4% voting share. *Source:* IMF, "Members' Quotas and Voting Power," accessed 2026.

131. AIIB: $100B authorized capital; 110 members. *Source:* AIIB 2024 Annual Report.

132. China $50K annual foreign-currency purchase limit. *Source:* SAFE, "Individual Foreign Exchange Management Measures."

. . .

CHAPTER 11

The Farmer's Blight

133. Births: 7.92M in 2025 (−17% YoY); fertility ~1.0; population shrunk 4 consecutive years. *Source:* National Bureau of Statistics of China, January 2026.

134. Women 20–34: projected 105M → 58M by 2050. *Source:* UN Population Division, World Population Prospects 2024.

135. Marriages: 6.1M in 2024 (−20.5%). *Source:* Ministry of Civil Affairs, PRC, 2024 Statistical Bulletin.

136. Property: Evergrande $330B debt; ~$4.7T household wealth destruction since 2021. *Source:* Hong Kong High Court liquidation order, January 29, 2024. Kenneth Rogoff and Yuanchen Yang, IMF Working Paper, 2024.

137. Savings: 160 trillion yuan. *Source:* PBOC, "Financial Statistics Report," December 2024.

138. C919: target 75, delivered 13; 50–60% Western components. *Source:* Aviation Week, January 2026. CSIS, 2025.

139. Youth unemployment >20%; publication suspended July 2023. *Source:* NBS suspended publication in July 2023 (21.3% in June 2023). Resumed with revised methodology, 2024.

140. Gordon Chang, The Coming Collapse of China. *Source:* Gordon G. Chang (New York: Random House, 2001).

141. SMIC 5nm covers ~80% of use cases (sustainment floor). *Source:* Author's analysis based on IC Insights, "Global Wafer Capacity by Node," 2024.

142. Tiangong: sole crewed platform post-~2030 ISS deorbiting. *Source:* NASA, "ISS Deorbit Plan," 2024.

· · ·

CHAPTER 12

The Kuttanadan Way

143. FAO Kuttanad Below Sea Level Farming System: GIAHS designation, 2013. *Source:* FAO, "Globally Important Agricultural Heritage Systems: Kuttanad Below Sea Level Farming System," 2013.

144. GI Bill: $7 in return for every $1 invested. *Source:* Joint Economic Committee, US Congress, 2013. US Department of Veterans Affairs.

145. DARPA: $3.5B annual budget; created ARPANET, GPS, mRNA foundations. *Source:* DoD FY2025 Budget Request. Sharon Weinberger, The Imagineers of War (New York: Knopf, 2017). Moderna S-1 filing, 2018.

146. Six adaptations totaling ~$600B over a decade. *Source:* Author's calculation: $200B Supply Sovereignty + $100B Quad Counter-BRI + $100B ARPA-X ($10B/yr × 10) + $200B National Investment Bank = $600B.

147. Iraq and Afghanistan: $2.3T. *Source:* Neta C. Crawford, Watson Institute, Brown University, updated September 2024.

148. KfW: operating since 1948. *Source:* KfW Group institutional history.

149. H-1B cap: current 85,000; proposed doubling to 170,000. *Source:* USCIS documentation. Proposed reform: author's policy recommendation.

150. NSF budget: ~$10B; proposed tripling to ~$30B. *Source:* NSF FY2025 Budget Request. Cold War R&D share: AAAS R&D Budget Program historical data.

151. Three Futures probability weightings: 30/40/30. *Source:* Author's scenario analysis. Probability assessments informed by: Graham Allison, Destined for War (2017); Hal Brands and Michael Beckley, Danger Zone (2022); RAND Corporation Taiwan contingency studies.

152. Burning Ghat has six phases: Price Compression through Ecosystem Colonization. *Source:* Analytical framework developed by the author. Phase-status assessments based on data documented in the preceding chapters, with sources cited therein.

· · ·

SELECT BIBLIOGRAPHY

Works cited across multiple chapters and foundational references.

Allison, Graham. Destined for War: Can America and China Escape Thucydides's Trap? Boston: Houghton Mifflin Harcourt, 2017.

Brands, Hal, and Michael Beckley. Danger Zone: The Coming Conflict with China. New York: W.W. Norton, 2022.

Carreyrou, John. Bad Blood: Secrets and Lies in a Silicon Valley Startup. New York: Knopf, 2018.

Chang, Gordon G. The Coming Collapse of China. New York: Random House, 2001.

Crawford, Neta C. "United States Budgetary Costs and Obligations of Post-9/11 Wars." Watson Institute, Brown University. Updated September 2024.

DeepSeek-AI. "DeepSeek-V3 Technical Report." arXiv:2412.19437. December 2024.

DeepSeek-AI. "DeepSeek-R1: Incentivizing Reasoning Capability in LLMs via Reinforcement Learning." arXiv:2501.12948. January 2025.

Hanna-Attisha, Mona. What the Eyes Don't See: A Story of Crisis, Resistance, and Hope in an American City. New York: One World, 2018.

Hevia, James L. English Lessons: The Pedagogy of Imperialism in Nineteenth-Century China. Durham: Duke University Press, 2003.

Hillman, Jonathan E. The Emperor's New Road: China and the Project of the Century. New Haven: Yale University Press, 2020.

Irwin, Douglas A. Peddling Protectionism: Smoot-Hawley and the Great Depression. Princeton: Princeton University Press, 2011.

International Energy Agency. World Energy Outlook 2024. Paris: IEA, November 2024.

International Federation of Robotics. World Robotics 2025: Industrial Robots. Frankfurt: IFR, September 2025.

Kalmoe, Nathan P., and Lilliana Mason. Radical American Partisanship. Chicago: University of Chicago Press, 2022.

Lazonick, William. "Profits Without Prosperity." Harvard Business Review, September 2014.

Lee, Kai-Fu. AI Superpowers: China, Silicon Valley, and the New World Order. Boston: Houghton Mifflin Harcourt, 2018.

Mason, Lilliana, and Nathan P. Kalmoe. Radical American Partisanship. Chicago: University of Chicago Press, 2022.

Muse Abernathy, Penelope. News Deserts and Ghost Newspapers: Will Local News Survive? Northwestern University, 2023.

Ringmar, Erik. Liberal Barbarism: The European Destruction of the Palace of the Emperor of China. New York: Palgrave Macmillan, 2013.

US Department of Defense. "Military and Security Developments Involving the People's Republic of China." Annual Report to Congress, various years through 2025.

US Geological Survey. Mineral Commodity Summaries 2025. Reston, VA: USGS, 2025.

Wang, Christoph Nedopil. "China Belt and Road Initiative (BRI) Investment Report 2025." FISF Fudan University, January 2026.

Weinberger, Sharon. The Imagineers of War: The Untold Story of DARPA. New York: Knopf, 2017.

Wilkinson, Endymion. Chinese History: A New Manual. 5th ed. Cambridge: Harvard University Asia Center, 2018.

. . .

NOTE ON COMPOSITE CHARACTERS

The following characters are composites created for narrative purposes. They are based on real patterns, industries, and demographic realities documented in the sourced data above. Still, they are not representations of specific individuals: Chen Yue, Zhang Mei, Liu Jing, Chen Liling, Wei Lin, Wang Sufen, Klaus Reinhardt, Diane Kessler, Maria Delgado (both Youngstown and Monterrey), Gerald, Marcus Chen, Sarah Kowalski, Kevin, Emma, Claire, Priya, and Jessica. The Singapore boardroom scene in the Preface is based on the author's personal experience with identifying details composited or changed.

. . .

End of Endnotes and Bibliography.

THEYYAM IMAGE CONTRIBUTORS

1. Saji Madapat

2. Pradeep Vellur
3. Abhijith Kanumarath
4. Shyamnath PV
5. Shahan Samad
6. Nikhil Raj
7. Sudeep AK
8. Bijith Thenhipalam
9. Vikas Kodakkad
10. Priyank Preman
11. Arjun Vadakara
12. Chetan Pardeshi

HUMBLE REQUEST TO REVIEW MY BOOK

I trust that you enjoyed reading this book. I'd like to hear from you and humbly request that you take a few minutes to post a review on Amazon. Your feedback and support will significantly improve my writing craft for future books and make this book even more commendable. This is a living manuscript and will continuously evolve based on your constructive feedback (contact @ https://www.theyyam.us/about or www.Tiger-Rider.com or

https://www.linkedin.com/in/goodtogreat/)

Proceeds from this book will be donated to the Mother Teresa Mission (Missionaries of Charity) or similar missions.